Attention Deficit Disorder

Attention Deficit Disorder

ADHD and ADD Syndromes

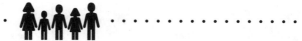

THIRD EDITION

Dale R. Jordan

pro·ed
An International Publisher

8700 Shoal Creek Boulevard
Austin, Texas 78757-6897
800/897-3202 Fax 800/397-7633
www.proedinc.com

An International Publisher
© 1998, 1992, 1988 by PRO-ED, Inc.
8700 Shoal Creek Boulevard
Austin, Texas 78757-6897
800/897-3202 Fax 800/397-7633
www.proedinc.com

Library of Congress Cataloging-in-Publication Data

Jordan, Dale R.
    Attention deficit disorder : ADHD and ADD syndromes / Dale R.
  Jordan.—3rd ed.
        p.   cm.
    Includes bibliographical references (p.   ) and index.
    ISBN 0-89079-742-0 (paperback : alk. paper)
    1. Attention-deficit hyperactivity disorder.
    [DNLM: 1. Attention Deficit disorder with hyperactivity.]
RJ506.H9J67   1998   97-35479
616.85′89—dc21   CIP

Printed in the United States of America

4   5   6   7   8   9   10   09   08   07   06   05   04   03

To my father, Jack,
who died when I was 11 years old,
but who left me a priceless model of parental love
that has influenced me all my life.
And to my mother, Gladys.
As a widowed parent of three children
during the Great Depression,
she taught me two biblical principles that have guided my life:
Seek first the Kingdom of God, and
whatever work your hands find to do,
do it with all your might.

Contents

Preface   *ix*

1   What Causes Attention Deficit Disorder?   *1*

2   Attention-Deficit/Hyperactivity Disorder Individuals   *19*

3   Attention Deficit Disorder Individuals   *45*

4   How ADHD and ADD Disrupt One's Life   *63*

5   Tag-Along Syndromes that Imitate ADHD and ADD   *97*

6   How To Help People with ADHD and ADD   *137*

Appendix A: Jordan Executive Function Index for Children   *157*

Appendix B: Jordan Executive Function Index for Adults   *175*

References   *193*

Index   *197*

Preface

In a time of drastic change, it is the learners who inherit the future. The learned usually find themselves equipped to live in a world that no longer exists.

(Hoffer, 1982, p. 83)

When the second edition of this work was published in 1992, these words from Eric Hoffer seemed prophetic of a time rather far away. Less than 10 years later as we peer through the opening door of the new century, Hoffer's lesson takes on more urgent meaning. During the past decade, neurological research has discovered amazing new information about the role that the brain plays in learning, remembering, controlling impulses, and paying attention. Those who ignore this new knowledge or do not learn these new lessons of neurology and body chemistry will be out of touch with the realities of what drives the ADHD and ADD behaviors. Those who continue to learn what research reveals will be equipped to offer effective help to individuals who cannot maintain attention or bring impulsive behavior under control. This third edition of *Attention Deficit Disorder* presents a clear, simple review of what we currently know about the neurological and biochemical causes of ADHD and ADD. This book is designed to guide teachers, parents, and counselors to recognize the many faces of attention deficit disorder and to know where to turn for help. It is my hope that this kind of new knowledge will stimulate fresh willingness on the part of instructors, employers, life partners, and parents to reach out compassionately to persons of all ages who struggle with the patterns described in these pages.

What Causes Attention Deficit Disorder?

1

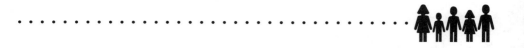

History of the Concept of ADHD and ADD

Even as far back in human history as the days of ancient Greece, physicians and philosophers wondered about the disruptive behaviors of children, adolescents, and adults who were impulsive, hyperactive, emotionally volatile, subject to wide mood swings, and unable to live by the rules of society. Greek writers speculated that such behavior might be caused by "body humors" being out of balance. Those ancient scholars had no idea just how close they were to understanding what causes such disruptive behaviors in many individuals.

Disruptive Behavior

During the nineteenth century, medical literature increasingly described behavior syndromes that disrupted personal and community lives through inattention, poor control of impulse, mood swings, explosive emotional patterns, and unexplained aggression and violence. Toward the end of the 1800s, William James became concerned about the socially disruptive presence of persons who had poor moral control, did not control impulses, and could not maintain full attention long enough to finish what they started. James developed the theory that such behavior must come from an underlying neurological deficit (James, 1890).

The first clinical description of what we now call ADHD was offered in 1902 when George Still delivered a series of lectures at the Royal College of Physicians in London, England. Still expanded the neurological theory proposed by James as he described disruptive behaviors of children who were aggressive, defiantly resistant to discipline, emotionally volatile, "lawless," spiteful and cruel, dishonest, and apparently without "inhibitory volition." In addition to being overly active, many of those disruptive children displayed chronic problems with maintaining attention. In the vocabulary of that day, Still reported that those youngsters had "a major deficit in moral control" (1902, pp. 1008–1009). In 1908 Alfred Tredgold elaborated on the work of James and Still by providing medical evidence that brain deficits contribute to disruptive behavior. Tredgold proposed a kind of special education for children who had impaired attention and inappropriate social behavior. By 1908 it was widely agreed that youngsters with disruptive behavior could be helped temporarily through medication and special education. Researchers believed that these special learners always would be impaired in social functioning (Weiss & Hechtman, 1993).

Brain Damage from Disease

Immediately following the close of World War I, an outbreak of *encephalitis lethargica* afflicted great numbers of children. After recovering from that illness, many victims of the disease displayed different behavior that was described as hyperactive, impulsive, inattentive, emotionally explosive, and socially inappropriate. During the 1920s special residential treatment centers were established to care for those children. Eli Kahn and Leonard Cohen (1934) concluded that those disruptive behavioral changes were caused by encephalitic damage to the brain stem. Kahn and Cohen introduced the concept that such disruptive behavior is "organically driven." This neurological concept was confirmed by William Bradley's work (1937) with new medication to reduce disruptive behaviors in "organically driven" children. The medication Benzedrine proved effective in reducing disruptive behavior that was attributed to brain stem deficits. Benzedrine was the first application of dextroamphetamine and levoamphetamine to inattention and hyperactivity.

Brain Damage and Behavior

During the 1930s Arthur Strauss conducted studies to differentiate between brain-damaged and non–brain-damaged children who were thought, at that time, to be mentally retarded. He described his brain-damaged population as having chronic problems with concept formation, language usage, emotional control, perception of new information and the world around them, and social behavior (Strauss & Kephart, 1955). Strauss further labeled these struggling children as distractible ("driven hither and yon by outside stimulation"), impulsive ("cannot master planful action"), perseverative ("perseveration obstructs the child's understanding of purposeful action"), and hyperactive ("motor disinhibition") (cited in Weiss & Hechtman, 1993, p. 5). Strauss also documented the difficulty this special population had with cognitive learning. By the end of the 1930s, the research by Kahn and Cohen, Bradley, Strauss, and others had produced the label "Minimal Brain Damage Syndrome."

Minimal Brain Damage Syndrome

During the decades of the 1940s and 1950s, the term "Minimal Brain Damage Syndrome" (MBDS) became the most widely used label for the cluster of behaviors that included hyperactivity, impulsivity, poor attention, mood swings, emotional explosiveness, and inappropriate social behavior. Labeling children as MBDS required neurological examinations based on electroencephalograms (EEG), even though many scientists realized that not all hyperactive children who struggled to learn had brain damage. During the 1940s the concept of "maturational lag" was proposed by Lauretta Bender (1942). This point of view suggested that the disruptive behaviors of MBDS might be caused by delayed maturity of portions of the central nervous system. If so, then children with MBDS might be expected to outgrow at least some of the symptoms as they passed through adolescence into early adulthood.

Hyperkinetic Impulse Disorder

In 1957 Morris Laufer, Ernest Denhoff, and George Solomons introduced the term "Hyperkinetic Impulse Disorder" (HID). HID syndrome labeled children who could not keep still. They were in some sort of constant motion, were always restless even in their sleep, and lived by impulse without thinking of the consequences. Laufer and Denhoff speculated that HID was caused by nerve pathway deficits in a portion of the midbrain (limbic system) called the diencephlon. In 1960 Stella Chess defined hyperactivity as follows: "The hyperactive child is one who carries out activities at a higher than normal rate of speed than the average child, or who is constantly in motion, or both" (p. 2379). During the 1970s Peggy Ackerman, Roscoe Dykman, and John Peters at the University of Arkansas also demonstrated that faulty attention and impulse control disorders are major ingredients of HID (Ackerman, Dykman, & Peters, 1977). In 1968 the second edition of the *Diagnostic and Statistical Manual of Mental Disorders* (DSM-II; American Psychiatric Association, 1968) introduced the diagnostic category "Hyperkinetic Reaction of Childhood Disorder." This new label largely replaced the earlier designation of MBDS in children and adolescents who could not keep still.

Minimal Brain Damage

By 1960 many diagnosticians and counselors agreed that the model of Minimal Brain Damage Syndrome was too narrow to continue to be useful as a diagnostic label. A broader point of view was needed. In 1962 Samuel Clements and John Peters at the Child Study Center in Little Rock, Arkansas, proposed the concept of "Minimal Brain Damage" (MBD). This new diagnostic model included consideration of a child's home environment, school performance, social behavior, health history, and emotional temperament. In presenting their new term MBD, Clements and Peters stated:

> It is necessary to take into account the full spectrum of causality from the unique genetic combination that each individual is to his gestation and birth experiences, to his interaction with significant persons, and finally to the stresses and emotional traumata of later life, after his basic reaction patterns have been laid down. (p. 195)

During the decade of the 1960s, MBD rapidly replaced MBDS as the label of choice for impulsive, disruptive, underachieving youngsters. The model of MBD was the guideline for establishing special separate classrooms for educating pupils with disruptive behavior, inability to pay attention, emotional volatility, hyperactivity, and inappropriate social conduct. However, many neurologists and psychologists were unhappy with the concept of Minimal Brain Damage. This opposing point of view was expressed in 1965 when Richard Gomez published the article "Minimal Brain Damage Equals Maximal Neurologic Confusion" (cited in Barkley, 1990). By the mid-1970s, a groundswell of professional opposition to MBD had developed. Yet those who criticized this point of view agreed that, fortunately, the concept of MBD kept attention focused on underlying neurological causes for disruptive behaviors.

Attention Deficit Disorder

In 1980 the third edition of the *Diagnostic and Statistical Manual of Mental Disorders* (DSM-III, American Psychiatric Association, 1980) replaced Hyperkinetic Reaction of Childhood Disorder with a new point of view regarding inattention and hyperactivity. DSM-III presented diagnostic criteria for Attention Deficit Disorder (ADD) with and without hyperactivity. The acronym ADD became the preferred clinical label in two variations: ADD+H (Attention Deficit Disorder with Hyperactivity) and ADD–H (Attention Deficit Disorder without Hyperactivity). DSM-III gave clinicians three categories of symptoms: (1) *inattention,* (2) *impulsivity,* and (3) *hyperactivity.* Neurologists and psychologists who were not satisfied with this new description of chronic inattention embarked on a flurry of research to support another point of view. During the early years of the 1980s, research teams lead by Russell Barkley, Jane Loney, Samuel Hinshaw, and others pursued the supposition that hyperactivity must be seen as separate from aggression (Barkley, 1990). Those scientists believed that the DSM-III criteria were inadequate to distinguish attention deficit disorders from conduct disorders. At the same time, Peggy Ackerman, Roscoe Dykman, and David Oglesby (1983) at the University of Arkansas studied the relationships between ADD+H/ADD–H and learning disabilities and reading difficulties. Their research showed important differences between hyperactive struggling learners (ADD+H) and quiet, passive, daydreaming struggling learners (ADD–H). Those and other studies established the need for new diagnostic criteria for attention deficit disorders (Barkley, 1990, 1995).

ADD Changed to ADHD

In 1987 a revised third edition of the *Diagnostic and Statistical Manual of Mental Disorders* (DSM-III:R, American Psychiatric Association, 1987) further changed the definition of attention deficit disorders. DSM-III:R replaced ADD+H/ADD–H with the new single label ADHD (Attention-Deficit/Hyperactivity Disorder). The category of ADD–H (Attention Deficit Disorder without Hyperactivity) was replaced with the label Undifferentiated ADD. This new point of view separated the quiet, passive, daydreaming behavior of ADD–H from the mainstream of attention deficit disorder (Barkley, 1990). Many research scientists now believed that ADD without hyperactivity was actually a different form of learning difficulty and should not be included as a subtype of attention deficit disorder.

In 1994 yet another redefinition of Attention Deficit Disorder appeared in the fourth edition of the *Diagnostic and Statistical Manual of Mental Disorders* (DSM-IV, American Psychiatric Association, 1994). DSM-IV presented new guidelines for labeling an individual as ADHD. The possibility of ADD–H (Attention Deficit Disorder without Hyperactivity) was brought back by this new set of diagnostic criteria. DSM-IV provided the following clinical categories of attention deficit:

314.01	Attention-Deficit/Hyperactivity Disorder, Combined Type
314.00	Attention-Deficit/Hyperactivity Disorder, Predominantly Inattentive Type
314.01	Attention-Deficit/Hyperactivity Disorder, Predominantly Hyperactive–Impulsive Type

DSM-IV restored ADD without hyperactivity as a subtype of attention deficit under the category 314.00, Attention-Deficit/Hyperactivity Disorder, Predominantly Inattentive Type.

This fourth effort by the American Psychiatric Association to define attention deficits continues to pose problems for diagnosticians, teachers, and parents. If an individual is quiet, passive, daydreamy, and continually off on mental rabbit trails instead of paying attention to the task, why must this person be labeled "hyperactive without hyperactivity"? It seems unlikely that this contradiction in terms will be resolved before the turn of the century.

Brain Structure and Attention Deficit Disorder

It would not be possible to name here all of the pioneers of neurological research who, since the 1960s, have studied the role of brain structure in human intelligence, learning, remembering, paying attention, controlling impulse, and expressing emotion. Among the leading scientists in this quest have been the late Norman Geschwind, Albert Galaburda, Antonio Damasio, Hanna Damasio,

Erin Zaidel, Frank Wood, and Alan Zametkin, to name a few. The advent of brain imaging science during the 1980s opened the way for researchers to watch the living brain at work. Brain imaging techniques, such as positron emission tomography (PET), magnetic resonance imaging (MRI), computed tomography (CT), brain electrical activity mapping (BEAM), and single photon emission computed tomography (SPECT), have permitted scientists to discover how the brain functions and which regions of the brain do what kinds of work. We can now see beneath the surface of the brain into previously hidden inner regions and discover how interior brain structures participate in thinking, learning, and remembering.

Emotions and Feelings

Basal and Higher Emotions

A major discovery related to attention deficit disorders is the role that emotions and feelings play in how the brain processes information. In his book *Descartes' Error,* Antonio Damasio (1994) presents a comprehensive description of how hundreds of substructures throughout the brain are linked to carry out the job of reasoning, thinking, and using what the brain has learned over one's lifetime. Damasio has documented the active roles of emotion and feeling in the thinking process. The seat of logic and commonsense reasoning is the prefrontal cortex at the front of the left brain (Figure 1.1). This region of the brain normally becomes the rational "parent" that guides the rest of the brain in thinking through issues, deciding what is best according to logic, and developing the safest or most efficient way to carry out a task. Historically, Western culture has placed a high value on logical reasoning that excludes emotions and feelings. Damasio has demonstrated how unrealistic that point of view is. In fact, it is impossible for individuals to do creative or productive thinking without incorporating emotions and feelings into the thought process.

Starting in early childhood, individuals who are not ADHD develop two centers of emotion that are critical in becoming successful adults. Strong (basal) emotions originate in the midbrain, or limbic system (see Figure 1.1). The amygdala, basal ganglia, pons, and medulla filter and regulate aggressive emotions such as fear, rage, hostility, the urge to kill, jealousy, and terror. Each of these potentially destructive emotions has a particular place in life, but they must be kept carefully in check if individuals are to be successful members of society. As the limbic system matures with age, most children develop the social skills of saying no to these strong emotions. At a certain developmental milestone during early childhood, the prefrontal cortex begins to exert control over strong basal impulses through the emergence of higher emotions, such as kindness, gentleness, thoughtfulness, patience, and compassion. Damasio has documented how the midbrain "child" learns to say no to strong emotional urges as the higher brain "parent" blends productive emotions with logical rea-

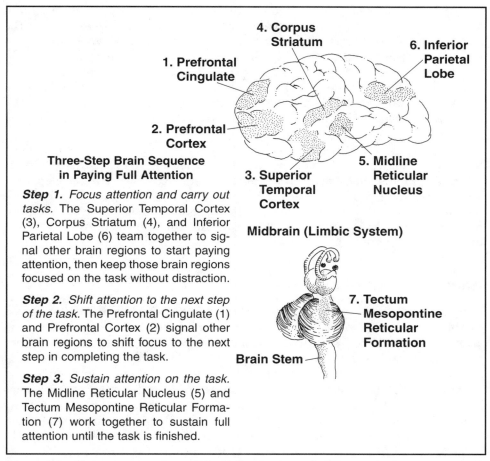

Figure 1.1. These seven regions of the higher brain and midbrain (limbic system) work together as a complex team to carry out attention tasks. When any of these links within the attention system fails to work on schedule or stops working too soon, attention deficits occur.

soning. Attention deficit disorder often makes it impossible for an individual to achieve this balance of controlling strong emotions and living by the guidance of higher emotions.

Feelings

In his book *Descartes' Error* Damasio (1994) also documents the critical role that feelings must play in mature, productive thinking. Feelings arise from body sensations that are triggered by emotion. When an emotional surge of uncertainty or fear begins, a person feels tightness in the chest and intestinal tract. When shy persons are surprised by praise, they feel a hot flush as the face blushes. When thoughtful individuals begin to sense that something is not right in a situation, they feel "warning signals" as emotions start to surge. Newly introduced individuals often feel an emotional surge of affection or "love" that colors how they regard the newcomer. Becoming a mature, rational adult means that individuals must learn how to blend emotions and feelings with logic. Attention deficit disorders directly interfere with this growing-up process.

In his book *Searching for Memory,* Daniel Schacter (1996) has described the complex interconnections between strong emotions and feelings of the midbrain and higher emotions of the prefrontal cortex as we develop memories and interpret past and present experiences. Being able to pay attention over periods of time requires incredibly complex cooperation between emotions, feelings, and logical thinking. To be successful, this neurological cooperation involves many regions of the brain.

Attention Control Systems

Figure 1.1 shows the many regions of the left brain, right brain, and midbrain (limbic system) that must work together as an integrated team to produce full attention over a period of time (Damasio, 1994; Schacter, 1996). If any of these attention-control systems stops working too soon, or if any of these attentional components is out of sequence, the brain loses its mental image and must start over with that attentional task. Attention deficit disorder occurs when members of this central nervous attention-control network do not or cannot function satisfactorily. Later chapters describe how cortical stimulant medication often provides a "fine-tuning" affect that allows out-of-sequence nerve pathways to work in harmony within this attention-control system.

How the Brain Receives New Information

Before the advent of brain imaging science in the 1980s, researchers generally believed that certain large regions of the brain did certain types of specialized work. For example, because the visual cortex at the back of the brain receives images from the eyes, it was assumed that reading is done by the visual cortex. Because the auditory cortex in the left brain interprets most of the oral language we hear, it was believed that this special region of the left brain controls spelling and word sounding. As Damasio (1994), Galaburda (1983), Schacter (1996), and others have demonstrated, language processing is much more complex than we originally believed. Brain imaging science has disclosed that hundreds of neuronal structures distributed throughout the brain work together to interpret and remember the countless bits of new information we learn during our lifetimes.

Visceral Information Pathways

How does the brain receive new information from the outside world? When most people are asked how many body senses we have, they usually name three or four, such as sight, hearing, touch, and smell. The brain does receive much new information through the eyes, ears, fingers, and nose. However, recent neurological research has proved that the brain receives new information through many other senses, most of which are related to the skin. Scientists use the term *viscera* to refer to organs inside the body cavity, such as the heart, lungs, spleen, liver, and digestive tract. The viscera also includes the skin, which is a giant single organ covering the outside of the body. Beneath the thin layer of outer skin are millions of nerve endings from the scalp to the soles of the feet. Each of these nerve endings is connected to one or more regions of the brain. Figure 1.2 shows how nerve pathways just under the outer skin send outside information to the brain stem and midbrain. The spinal cord, brain stem, and midbrain receive and begin to process millions of bits of visceral data per minute from the skin and the internal organs. The skin constantly generates data related to air temperature, texture of clothing, pressure from shoes and other garments, insect bites, scrapes and scratches on the skin, the sting of corrosive liquids, and so forth. Internal organs dispatch information about such body

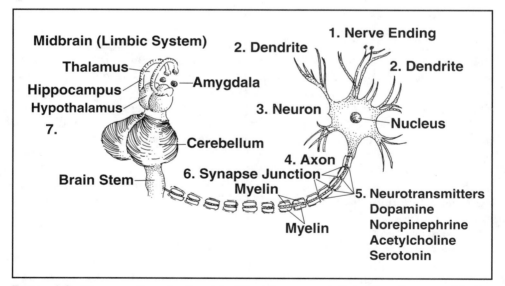

Figure 1.2. Nerve endings in the skin (1) pick up new information from outside the body and send it along dendrites (2) into the neuron (3). This information is then sent down axon pathways (4) by neurotransmitters (5) that fire from one synapse junction (6) to the next until the message reaches the receiver cell. This chain of events is repeated until the new information reaches the midbrain (limbic system) [7].

issues as heart beat, rate of breathing, blood pressure, and things happening inside the digestive tract. As Figure 1.2 illustrates, this information goes first to various members of the limbic system (brain stem, cerebellum, amygdala, hippocampus, thalamus, and hypothalamus) (Blakeslee, 1995).

Each of these limbic system organs is like a computer chip that specializes in processing certain kinds of data. Once each limbic system member has done its job, that information is sent on to relay centers within the higher brain. These relay centers decide where each partly processed bit of data should go next. This new information is then fired toward its final destination somewhere in the right and left brain hemispheres (Damasio, 1994; Schacter, 1996).

Neurotransmitters

One of the amazing facts of brain structure is how information is transmitted along nerve pathways. As Figure 1.2 shows, individual nerve cells put out two types of long fibers that connect each cell to many others. Some of these connecting fibers are *dendrites*. They pick up bits of information and bring that data into the nerve cell. The other connecting fibers are *axons*. These are often very long transmission lines that connect cells throughout the brain and spinal cord. Dendrites and axons are not single continuous strands like wire or optic fibers in telephone lines. Instead, they are composed of short segments that lie in long lines, much like a pontoon bridge over a river. Spaces between the axon segments are called *synapse junctions*. The brain sends and receives information by spurts of electrical energy called *firing*. Electrical impulses at the sending end of each axon segment fire across the synapse to the receiving end (*receptor*) of the next axon segment in the chain. When the electrical charge reaches the tip of each axon segment, a tiny chemical explosion occurs. This explosion causes the receiving axon segment to generate specialized chemical compounds called *neurotransmitters*. The brain uses many different neurotransmitters, each of which is designed to perform a unique function in passing and receiving information. Among the most common neurotransmitters are dopamine, serotonin, acetylcholine, and norepinephrine.

Several neurotransmitters play major roles in emotional control. For example, when norepinephrine is lacking, the individual tends to slide into a state of depression. If serotonin is in short supply, the person becomes overly aggressive or even violent. Individuals who do not have enough dopamine tend to develop insatiable behavior that causes them always to want more. Dopamine regulates attention span and also brain functions during moments of stress. When acetylcholine is limited, long-term memory is erratic and unpredictable. Recent research has verified that attention deficit disorders are often linked to low levels of dopamine (Ratey & Johnson, 1997). Cortical stimulant medications such as Ritalin and Cylert increase the level of dopamine in the brain, which causes a reduction in symptoms of attention deficits.

The Bloodstream

A second source of body information constantly sends other types of data to the brain. The bloodstream bathes and feeds each of the several billion cells in the human body. The bloodstream carries enzyme messages, hormone cues, and body chemistry data from internal organs and individual cells to the brain, then from the brain back to organs and cells. The bloodstream supplements the central nervous system as an information highway, supplying new data to the brain and taking chemical messages back to all the body parts (Damasio, 1994).

How the Brain Processes New Information

Limbic System Filtering

As the midbrain receives new data from nerve pathways, specialized regions of the limbic system filter out irrelevant information and make decisions about where to send new data that the brain needs to receive. At the same time, these limbic system organs discard unnecessary data that the higher brain does not need. Figure 1.3 illustrates how the midbrain distributes this filtered information. Much of the new data goes first to the parietal lobes in the middle of each brain hemisphere. The parietal lobes are relay stations that gather new information and send it to other regions of the brain that specialize in interpreting and using that kind of knowledge. New data that relates to body movement goes to the motor cortex. Information related to body sensations is sent to the sensory cortex. New information that involves visual perception goes to the occipital lobe. Data that pertains to spoken language is sent to the temporal lobes. Information related to higher thinking is dispatched to the frontal lobes (Damasio, 1994; Schacter, 1996). Persons with attention deficits and disruptive behaviors do not have consistent filtering within their limbic systems. Too much unnecessary information slips through the midbrain screen into higher regions of the brain. That irrelevant data triggers distraction, confusion, and mistakes in perception and decision making.

Coordinated Firing Rhythms

Brain research during the 1990s discovered that all neurological transactions happen very quickly in a series of firing rhythms that carry new data in precisely timed waves throughout the brain. Neurologists speak of *timing* as neurons fire their messages down axon pathways (Damasio, 1994). Brain research conducted by Nancy Kopell, Christof Koch, Charles Gray, Gyorgy Buzsaki, and others has produced a new model of how the brain times its sending and receiving of information along neuronal pathways (Blakeslee, 1995). If these timing sequences become irregular or off schedule, the brain becomes confused

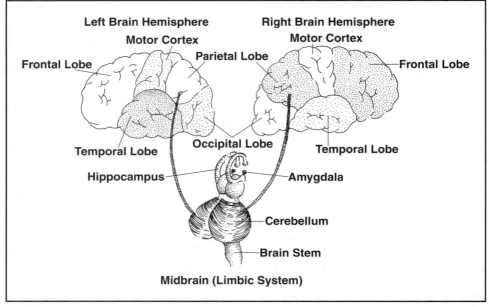

Left Brain Hemisphere
Motor Cortex
Parietal Lobe
Frontal Lobe

Right Brain Hemisphere
Motor Cortex
Frontal Lobe

Occipital Lobe
Temporal Lobe
Temporal Lobe

Hippocampus ── **Amygdala**

── **Cerebellum**

── **Brain Stem**

Midbrain (Limbic System)

Figure 1.3. After new information reaches the brain stem, it is quickly filtered and sorted by the cerebellum, amygdala, and hippocampus. Unnecessary data is filtered out and discarded. Necessary information is organized, then sent on to the parietal lobes in the right and left brain hemispheres. From there the new data is distributed to the temporal lobes, occipital lobes, frontal lobes, or motor cortex for final interpretation.

and cannot complete its work. In attention deficit disorders, firing sequence and timing of brain transmissions are unpredictable and off schedule.

During the mid-1990s, Rodolfo Llinas (1993) measured the speed of cell firing in the brain stem. His research estimated that cells within the brain stem fire at the rate of 10 cycles per second. Llinas described this rhythm of cell firing as a "fluid motion" that transmits data in a steady, continuous stream to other midbrain regions, such as the cerebellum (Blakeslee, 1995). Llinas and his colleague Urs Ribary also measured a different rate of cell firing in regions of the cerebral cortex in the left and right brain hemispheres. During deep sleep, the cerebral cortex cells fire at the slow rate of 2 cycles per second. During moments when the brain is daydreaming or "coasting along in neutral," the cerebral cortex cells fire at a somewhat faster rate of 10 cycles per second. When the brain is wide awake or dreaming vividly, the cell firing rate increases to 40 cycles per second. These 40-cycle-per-second waves sweep the brain from front to back the way that radar sweeps the atmosphere in weather forecasting. Llinas and Ribary estimate that these bursts of cell firing occur every 12.5-thousandths of a second (Blakeslee, 1995). Later chapters describe how attention deficit disorders interrupt these brain wave cycles. We now know that learning disabilities and attention deficit disorders are related to differences in how the central nervous system receives and processes new information.

Right Brain Monitors Left Brain

During the 1980s, several scientists reported evidence that regions of the right brain keep track of what occurs while the left brain processes language information. For example, Erin Zaidel at the University of California in Los Angeles described the "Oops center" he had found in the right brain sensory cortex (Zaidel & Zaidel, 1979). This right brain center monitors language usage by the left brain. Even though the right brain is "illiterate" (does not read words), the "Oops center" signals the left brain when a mistake has been made in spelling, sentence structure, punctuation, and other errors in language usage or in reading. Zaidel's research explained how children develop self-correcting skills as they reach certain developmental milestones in academic learning. As the brain matures, the right brain becomes the "editor" that helps the left brain spot its mistakes and correct them. In attention deficit disorders and learning disabilities such as dyslexia, this right brain monitoring is incomplete. Individuals with ADHD, ADD, and dyslexia often do not recognize their own errors and, hence, do not self-correct, because links between the right brain and left brain are incompletely developed.

Balance of Positive and Negative Emotions

In his research with brain-damaged stroke patients, Vilayanur Ramachandran (1993) at the University of California in San Diego discovered how the right brain "keeps the left brain honest" in interpreting emotions and feelings generated by events in one's life. In a general way, the left brain regulates positive, optimistic emotions and attitudes. In contrast, the right brain deals with negative interpretations of life events. The right brain scans the environment to identify negative or potentially harmful events, while the left brain seeks out positive events that will benefit the individual. When positive and negative emotions are in good balance, the brain sees both optimistic and pessimistic factors realistically so that persons do not overinterpret life in either emotional direction.

Unidentified Bright Objects

When individuals have difficulty keeping positive and negative feelings and emotions in balance, brain scans often show bright spots along axon pathways. These bright spots are called unidentified bright objects (UBOs). These UBOs appear to be breaks in the myelin sheath that surrounds axon segments. When the myelin sheath is broken, brain fluids seep into the axon pathway, the way moisture enters electrical lines through broken insulation. UBOs create "short circuits" along axon pathways, causing incomplete processing of information and thought patterns. Ramachandran has charted the influence of right-brain lesions seen in brain scans of stroke patients who develop an unbalanced emotional state called *anosognosia*. These individuals live in a state of denial regarding their physical disabilities caused by stroke. Anosognosia disrupts the monitoring relationship between right-brain realism and left-brain optimism. During the phase of anosognosia, persons who are paralyzed on the left side deny that they have any physical impairment. This interrupted connection between brain hemispheres makes it impossible for the right brain to "keep the left brain honest" in interpreting emotions and feelings about what is happening in an individual's life.

How the Brain Remembers

Inner Voice

Damasio (1994), Schacter (1996), and others have described how the brain builds memory images of what we have experienced, learned, dreamed, or imagined. Beginning in early childhood, the brain develops an *inner voice* that permits a type of inside-brain communication. In a way, the brain regions talk to each other. In 1977 Jacob Bronowski developed an intriguing model of how this "brain language" separates human beings from animals. Bronowski believed that before the brain sends action signals to the rest of the body, various brain regions hold a "mental language conference" that forces a pause between impulse and action. During this pause for mental conversation, regions of the brain that do logical reasoning confer with other brain regions that control emotion and feeling. According to Bronowski's model, a mature brain with a good balance between logic and emotion quickly comes to reasonable, commonsense conclusions that take into account the consequences of any action. This brain network conversation asks: "If we do this, what will be the consequences? If we don't do this, then what will be the consequences?" In milliseconds the brain decides on the safest, most reasonable course of action. Signals then are sent to activate the body to carry out that internal decision or to refrain from doing so.

Chapter 2 describes Russell Barkley's new definition of ADHD (Attention-Deficit/Hyperactivity Disorder), which is based upon Bronowski's model of inner brain conversation. According to Barkley's point of view, attention deficit disorder is caused when the brain cannot carry on the inner voice dialogues proposed by Bronowski. When this mental voice deficit is mild or moderate, attention deficit disorders occur. When the inner voice deficit is extreme, oppositional-defiant behavior and conduct disorders arise.

The Noisy Brain

In their book *Shadow Syndromes,* John Ratey and Catherine Johnson (1997) describe the "noisy brain" that chatters on and on and cannot be still. When the brain cannot stop talking to itself, the individual is handicapped by a life-long inability to pay full attention to the outside world. Ratey and Johnson demonstrate how the noisy brain that never stops chattering is the cause of a variety of dysfunctions, including obsessive/compulsive disorder, intense self-focus that may evolve into narcissism, or even chronic depression that causes the person to withdraw into a self-contained private world of noisy emotional misery. Chapter 6 describes how medication can help to rid the brain of excess noise so that the inner voice can function without distraction.

Emotional Memory

The brain's inner voice plays a major role in how the central nervous system recalls knowledge and builds memory images. When old information must be recalled, the left frontal lobe searches its database and locates part of that knowledge. At the same time, other regions throughout the brain conduct their own search for data that is related to the information the frontal lobe is activating. However, the brain never simply calls up facts or figures as a computer does. Commands for memory material also activate emotions and feelings that were present when that event occurred, or when that old information was first encountered.

In his book *Searching for Memory*, Schacter (1996) documents the impact that emotions and feelings have on the memory images brought forth by various brain regions. As new information enters the brain, that data is segmented into codes that are stored throughout the brain in specialized neuron clusters. These neuron clusters, called *engrams*, are like computer memory chips that hold analog or binary code patterns for future use. Every bit of information the brain receives is encoded in a series of interconnected engrams that are scattered throughout the right and left brain hemispheres (see Figure 1.3). When the brain needs to activate any stored information, a locater signal is broadcast in waves throughout the brain. Those engrams holding portions of that data become active and form a neurological network that brings that mental image alive. If the original event related to the emerging memory was peaceful, then the brain reproduces a peaceful mental image. If the original event was traumatic or threatening, then the brain brings up an image that is colored by strong emotions and urgent feelings (Damasio, 1994; Schacter, 1996).

Changes in Memory

Contrary to popular belief about the accuracy of human memory, the brain never recreates the same memory image twice. Each time the brain develops memory images of knowledge or experience, the new image differs somewhat from other times when that event or set of facts was recalled (Damasio, 1994; Schacter, 1996). Ratey and Johnson (1997), Schacter (1996), Damasio (1994), and others have described how strong emotions that are governed by the amygdala in the midbrain, and higher emotions that are governed by the left frontal lobe, change with time. As persons mature and become wiser, or as individuals fail to mature or become neurotic, emotions and feelings linked to early experiences change. Memory images evoked at age 14 are often quite different from memories of those same events when one is age 40 or 55. There is much evidence that memory cannot be held to fully logical or factually correct standards. As we call up memory images of past events, those recollections may be no more historically or factually accurate than the symbolic images of a dream.

A classic example of how memories of the same event vary in retelling is found in the New Testament accounts of the Apostle Paul's miraculous conversion on the road to Damascus. Paul tells this story five times in his New Testament writings, and each time he tells the story somewhat differently. This kind of changing of the story each time it is recalled is exactly how the brain handles old information. As Damasio (1994) and Schacter (1996) have demonstrated, it is never possible for individuals to remember situations the same way twice. Attention deficit disorders make it even more difficult for ADHD or ADD individuals to recall what they know without cluttering the story, scrambling the sequence, or leaving out important parts of the original event. This variation of memory is not lying, as critics often declare when ADHD or ADD individuals tell their stories differently. The brain and emotions reproduce different versions of old events, depending on the feelings experienced when the original event took place, as well as maturational changes that occur as the individual grows older.

Memory and Attention Deficit

This new understanding of how the brain learns and remembers greatly enhances our understanding of the impact of attention deficit disorders, learning disabilities, obsessive/compulsive behavior, and other types of socially disruptive lifestyles. As later chapters describe, difficulties in learning and remembering become strongly emotional events for struggling learners, classmates, teachers, and families. The more negative the first learning event was, the more unsettling and unreliable each future memory of that event will be. In the book *Overcoming Dyslexia in Children, Adolescents, and Adults,* I have described patterns of school phobias, panic attack, and chronic anxiety that many struggling learners display when asked to do schoolwork (Jordan, 1996a). Schacter (1996), Damasio (1994), Ratey and Johnson (1997), and others have demonstrated how strong emotions, that are largely controlled by the amygdala in the limbic system, and feelings that cause tightness of the chest and contractions of the digestive tract, actively block the brain's work in individuals who have attention deficit disorder.

Family Patterns of Attention Deficit Disorder

Inherited Attention Deficit Disorder

In his book *Taking Charge of ADHD,* Russell Barkley (1995) summarized the findings of research into attention deficit disorder since the early 1970s. In reviewing more than 7,000 published reports, Barkley found consensus among scientists that attention deficits tend to run down family lines. In 1990 Joseph Biederman and his colleagues at Massachusetts General Hospital reported that if a child has ADHD, his blood relatives are 500% more likely also to have ADHD than the non-ADHD population (Biederman, Faraone, Keenan, & Knee, 1990). In their comprehensive study of twins, Jacquelyn Gillis and her associates at the University of Colorado discovered that if one identical twin has ADHD, the other twin also has ADHD 79% of the time. If one fraternal twin has ADHD, the other twin is 32% likely also to have ADHD (Gillis, Gilger, Pennington, & Defries, 1992). At least two genetic markers linked to the heritability of attention deficit disorder have been identified: chromosomes 6 and 15 (Gillis et al., 1992; Jordan, 1996a). These genetic markers are also linked to dyslexia. Later chapters describe the frequent presence of learning disabilities, including dyslexia, when ADHD exists.

Lifestyle of ADHD Families

In reviewing 25 years of research of ADHD, Barkley (1995) found evidence that adults with ADHD drink more alcohol than non-ADHD adults. Women who have ADHD are more likely to drink alcohol during pregnancy than non-ADHD mothers. Adults with ADHD are more likely to smoke cigarettes in the home or while driving the family car than non-ADHD adults. Children born into families who frequently smoke and drink are more likely to be hyperactive and have problems with controlling attention. Research since the 1970s also shows a much higher rate of attention deficit disorders in low-birthweight children, even those who are delivered at or near due dates. The mother's nutrition during pregnancy, especially during the first trimester, is linked to attention deficit in children. Decisions by mothers to smoke, drink alcohol, consume too much caffeine, or eat nutritionally imbalanced foods during pregnancy increase the likelihood that the child will develop attention deficit symptoms early in life, or later when the stress of formal education is encountered (Barkley, 1995; Jordan, 1996a).

Attention-Deficit/ Hyperactivity Disorder Individuals

2

> *I often wonder if people without ADHD have any real idea of the amount of energy one with ADHD expends in just keeping above the tidal flood of their minds. When one's thoughts change faster than the stock market. The work of just writing a letter that begins to make sense. Of sitting down and trying to study and learn. People without ADHD think they have it hard. Let them trade places with me for a week. They couldn't handle it for a day, let alone a week.*
>
> —Robert Vaughan, who has lived 42 years with ADHD

Chapter 1 described how the twentieth century opened with confusion about disruptive learners who could not settle down, pay attention, or obey the rules. At the turn of this century, scientists faced a thicket of impressions about the nature of attention deficits, poor decision making, and inappropriate social behaviors. As the twentieth century moved forward, neurologists and educators began to separate the overlapping branches of the thicket surrounding the issue of attention deficit disorders. Technology that was developed during the last half of the twentieth century revealed the underlying neurological and biochemical reasons why 5% (Barkley, 1995) to 13% (Jordan, 1992, 1996a) of the general population have chronic difficulty maintaining attention and following through on tasks without supervision.

Two Branches of Attention Deficit

Although the twentieth century began with just a thicket of impressions regarding attention deficit disorders, the century is ending with a more clearly defined tree of knowledge about this socially disruptive syndrome. The invisible roots of poor attention lie below the surface of an ADHD individual's behavior. Brain imaging science provides a clear view of these root causes of ADHD within the central nervous system. From the neurological root structure of inattention grows a determined stem or trunk that supports two main branches of this disorder. One branch is constantly in motion. It trembles, shakes, and rustles noisily so that observers do not miss the fact that behavioral and attentional problems exist. This branch in motion has been labeled in numerous ways: "deficit in moral control," minimal brain damage, minimal brain dysfunction, ADD+H (Attention Deficit Disorder with Hyperactivity), and ADHD (Attention-Deficit/ Hyperactivity Disorder). The other branch of the inattention tree is quiet and passive so that observers often do not readily recognize an underlying problem with attention control. In fact, many specialists believe that this nonhyperactive branch should be removed from the ADHD tree because it seems to belong to another species of behavioral difference. Chapter 3 explores this passive form of inattention that arises from the same root system that produces ADHD.

What Is ADHD?

There is no simple answer to the question "What is ADHD?" ADHD is many things, all of which trigger disruptions in personal relationships, workplace performance, classroom learning, and group activities. ADHD has many faces so that what appears in one situation might not be seen in different circumstances. ADHD occurs at different levels of severity. The following severity scale shows the range of ADHD symptoms an individual might display.

1 2 3 4 5 6 7 8 9 10
mild   moderate severe

Mild ADHD   This individual displays some, but not all, of the faces of ADHD presented below. He or she becomes restless soon after starting a task. Body motion emerges and increases after a few minutes. The individual fails to comprehend all that he or she hears. Reading comprehension is spotty and unpredictable. The mildly ADHD individual must be reminded to stay on task or to finish what is started. With supervision and reminding, this person can finish tasks and make good grades in school. This individual can succeed in the workplace if enough supervision is given. At the mild level, ADHD is more a nuisance than a serious problem. The mildly ADHD individual can develop self-reminder strategies so that he or she can finish tasks without always needing outside help.

Moderate ADHD   This person continually displays most of the faces of ADHD presented below. He or she continually jumps track and fails to follow through on tasks without frequent reminding. The moderately ADHD person must have supervision to succeed in the classroom or the workplace. With adequate supervision and guidance, he or she can succeed most of the time. This individual continually struggles in social relationships, in workplace performance, and in classroom learning. He or she lives emotionally more than logically. This person has always been regarded as "difficult," but success is possible if others show enough patience and willingness to overlook the irritating habits described below.

Severe ADHD   Persons with severe ADHD face almost impossible challenges in social relationships, classroom performance, and workplace competency. At the severe level, it is not unusual to find all of the faces of ADHD that are described below. The severely ADHD individual is a very difficult person at home, at school, at work, and in the community. This individual has volatile emotions that flare under the slightest criticism or challenge. The severely ADHD person is undependable, overly touchy and irritable, and generally irresponsible. In most instances, severely ADHD individuals become social misfits because of aggressive, self-focused, and immature behavior. As time goes by, they do not learn from their mistakes or from the advice of others.

Defining ADHD

In spite of the wealth of recent neurological insight into the root causes of ADHD, our society has failed to achieve a unified definition of this chronic difference in behavior.

DSM-IV Criteria

The most widely acknowledged current definition of ADHD is provided by the fourth edition of the *Diagnostic and Statistical Manual of Mental Disorders* (DSM-IV; American Psychiatric Association, 1994). Table 2.1 lists the criteria that DSM-IV requires for making a clinical diagnosis of ADHD. In determining the presence of ADHD, DSM-IV looks at two varieties of behavior: (1) *inattention* and (2) *hyperactivity-impulsivity*. Herein lies a problem with this point of view. The DSM-IV definition of ADHD contains two major contradictions. According to these guidelines, it is possible for a person to show inattention without being hyperactive-impulsive. In that case, the individual is labeled with the diagnostic code 314.00, Attention-Deficit/Hyperactivity Disorder, Predominantly Inattentive Type. This contradictory terminology poses problems as counselors try to

Table 2.1

The Guidelines for Diagnosis of ADHD from DSM-IV

A. Either (1) or (2):

(1) six (or more) of the following symptoms of **inattention** have persisted for at least 6 months to a degree that is maladaptive and inconsistent with developmental level:

Inattention
(a) often fails to give close attention to details or makes careless mistakes in schoolwork, work, or other activities
(b) often has difficulty sustaining attention in tasks or play activities
(c) often does not seem to listen when being spoken to directly
(d) often does not follow through on instructions and fails to finish schoolwork, chores, or duties in the workplace (not due to oppositional behavior or failure to understand instructions)
(e) often has difficulty organizing tasks and activities
(f) often avoids, dislikes, or is reluctant to engage in tasks that require sustained mental effort (such as schoolwork or homework)
(g) often loses things necessary for tasks or activities (e.g., toys, school assignments, pencils, books, or tools)
(h) is often easily distracted by extraneous stimuli
(i) is often forgetful in daily activities

(2) six or more of the following symptoms of **hyperactivity–impulsivity** have persisted for at least 6 months to a degree that is maladaptive and inconsistent with developmental level:

Hyperactivity
(a) often fidgets with hands or feet or squirms in seat
(b) often leaves seat in classroom or in other situations in which remaining seated is expected
(c) often runs about or climbs excessively in situations in which it is inappropriate (in adolescents or adults, may be limited to subjective feelings of restlessness)
(d) often has difficulty playing or engaging in leisure activities quietly
(e) is often "on the go" or often acts as if "driven by a motor"
(f) often talks excessively

Impulsivity
(g) often blurts out answers before questions have been completed
(h) often has difficulty awaiting turn
(i) often interrupts or intrudes on others (e.g., butts into conversations or games)

B. Some hyperactive–impulsive or inattentive symptoms that caused immediate impairment were present before age 7 years.

(continues)

Table 2.1. *Continued*

C. Some impairment from the symptoms is present in two or more settings (e.g., at school [or work] and at home).

D. There must be clear evidence of clinically significant impairment in social, academic, or occupational functioning.

E. The symptoms do not occur exclusively during the course of a Pervasive Developmental Disorder, Schizophrenia, or other Psychotic Disorder, and are not better accounted for by another mental disorder (e.g., Mood Disorder, Anxiety Disorder, Dissociative Disorder, or a Personality Disorder).

Code based on type:

314.01 **Attention-Deficit/Hyperactivity Disorder, Combined Type:** if both Criteria A1 and A2 are met for the past 6 months

314.00 **Attention-Deficit/Hyperactivity Disorder, Predominantly Inattentive Type:** if Criterion A1 is met but Criterion A2 is not met for the past 6 months

314.01 **Attention-Deficit/Hyperactivity Disorder, Predominantly Hyperactive–Impulsive Type:** if Criterion A2 is met but Criterion A1 is not met for the past 6 months

Coding note: For individuals (especially adolescents and adults) who currently have symptoms that no longer meet full criteria, "In Partial Remission" should be specified.

From American Psychiatric Association (1994), *Diagnostic and statistical manual of mental disorders* (4th ed.). Washington, DC: Author. Copyright 1994 by the American Psychiatric Association. Reprinted with permission.

explain to frustrated parents why their quiet, passive, inattentive child must be labeled "hyperactive." DSM-IV presents a further contradiction by labeling certain persons with code 314.01, Attention-Deficit/Hyperactivity Disorder, Predominantly Hyperactive-Impulsive Type. Again counselors face the challenge of explaining how a hyperactive-impulsive child can be placed in the attention deficit category if he or she does not pass the test for inattention. DSM-IV has not yet achieved a clear enough definition of the hyperactive branch of the attention deficit tree.

ADHD: Poor Self-Regulation

Among the scientists who are dissatisfied with the DSM-IV definition of ADHD is Russell Barkley at the University of Massachussets Medical Center. Since the early 1980s he has insisted that the problem of ADHD is more than, or possibly different from, lack of attention control. In 1990 Barkley and his colleagues documented the frequent overlap (comorbidity) of different types of disruptive behavior that were often seen with the diagnosis of ADHD (Barkley, Spitzer, & Costello, 1990). Barkley's research indicated that 65% of those diagnosed as ADHD also display symptoms of Opposition Defiant Disorder. Barkley also found that another type of disruptive behavior, Conduct Disorder, accompanies ADHD 30% of the time. These syndromes are described in Chapter 5 (see pages 97–103).

As he and his colleagues continued to separate the branches of the thicket surrounding attention problems, Barkley developed a definition of ADHD that was not based on inattention as such. In his book *Taking Charge of ADHD,* Barkley (1995) presented a new model for understanding this form of disruptive behavior:

> ADHD probably is not primarily a disorder of paying attention but one of *self-regulation:* how the self comes to manage itself within the larger realm of social behavior. ADHD is . . . a disturbance in the child's ability to use self-control with regard to the future . . . an inability to use a sense of time and of the past and future to guide . . . behavior. What is not developing properly . . . is the capacity to shift from focusing on the here and now to focusing on the future. (p. viii–ix)

This point of view recognizes the major difficulty that ADHD persons have over time in coping with workplace requirements, classroom expectations, family responsibilities, personal relationships, and community standards for public behavior. If the individual is "time blind," he or she cannot see the past, present, and future as a logical sequence or unbroken continuum. Because of this chronic deficit in comprehending time, ADHD individuals cannot develop appropriate behavior to fit into society without disruption. Being "time blind" is much more crippling than simply not paying attention well enough.

ADHD Individuals Cannot Wait

A major component of Barkley's model of ADHD is what he has called *disinhibition.* By this Barkley and his colleagues mean that the ADHD individual cannot wait. Chapter 1 (see page 14) reviewed Jacob Bronowski's concept of "brain language," which permits the frontal lobes, where logical thinking originates, to communicate with the rest of the brain in making decisions. A major component of Bronowski's model was the critical role of time (taking time before deciding) that this brain language plays. Bronowski reasoned that before acting, the brain regions conduct a rapid conversation in which the consequences of each possible action are considered. This brain conversation inserts time into the decision-making process. By pausing before acting, the brain follows logic more than emotion. The individual whose brain conducts this intrabrain communication lives by logical reasoning instead of acting on impulse.

Disinhibition

Barkely's model of ADHD is based on Bronowski's notion that the mature brain takes time to pause and reflect before acting. The ADHD brain does not. An unfortunate factor in ADHD is the tendency for individuals to act on impulse instead of pausing to consider consequences. This impulsive lifestyle (disinhibition) does not separate facts from feelings, according to Barkley's model of ADHD. This impulsive ADHD person does not develop a sense of past, present, and future that guides most individuals in making choices and decisions. Disinhibition keeps ADHD persons from learning from their mistakes. Each new impulse arises anew with no automatic logical link to past experience. Barkley insists that impulsivity (disinhibition) is the root problem with ADHD, not short attention span.

The Many Faces of ADHD

Like a diamond, ADHD has many faces that often seem to change as they are viewed in different situations. Individuals who are severely ADHD often display each of the following faces, especially when they are under pressure to perform or to maintain self-control. In moderate ADHD, persons may display only some of those faces, depending on the situation. In mild ADHD, it is not unusual for individuals to hide their poor attentional patterns for brief periods of time. To see ADHD clearly, we must look at severe manifestations of each of the following faces of attention disorder. Moderate or mild ADHD displays these tendencies at less disruptive levels.

ADHD Individuals Are Too Noisy

Chapter 1 presented John Ratey and Catherine Johnson's concept (1997) of "the noisy brain." This model of ADHD is based on the fact that the ADHD brain is filled with "noise" that is similar to static in an overloaded radio broadcast. The noisy brain is never quiet. Chapter 1 described the brain's inner voice, which carries on a kind of dialogue, enabling the many brain centers to communicate. In the ADHD brain, this inner voice does not stay quiet long enough to listen well. The overly verbal (hyperlexic) brain fails to pay attention to important new data that enters from the limbic system. The overly talkative brain attends to bits and pieces of data instead of hearing complete streams of new information. Without waiting to process the full incoming message, the noisy brain jumps to conclusions before all the data is in. The overly verbal ADHD brain continually makes mistakes in judgment because the chattering inner voice interrupts the frontal lobe as it tries to think things through. The noisy brain becomes sidetracked by emotions and feelings that surge beyond normal levels. The voice of the ADHD brain clamors on and on, demanding immediate action instead of becoming still enough to think things through from start to finish. Cascades of emotion overwhelm logic, triggering impulsive behavior that does not think of consequences. Decisions are based on part of the evidence because the brain is talking too much to hear the rest of the story. The motor cortex sends premature signals that create inappropriate body activity. The ADHD brain talks too much, keeps the body in constant motion, and over-reacts with stronger emotions than the situation demands.

ADHD Individuals Are Too Quickly Bored

Low Brain Sugar Metabolism and Slow Blood Flow

Barkley (1995), Jordan (1992, 1996a), and Ratey and Johnson (1997) have described the disruptive impact of boredom in ADHD behavior. Among class-room teachers, it is common knowledge that children with attention deficits display boredom much sooner and more often than classmates who have long attention spans. Parents of ADHD youngsters struggle to keep restless ones focused from start to finish on routine homework and chores. In his book *Descartes' Error,* Damasio (1994) documents the powerful influence of the left frontal lobe (prefrontal cortex) on how long the brain pays attention before shifting to another issue. The ADHD brain shows deficits in prefrontal cortex functions. Chapter 1 reviewed the importance of firing rhythms as brain systems coordinate thinking and deciding (see pages 11–13). Llinas discovered that the wide awake, fully alert frontal cortex fires at the rate of 40 cycles per second (Blakeslee, 1995). When blood flow and sugar metabolism fall below normal rates, the firing rhythm in the frontal cortex drops below 40 cycles per second. This reduction in firing rhythm sets off a chain reaction that produces sluggish communication between brain regions.

Figure 2.1 shows the region of the frontal lobe (superior prefrontal cortex) where the ADHD brain metabolizes sugar too slowly. This discovery by Alan Zametkin and his colleagues helped to explain why persons with ADHD do not maintain focused attention for longer than brief periods of time (Zametkin, Nordahl, Gross, Semple, Rumsey, Hamburger, & Cohen, 1990). Added to the problems of low blood sugar metabolism and slower firing rhythm is the factor of slow blood flow in the superior prefrontal cortex and the premotor cortex (Figure 2.1). Frank Wood (1991) at Bowman-Gray School of Medicine has doc-umented how slow blood flow robs the higher brain of its normal energy sup-ply. This combination of low sugar metabolism, slow blood flow, and slow firing rhythm creates a condition called *underarousal.* Underarousal is much like becoming drowsy when one is driving a car or sitting still during a lecture. As the sleepy driver or drowsy listener starts to nap, the body jerks to wake up the sluggish person. A similar "wake-up call" sweeps the sleepy ADHD brain. To overcome low energy levels caused by low blood sugar metabolism, the motor cortex fires signals to muscle systems to make the body active. This "wake-up call" is sent over and over when the frontal cortex begins to fall asleep. Hyperactive behavior of many ADHD persons is the brain's way of making up for irregular sugar metabolism and blood flow.

Underarousal and Boredom

A disruptive by-product of underarousal in the left frontal lobe is quick boredom. The sluggish frontal lobe of the ADHD brain must have frequent stimulation to stay alert. As the frontal lobe loses interest, the brain searches for a more exciting, interesting, or faster moving activity. This is why ADHD learners soon become restless and wiggly doing passive paper-and-pencil activities. The understimulated brain needs more excitement, so attention shifts from the task that has become too passive and boring to another event that engages the whole body in movement and new excitement. Looking around to see what others are doing, along with heavy yawning, stimulates the brain more than continuing to solve arithmetic problems. Squirming in the chair or standing up stimulates the brain more than sitting quietly. Going across the room to the pencil sharpener is much more interesting than continuing to sit still. Looking

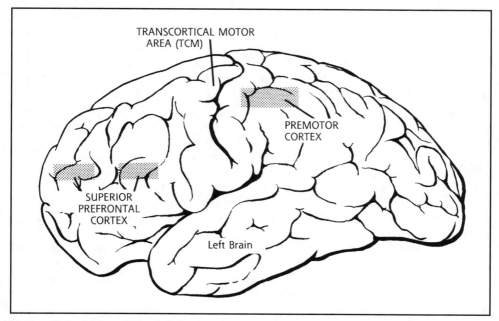

Figure 2.1. Areas of the left brain where sugar usage (brain glucose metabolism) is lower in persons who have ADHD than in those who do not have ADHD patterns. (Based on the model reported by Alan Zametkin et al., 1990.)

out the window brings the brain more stimulation than staring at a book page or worksheet on the desk. Stopping to play with a ball is more exciting than carrying out trash. As the ADHD brain becomes bored, the person's attention seeks out more interesting and stimulating activity.

ADHD Individuals Are Aggressive

Perhaps the most disruptive face of ADHD is aggressive behavior. Inner drives that push the ADHD person into hyperactivity also cause the ADHD brain to ignore the privacy of others. As most individuals mature, they learn to look for boundaries that mark the privacy of others. In a society that is governed by rules of politeness, most young children begin to notice social signals that say they should stop and not press further. Everyone has a natural need for privacy inside a personal inner space. Individuals who are very private, even shy, must have a wide boundary zone that keeps others at a distance. Persons who need a lot of privacy give many signals that they want to be left alone, or that they must know ahead of time when someone plans to enter their private space. Outgoing people who talk a lot and want to be with others have much less need for privacy. Yet everyone sets limits on when outsiders are welcome to come into personal private space. Children are taught to recognize privacy signals to know when they are welcome to come close, or when they should back away and leave others alone. During early childhood most youngsters learn to read privacy signals in the faces of adults and older siblings. A warm smile means "Come on in. You are welcome." A stern face, or a frown, means "Stay out of my space right now. You are not welcome." Body language sends clear signals that invite others in or warn others to stay outside private space. Arms crossed over the chest with the body standing stiffly or slightly turned away send the message "Don't come near me right now." Arms open and moving with the body standing in a relaxed way tell others that the gate is open and they are welcome to enter private territory. A stern unemotional voice sends the signal to stay away. A warm, affectionate voice welcomes outsiders to come in.

The ADHD brain that is driven by churning emotions and hyperactive mental images does not read these and other privacy signals. Impulsive ADHD individuals bound through closed gates, intruding into private space with no regard to the nonverbal signals to stay out. Individuals with ADHD are aggressive and intrusive. The ADHD brain does not learn the nonverbal language of reading social signals. This aggressive tendency quickly irritates and offends others who wish to be left alone. ADHD aggression triggers resentment toward the hyperactive intruder, setting off a cascade of negative emotions that turn encounters into confrontations. Teachers, employers, and relatives of ADHD individuals must deal continually with disruptions caused by aggressive, thoughtless disregard for the privacy of others. ADHD behavior includes social blindness, often referred to as "social dyslexia," that does not read the signals that guide polite relationships.

ADHD Individuals Are Too Easily Distracted

It is impossible for the ADHD brain to ignore what goes on nearby. Attention darts to nearby movement to see what is happening. An ADHD person's attention leaps toward every new sound to find out what is going on. Any unusual odor is an irresistible attraction that must be explored. Visceral signals that air temperature has changed capture the brain's attention, jerking it away from the task before finishing. Pressure of clothing on the thighs or buttocks triggers squirming and tugging that cannot be postponed. An itch starts somewhere on the skin and must be scratched. The eyes glimpse something on the edge of vision, and the head turns to examine that new visual image. An ear picks up a sound that draws the brain's attention to that new event. Feelings emerge inside the body as gas bubbles work through the digestive tract or a belch erupts. These visceral feelings cannot be ignored. Anything new or different in the ADHD person's environment calls for immediate investigation. The ADHD brain cannot ignore interesting or exciting temptations to abandon tasks that have become boring.

ADHD Individuals Are Poor Listeners

ADHD individuals cannot stay on track when listening. When a flow of new oral information comes their way, they cannot absorb the full message. Only bits and pieces of what the ADHD person hears moves from the hippocampus, where long-term memory begins, into higher brain regions where permanent memory is established (see Figure 1.1). When a listening experience is over, the ADHD person clamors, "What? What did you say? Tell me again." Later the ADHD listener claims, "You didn't tell me that!" or "I didn't hear you say that." As a rule, the ADHD brain absorbs and retains less than 30% of oral information the first time it comes through listening (Jordan, 1992, 1996a).

ADHD Individuals Are Unable To Finish What They Start

An earmark of ADHD is the trail of unfinished tasks and projects that are continually left behind. ADHD persons seldom finish what they start without repeated reminding and close supervision. Classroom assignments are started but seldom finished. Household chores are begun but invariably are left uncompleted. The first line of math problems is worked accurately, but the rest of the page is left unfinished. The first few items on a worksheet are done well, but the rest of the page is left blank. Yet ADHD individuals insist that they finished their work. Many arguments erupt when adults ask why work was not finished, and the ADHD worker responds, "I did too finish. You always blame me for not finishing. I did all of it!" Figures 2.2 and 2.3 show examples of how

ADHD interrupts math assignments. Students with ADHD are seldom aware when their attention leaves a task. The stimulation of jumping to a new track erases the short-term memory of laying aside an old task that has become too boring and uninteresting.

ADHD Individuals Are Impulsive

One of the major tasks of the higher brain is to control impulses that are generated by regions of the midbrain. The brain stem, amygdala, medulla, and basal ganglia are the first brain regions to deal with high-energy issues that demand immediate satisfaction. As new, unfiltered visceral and environmental information enters the midbrain, a lot of stimulating, exciting possibilities clamor for the higher brain's attention. Odors that signal something pleasant or unpleasant call out for immediate response. New sounds that promise interesting relief from the now-boring task demand investigation. A nearby comment is so enticing that the listener simply must reply. An invitation from friends to go do something exciting cannot be postponed. As these calls for action enter the brain, the frontal cortex has the responsibility to say no. The frontal cortex is the higher brain's logical adult to the limbic system's emotional child. In its logical way, the frontal cortex must maintain control over the midbrain's whims and impulses if the person is to live a self-regulated life.

$$
\begin{array}{cccccc}
\begin{array}{r} 1 \\ +3 \\ \hline 4 \end{array} &
\begin{array}{r} 5 \\ +4 \\ \hline 9 \end{array} &
\begin{array}{r} 47 \\ +\ 2 \\ \hline \end{array} &
\begin{array}{r} 7 \\ +9 \\ \hline 14 \end{array} &
\begin{array}{r} 66 \\ +\ 4 \\ \hline \end{array} &
\begin{array}{r} 86 \\ +29 \\ \hline 115 \end{array}
\end{array}
$$

Figure 2.2. Math assignment of a 14-year-old boy who has ADHD. Although he intended to finish the addition problems when he skipped them, he became distracted and failed to do so. He turned in his paper thinking that he had finished the assignment.

$$
\begin{array}{cccccc}
\begin{array}{r} 5 \\ -3 \\ \hline 2 \end{array} &
\begin{array}{r} 8 \\ -2 \\ \hline 6 \end{array} &
\begin{array}{r} 76 \\ -12 \\ \hline 64 \end{array} &
\begin{array}{r} 14 \\ -\ 6 \\ \hline 12 \end{array} &
\begin{array}{r} 25 \\ -16 \\ \hline 11 \end{array} &
\begin{array}{r} 370 \\ -\ 82 \\ \hline 312 \end{array}
\end{array}
$$

Figure 2.3. Math work of a 10-year-old girl who has ADHD. She began to subtract, and then became distracted. When she returned to her work, she did not notice the subtraction signs. By this time, she was too confused and disorganized to think clearly. To fill the answer spaces, she partly added and partly subtracted the remaining problems.

In the ADHD brain, the frontal cortex cannot stay in charge of the emotional appeals from the limbic system. As the frontal cortex loses these internal arguments, emotions and impulses take control of the ADHD person's behavior. He or she does not think of consequences as tasks are abandoned and the person's attention darts off to a more interesting or exciting venture.

ADHD Individuals Are Poor Organizers

In their book *Driven to Distraction,* Edward Hallowell and John Ratey (1994a) tell many stories of disruptions that occur in personal relationships, the workplace, and within families because of poor organizational habits in ADHD. The ADHD brain does not develop a comprehensive sense of when things are organized or remain disorganized. Individuals with ADHD do not notice when things are out of order or in the wrong place. Parts of a situation do not fit together into a complete organized mental image. An ADHD child does not see when his or her room is jumbled and overly cluttered. Most ADHD adults drive messy vehicles that are littered with trash the driver rarely tidies up. An ADHD employee works in a messy space with job stuff scattered around or loosely piled in overflowing stacks. An ADHD student is unaware that his or her locker and desk are crammed with old papers, lunch wrappers, and clothing from last season. The ADHD brain does not see a mess. Persons with ADHD perceive only one or two individual items at a time. They do not form a mental image that work space, living areas, or vehicle interiors are cluttered and disarrayed. Those who are ADHD live in a cluttered, untidy world without a clue that they are guilty of disorganization. They are bewildered when their unorganized lifestyle frustrates and irritates others. Being untidy seems normal to most ADHD persons who see no problem with being poorly organized. They do not understand why their scattered lifestyle drives parents, teachers, employers, lovers, and friends to distraction.

ADHD Individuals Are Too Emotional

Chapter 1 reviewed Damasio's and Schacter's discoveries of the link between strong emotions and attention deficits (Damasio, 1994; Schacter, 1996). Figure 1.1 shows the midbrain structures that regulate the rise and flow of strong emotions (see page 7). In young children who do not have ADHD, the emotion centers of the limbic system (amygdala, basal ganglia, pons, and medulla) begin to mature during early childhood at the same time the frontal cortex gradually takes charge of the brain's emotional stability. By age 3 or 4, the prefrontal cortex has begun to exert higher emotions that govern polite social behavior, such as patience, kindness, compassion, gentleness, and foregiveness. By age 4 most children have begun to say no to strong emotions and yes to gentler emotions that make society pleasant and safe.

As children develop fluency in oral language and begin to read, they usually learn to stop urges to become angry, to cry over little bumps and bruises, or to crowd aggressively in front of others to be first in line. This development of socialization skills and control of emotional aggression lags behind schedule for ADHD youngsters. These individuals continue to have emotional eruptions that are no longer appropriate for their age. They disrupt group activities with temper tantrums when they fail to get their own way. They clamor for more when treats are given by adults. They aggressively "want what they want when they want it" without having a sense of politeness or waiting one's turn. ADHD children, adolescents, and adults deal with life on a strongly emotional level rather than staying calm and thinking things through. The prefrontal cortex lags behind in being able to remind the limbic system to stop strong emotional surges.

ADHD Individuals Are Insatiable

One of the signs of social maturity is the ability to be satisfied. The ADHD brain seldom is satisfied. Self-focused emotions yearn for more. When logical, commonsense reasoning from the frontal lobe says "That is enough for now," aggressive emotions from the limbic system struggle for more. "He got more than I did," clamors the ADHD individual. "I didn't get my fair share." "You always give my sister more than you give me," shouts the ADHD adolescent male as he starts the vehicle his parents bought for his 16th birthday. He ignores the fact that his sister had to wait until age 18 for her first car. "I'm going to quit this stupid job," grumbles the ADHD adult. "I can't ever please the boss. He always treats everyone else better than me." Jealousy is an active part of being insatiable. Envy eats away the heart of relationships as the insatiable ADHD attitude holds grudges against others. Insatiable ADHD persons display the lifestyle of grumbling, complaining, and accusing others of receiving more. "Life is not fair" could be the motto of ADHD individuals who are never satisfied. The aggressive habit of being insatiable disrupts family life, classroom environments, workplace cooperation, and personal relationships between friends and lovers.

ADHD Individuals Are Overly Sensitive

As children mature, they normally learn to welcome guidance and constructive criticism. Part of growing up should be to learn from one's mistakes and the advice offered by wiser, older persons. One of the most disruptive characteristics of ADHD is being overly sensitive to criticism. ADHD children, adolescents, and adults cannot accept criticism without reacting aggressively in self-defense. Instead of listening to advice on how to do the task better next time, the ADHD person erupts in an overly emotional protest that is designed to stop the flow of criticism. Without thinking of the consequences, the ADHD brain leaps to self-defense that involves strong argument, denial, and blaming someone else. "There you go criticizing me again!" the ADHD individual blurts out. "No matter how hard I try, you always tell me I'm wrong. You never pick on anyone else. It's not my fault." In the workplace, the ADHD employee blames equipment for ruining that piece of work. Or it is the custodian's fault for not cleaning the work area last night. Or it is the foreman's fault for changing the rules and not telling the worker. At home, parents are bombarded by aggressive verbal tirades about how the ADHD child is always the victim of another person's carelessness. In the community, an ADHD driver rails at the police officer who is issuing a speeding ticket. "It's not my fault I was going 70 miles an hour through that school zone. Someone took down the speed limit sign. Besides, you cops just pick on guys who drive four-wheel-drive trucks." In a dating relationship, the ADHD partner has a tantrum when a suggestion is made that he or she figure out a system to be on time for dates and appointments. "There you go again blaming me!" the ADHD partner yells. "It's not my fault I'm late. You just can't make up your mind when we're suppose to meet." Of all the faces of ADHD, being so overly sensitive to constructive criticism is one of the most disruptive and costly traits of poor socialization skills.

ADHD Individuals "Jump Mental Tracks"

Chapter 1 reviewed Damasio's and Schacter's descriptions of how the brain calls up old memories, adds new knowledge to old information, and thinks through new ideas (see pages 7–8). First, the limbic system sends filtered information to the parietal lobes (see Figure 1.3). From there the new data is fired to other brain regions where the information is processed. Finally the frontal lobes (prefrontal cortex) receive the refined information and supervise the brain in building engrams that hold permanent memories (Damasio, 1994; Schacter, 1996). In order for the brain to think from start to finish, attention must remain fixed on specific idea tracks. The ADHD brain cannot stay fixed on an idea track longer than a few seconds. Without warning, the ADHD listener jumps to a different track, leaving the original thought pattern unfinished. This is similar to surfing channels on a television set by holding down the change-channel button or by repeatedly pressing the change button to see another channel. Many ADHD persons jump track when their brains pick up a new signal from a word that is heard or something that is seen. For example, an ADHD individual might be listening to a conversation in which the speaker mentions "four-wheel-drive truck." Without warning the ADHD listener jumps from listening to the conversation to thinking about four-wheel-drive vehicles. The ADHD brain is now fixed on rapid images of high-energy vehicles instead of continuing to listen to the original idea track. Sometimes the ADHD listener sees something out of the corner of the eyes or whiffs a new aroma. Suddenly the brain jumps track to that visual or olfactory event. It is not unusual for an

ADHD person to begin a mental cascade of images that start on a newly trig-gered track, leap to still another track, then jump to still a different track in a rapid mental sequence. Within seconds the ADHD brain has leap-frogged far from the original mental activity, and none of the new mental processes is fin-ished. Inside the ADHD brain, countless interrupted idea tracks are started but never completed.

ADHD Individuals Have Active Fantasies

When the ADHD brain jumps away from the reality of task performance, regions of the right and left brain that host imagination take over the person's thinking. Suddenly thoughts are off into the world of fantasy or make-believe. "What if I had a four-wheel-drive truck? Especially that red one with the chrome roll bars I saw last night. Man, I would put in the biggest boom box in town. I would paint flame stripes down the sides. I would get mag wheel covers and put in purple shag upholstery. I would jack it up with the highest struts in town. Everybody would be pea-green jealous and want to ride with me. All the girls would be nice to me for a change." This type of high-energy magical thinking is commonly found in persons with ADHD. Over time, a great deal of mental energy goes into fantastical make believe instead of into the realities of life. Magical thinking or active fantasy is a highly desirable part of early childhood. Make-believe play is the first work of growing up. However, when fantasy continues to preoccupy the thoughts of older children, adolescents, and adults, the result is lost productiv-ity and separation from the rest of society.

ADHD Individuals Are Immature

Individuals who have ADHD are noticeably less mature than others their age. As a rule, intelligence is far ahead of emotional development. Most persons with ADHD are quite bright, but that intelligence is not available for consis-tent use. In an important way, ADHD individuals are upside down in their emotional maturity. The following maturity profile illustrates this frustrating imbalance between ability and behavior. The first column shows certain areas of behavior or skill level. The second column shows the age at which that skill would be measured. The third column shows what grade level this behavior or skill would fit.

Oral vocabulary age (ability to make conversation, use words correctly)	18	Adult level
Mental age (ability to do problem solving and logical thinking when the brain is fully focused)	17	12th grade
Reading age (ability to glean the full meaning of printed material)	17	12th grade

Spelling age (ability to spell words correctly from memory or dictation)	16	11th grade
Chronological age	14	9th grade
Math age (skills in arithmetic computation and number problem solving)	13	8th grade
Attention span age (how long attention can remain fully focused without jumping to another track)	8	3rd grade
Emotional maturity age (has tantrums, is self-centered, has no patience, is thoughtless, is very impulsive and overly emotional)	7	2nd grade

ADHD individuals with this kind of difference between verbal ability, intelligence, and control of basal emotions are highly disruptive in most situations. Having the oral skills of a young adult while behaving like a spoiled child sabotages all relationships and fosters a lifestyle of failure.

ADHD Individuals' "Plugs Keep Falling Out"

As I prepared to retire from private practice in the diagnosis and treatment of learning disorders, I spent a day with an 11-year-old girl with severe ADHD. Her maturity profile resembled the one above. Heather's hyperactive behavior had exhausted her parents, and her disruptive behavior kept the classroom in an uproar. Yet adults agreed that she seemed to be highly intelligent. My office was well equipped for Heather's aggressive ADHD behavior. Heavy carpet was supported by thick foam padding. Chairs were on rollers. The work table was made of solid oak lumber sturdy enough to support an elephant. A large fuzzy beanbag sat at one end of the room, ready to absorb the energy of belly flops and flying leaps. As Heather and I worked through the diagnostic tests, she rolled on the floor, dived onto the beanbag, scooted around in chairs, and lay on her back kicking the underside of the table. With this freedom to discharge excess energy, she did not miss a beat in listening and responding to test questions. At the end of the day Heather still was bursting with energy, but she had demonstrated oral language development far above her age. I could talk with her on a young adult level.

As I prepared to review the day's work with Heather's parents, I asked her to tell me what it is like to have ADHD. While performing acrobatic leaps and bounds around the office, she told me of an experience she and her brother had had the previous summer. Their grandmother had taken them to Silver Dollar City in Missouri. There the children had enjoyed reconstructions of life in the early 1900s. Heather's favorite historical display was the telephone office where a lady sat on a tall stool and plugged cords into the switchboard as she said, "Number please." Heather stopped bounding and leaping long enough to explain that having ADHD is like that old-fashioned telephone exchange. "I put in all my plugs," she said, "but my plugs keep falling out." I have never heard a better explanation of what it is like to have ADHD.

This lifestyle of mental plugs falling out explains many of the irregular patterns we see when ADHD individuals take certain kinds of tests. For example, Figure 2.4 shows the irregular, seesaw pattern of subscores on the *Weschler Intelligence Scale for Children (WISC–III)* that signals attention deficit disorder. The higher scores show where the plugs stayed in all the way through the subtest activities. The lower scores show where the student's plugs kept falling out, making it impossible for the ADHD individual to maintain full attention. Figures 2.5, 2.6, 2.7, and 2.8 show an ADHD student's irregular performances on the school's standardized achievement tests over four years time. The wide range between highest scores and lowest scores show where his plugs fell out and kept him from concentrating from start to finish on several subtests. Wide differences between top and bottom scores signal ADHD interference as the brain tries to hold mental images from start to finish.

Is ADHD Ever Outgrown?

Opinions differ strongly as to whether ADHD is ever outgrown. Scientists who develop diagnostic criteria for the American Psychiatric Association are not in full agreement on this issue. The third edition of the *Diagnostic and Statistical Manual of Mental Disorders* (DSM-III; American Psychiatric Association, 1980) included a subtype of attention deficit disorder under the code 314.80, Attention Deficit Disorder, Residual Type. Three possible diagnostic protocols were provided:

1. The individual once met the criteria for Attention Deficit Disorder with Hyperactivity.

2. Signs of hyperactivity are no longer present, but other signs of the illness have persisted to the present without periods of remission, as evidenced by signs of both attentional deficits and impulsivity (e.g., difficulty organizing work and completing tasks, difficulty concentrating, being easily distracted, making sudden decisions without thought of the consequences).

3. The symptoms of inattention and impulsivity result in some impairment in social or occupational functioning.

DSM-III did not estimate how many adults fit this residual category. The category of Attention Deficit Disorder, Residual Type, was deleted from the revised 1987 guidelines (DSM-III:R; American Psychiatric Association, 1987). However, from 1980 to 1987 the official diagnostic view of attention deficit

(*text continues on page 40*)

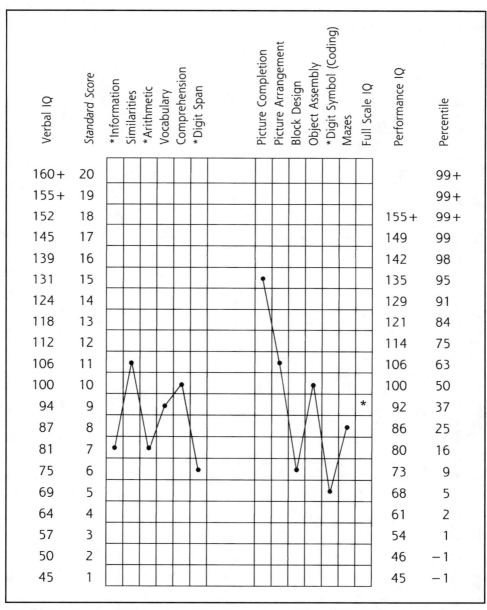

Figure 2.4. Typical ACID (sawtooth) pattern of a student with ADHD or ADD. This boy is 12 years, 8 months old in grade 6.3. He struggles in all areas of formal academic work.

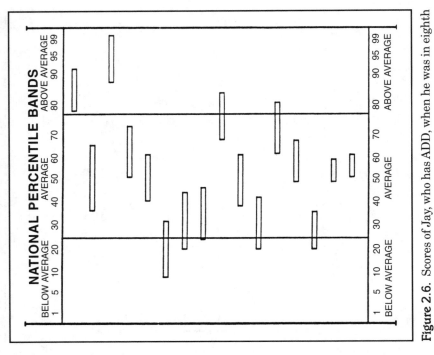

Figure 2.6. Scores of Jay, who has ADD, when he was in eighth grade.

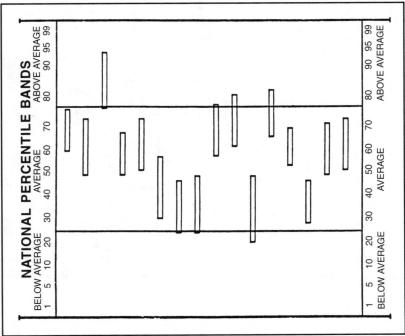

Figure 2.5. Scores of Jay, who has ADD, when he was in seventh grade.

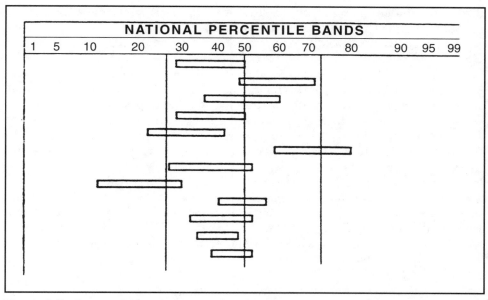

Figure 2.7. Scores of Jay, who has ADD, when he was in ninth grade.

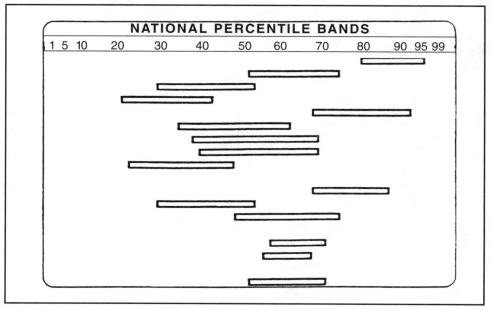

Figure 2.8. Scores of Jay, who has ADD, when he was in 10th grade.

disorder included the concept that at least some ADHD children outgrow most of their childhood or early adolescent symptoms.

Pages 20–21 describe different levels of severity of ADHD. In his book *Taking Charge of ADHD,* Barkley (1995) estimated that 70% of individuals with moderate or mild ADHD lose most of their childhood symptoms by early adult years. This reduction in ADHD symptoms permits these persons to become well-educated and productive adults. During my 40 years of professional life, I have worked one-on-one with several thousand ADHD individuals. I have remained involved in many of their lives and have met children and grandchildren of the first ADHD youngsters I met. This multigenerational experience has allowed me to observe firsthand the developmental progress of two generations of struggling learners. On reflection, I estimate that 80% of all children with mild or moderate ADHD eventually outgrow most of their early attentional deficit symptoms. Sadly, the remaining 20% of this special population emerge into their adult years still handicapped by many faces of ADHD. As Chapter 6 describes, medication often reduces negative behavior and ADHD symptoms enough to let these residual-type adults earn a moderate living and enjoy some of the blessings of adulthood. Those who do not outgrow childhood ADHD struggle all their lives with the disruptive patterns described in this chapter.

Checklist of ADHD Behaviors

Hyperactivity

_____ Excessive body activity

_____ Cannot ignore what goes on nearby

_____ Cannot say "no" to impulses

_____ Cannot leave others alone

_____ Cannot spend time alone without feeling nervous or left out

_____ Cannot keep still or stay quiet

Short Attention Span

_____ Cannot keep thoughts concentrated longer than a short period of time

_____ Continually is off on mental rabbit trails

_____ Continually must be called back to the task

Loose Thought Patterns

_____ Cannot maintain organized mental images

_____ Cannot do a series of things without starting to make mistakes

Poor Organization

_____ Cannot keep life organized without help

_____ Cannot stay on schedule without supervision

_____ Lives and works in a cluttered space

_____ Cannot straighten up own space without help

_____ Cannot do homework or silent projects without supervision

Change of First Impression

_____ First impressions do not stay the same

_____ Mental images immediately change

_____ Continually is surprised or startled as things seem different

Poor Listening Comprehension

_____ Cannot get the full meaning of what others say the first time

_____ Continually says "What?" or "What do you mean?" as speaker finishes an oral message

_____ Interrupts speaker by clamoring "What?" or 'Huh?" or "What do you mean?"

_____ Cannot follow oral instructions without hearing again

_____ Does not keep on listening

_____ Attention darts away before speaker has finished talking

_____ Later insists "You didn't say that" or "I didn't hear you say that"

Overly Sensitive

_____ Immediately has defensive reaction to criticism or correction

_____ Spends a great deal of emotional energy defending self and blaming others

_____ Flies into tantrum when criticized

_____ Jumps the gun; does not wait to receive all the information before becoming angry or defensive

_____ Leaders must spend a lot time restoring calm and soothing hurt feelings

Unfinished Tasks

_____ Does not finish any task without supervision

_____ Leaves several unfinished tasks scattered around

_____ Thinks task is finished when it is not

_____ Does not realize when more is yet to be done to finish task

Trouble Fitting In Socially

_____ Cannot fit into group situations without conflict

_____ Whines and clamors for own way

_____ Fusses about rules not being fair

_____ Storms out of game when not winning

_____ Wants to quit and do something else before others are finished

_____ Tends to be abrupt, rude, impolite in expressing opinions

_____ Is overly critical of how social events are managed

_____ Keeps conflict going over unimportant issues

_____ Displays self-centered attitude instead of noticing needs of others

_____ Is aggressive and domineering in order to get own way

Easily Distracted

_____ Attention continually darts to whatever is going on nearby

_____ Cannot ignore nearby events

_____ Continually stops work to see what others are doing

_____ Is overly aware of nearby sounds, odors, movement

_____ Cannot ignore own body sensations

Immaturity

_____ Behavior is obviously less mature than expected for this age

_____ Behaves like much younger person

_____ Cannot get along well with age-mates

_____ Prefers to play or be with younger persons

_____ Has the interests and thought patterns of much younger persons

_____ Does not make effort to "grow up"

_____ Refuses to accept responsibility

_____ Behavior is impulsive/compulsive

_____ Acts on spur of the moment instead of thinking things through

_____ Refuses long-term goals

_____ Insists on immediate satisfaction of wishes and desires

_____ Puts self ahead of others

_____ Blames others for own mistakes

_____ Triggers displeasure of companions

_____ Is often disliked by others

Insatiability

_____ Desires are never satisfied

_____ Clamors for more

_____ Cannot leave others alone

_____ Demands attention

_____ Is quickly bored and wants something different

_____ Complains that others get larger share

_____ Blames parents and leaders for not being fair

_____ Drains emotions of those who must be involved in this person's life

_____ Triggers desire in others to push this person away

_____ Is often dreaded by others

_____ Becomes target of rejection by others

Impulsivity

_____ Does not plan ahead

_____ Acts on spur of the moment

_____ Shows no common sense in making decisions

_____ Does not think of consequences

_____ Demands immediate satisfaction of wishes and desires

_____ Cannot put off desires or wishes

Disruptiveness

_____ Is a disruptive influence in group

_____ Keeps things stirred up

_____ Triggers conflict within group

_____ Disturbs neighbors during study time or work time

_____ Causes others to complain about how this person behaves

_____ Others are relieved when this person is absent

Body Energy Overflow

_____ Some part of body is in continual motion

_____ Cannot sit still

_____ Cannot be quiet

_____ Can hold body motions under brief control, but overflow starts again soon

Emotional Overflow

_____ Emotions are always near the surface

_____ Clamors in an emotional way

_____ Is easily triggered into an hysterical or overly emotional state

_____ Tantrums are always near the surface

Lack of Continuity

_____ Lifestyle does not have continuity

_____ Lives life in unconnected events

_____ Must have supervision and guidance to stay with a course of action

_____ Is continually surprised by each new task requirement, no matter how many times the routine has been done

Attention Deficit Disorder Individuals

3

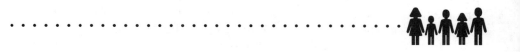

The child with an attention deficit can pay attention. But it takes that child 100 percent motivation to do what a normal child can do with 55 percent motivation. . . . If you follow these children around throughout an ordinary day, the number of nos and stops and don'ts they hear is astronomical.

—Allan Phillips, Department of Psychiatry, University of California at Los Angeles
(cited in Ratey & Johnson, 1997, pp. 158, 210)

In spite of recent enormous gains in understanding attention deficit disorders, scientists remain divided on the issue of hyperactivity. As our society approaches the twenty-first century, a persistent question remains: Can attention deficit disorder exist without hyperactivity? In answer to that question, four editions of the *Diagnostic and Statistical Manual of Mental Disorders* of the American Psychiatric Association first said yes, then no, then perhaps. Many prominent researchers insist that a nonhyperactive population with attention deficits exists (Copeland & Love, 1991; Hallowell & Ratey, 1994a; Jordan, 1992, 1996a, 1996b; Weiss & Hechtman, 1993). Other equally prominent specialists doubt the presence of nonhyperactive attention deficit disorder (Alexander-Roberts, 1995; Bain, 1991; Barkley, 1995; Green & Chee, 1994; Ingersoll & Goldstein, 1993; Jasuja, 1995; Parker, 1989; Warren & Capehart, 1995). Using the label ADD to designate Attention Deficit Disorder with Hyperactivity adds much confusion to this issue. For example, *You and Your A.D.D. Child* (1995) by Paul Warren and Jody Capehart, and *Understanding ADD* (1994) by Christopher Green and Kit Chee address only the issues of ADHD described in Chapter 2. The use of contradictory labels for attention deficit disorders contributes to confusion about the two branches of the attentional deficit tree.

What Is ADD?

I began my career of teaching and diagnosing struggling learners in 1957 when the disruptive behaviors now called ADHD were labeled MBDS (Minimal Brain Damage Syndrome) and HID (Hyperkinetic Impulse Disorder). During the 1960s my generation largely accepted the newer label MBD (Minimal Brain Dysfunction). During the 1980s we changed to using the new labels ADD+H (Attention Deficit Disorder with Hyperactivity) and ADD–H (Attention Deficit Disorder without Hyperactivity). To the dismay of most diagnosticians, 1987 brought still another shift to the single label ADHD (Attention-Deficit/Hyperactivity Disorder). In 1994, diagnostic specialists were asked to switch to yet another set of diagnostic labels that stipulated hyperactivity while permitting nonhyperactive forms of ADHD. The arguments for labeling all forms of attention deficit as ADHD are largely academic. Supporters of this point of view usually are scientists who accept only what can be measured by standard technology as being truly attention deficit disorder. This rigid diagnostic model often fails to include quietly disruptive behaviors that fall through the cracks of standard evaluation for attention deficit disorders.

The Existence of ADD Without Hyperactivity

As a hands-on teacher, diagnostician, and counselor of struggling learners for 40 years, I came face to face with the fact that not all persons who have attention deficits are hyperactive. In fact, my experience with several thousand struggling learners from around the world convinced me that fewer than half of all attention deficit individuals are hyperactive. If hyperactivity is required for diagnosis of attention deficit disorder, then Russell Barkley and others are correct when they estimate that 5% percent of the population are ADHD (Barkley, 1995). This means that only 5 individuals out of 100 display the faces of ADHD described in Chapter 2. However, if nonhyperactive ADD is included as a form of attention deficit disorder, then 10% (Green & Chee, 1994) to 13% (Jordan, 1992, 1996a) of the human population have attentional disorders. This chapter explores the many faces of ADD (Attention Deficit Disorder without Hyperactivity) that quietly disrupt families, classrooms, personal relationships, and the workplace around the world.

ADD Individuals Are Passive

Lack of Body Motion

In stark contrast to the hyperactive (ADHD) branch of the attention deficit tree, persons with ADD exhibit no noticeable movement. Outwardly, this branch of the tree is still. There is no squirming, bouncing, or leaping about to attract attention.

Individuals with ADD often sit quietly for long periods of time with no display of excess energy. Nothing on the surface reveals the internal loss of attention that interferes with the ADD person's interaction with his or her environment. ADHD individuals make a lot of noise and get right up in the face of others. ADD individuals drift through life making very little noise and experiencing infrequent confrontations. This passive exterior causes many parents, teachers, diagnosticians, and job supervisors to miss the subtle signs of underlying loss of attention.

Passive/Aggressive Personality Style

It is possible to provoke ADD persons to the point of triggering a strong emotional response. Passive individuals absorb great amounts of pressure and stress without responding openly. In fact, before the mid-1970s, passive/aggressive tendencies were regarded as a type of emotional disorder. Mental health specialists thought that holding in one's strong emotions was a sign of emotional disturbance. But being able to absorb insult and stress without becoming angry is a positive trait, up to a point. The world's peacemakers and diplomats usually are passive/aggressive persons who automatically soak up insult without handing it back through confrontation. The habit of absorbing criticism, rejection, or unfair discipline, however, can become a problem for the ADD brain.

The quiet, passive exterior of ADD often misleads aggressive persons into thinking that it is fine to continue to push ADD strugglers. At a certain point of stress, the ADD limbic system shouts "Enough!" Without warning, a storm of aggressive emotions boil out of the ADD individual. These delayed, infrequent reactions to stress always shock parents, teachers, and employers who did not see the aggressive storm coming. When passive/aggressive ADD persons reach their limit of accepting stress, they react in one of two ways. Either the exasperated individual blasts the environment with explosions of temper, hostility, and old grievances, or the explosion is kept inside, sending the insulted person into very active magical thinking that unplugs the prefrontal cortex from the world. Inside this private battlefield of make-believe, the angry ADD person broods, sulks, and role-plays how to get revenge. Many ADD individuals who explode internally start a crusade of hidden vengeance to get even with the person who triggered the aggressive blast. It is not unusual to see such ADD aggression destroy things that belong to the enemy, or sabotage the enemy's vehicle, or send anonymous mail that tries to damage the other person's reputation. Aggression that is held inside comes out in quietly destructive ways that outsiders did not suspect could happen. In some instances, murders have occurred when the totally aggrieved ADD individual decided to remove his or her adversary from the face of the earth.

ADD Individuals Are Quietly Confused

Internally, the ADD brain is as filled with noise as the ADHD brain. Plugs quietly drop out of thought patterns, in contrast to the commotion created when

ADHD plugs fall out. Continual "short circuits" occur as the prefrontal cortex tries to communicate common sense to the limbic system and brain stem. The ADD brain fails to absorb or comprehend much of the new information received by the midbrain. Individuals who are ADD rarely follow streams of oral or visceral information from start to finish. Too many bits of data fail to register to allow the ADD brain to stay involved with what goes on nearby. When ADD individuals describe their mental images, they reveal constant confusion. "I don't get it," the ADD brain says. "What do you mean?" Then the ADD person gives up trying to comprehend and drifts away into a world of invisible make-believe.

ADD Individuals Are Slow in Processing

The ADHD brain races ahead, darts off on side trails, and jumps to conclusions. Body movement follows these sudden changes in the brain. ADHD moves too fast with too much disruption. In contrast, ADD moves forward too slowly in thinking things through and deciding what to do next. Many ADD individuals need two or three times longer than their neighbors to do the same amount of work. Making decisions is a slow, frustrating process. If outsiders apply pressure to make the ADD brain work faster, the slow processing person loses mental images and comes to a standstill. If the plugs stay in, he or she must back up and start the thought process again. If plugs fall out under pressure to hurry, the ADD individual gives up in silent confusion and stops trying. Yet the body does not signal this breakdown in mental processing. Careful observers see the eyes of the ADD person slowly shift away to "star gaze" toward the ceiling or out the window. The ADD brain cannot speed up to stay on the schedules set by faster thinkers and planners.

ADD Individuals Are Forgetful

Parents of ADD children tell many stories of their frustrations in keeping track of all the things ADD youngsters forget. The ADD brain does not keep mental lists of objects to be transported, schedules to be kept, projects to be started or finished, or commitments to be honored. Parents, teachers, and supervisors constantly must monitor ADD individuals to make sure they remember. Children and adolescents who are ADD leave trails of lost clothing, school supplies, sports equipment, and tools. The ADD brain does not keep track of where things were last seen or set down. Later the ADD person cannot remember what happened to a jacket, pair of shoes, dad's tools from the garage, school books needed for homework, or homework to be turned in next day. Adults with ADD are forever losing car keys, wallets or purses, workplace items, shopping lists, and even the family car that was parked somewhere on a parking lot. Money management often is impossible because ADD individuals forget to record checks written, or they lose important receipts for purchases. This chronic forgetfulness triggers conflict and frustration in those who must share space or life with one who is ADD.

ADD Individuals Are Poor Organizers

The ADD brain does not keep track of time, nor does it keep track of sequence. Internally there is no "clock" that tells the ADD brain how much time has passed or how much time remains before the next event begins. ADD individuals do not think in start-to-finish segments. Those who have ADD deal with one issue at a time, slowly thinking about it until attention drifts away to a new idea. As the ADD brain leaves an unfinished thought and moves to another, the individual is unaware of any sequence. Mental images occur alone without connection to what went before and what is to follow. Consequently the ADD person's lifestyle is disorganized. Personal space becomes cluttered with forgotten items scattered about. Conversations are left unfinished. Tasks are partly done. Responsibilities are only partly carried out. Formal learning is spotty and filled with gaps in knowledge. Skill development is incomplete. The ADD brain wanders here and there, leaving an untidy trail of unorganized business. Memory for detail is ragged and full of holes. The ADD person often is poorly groomed because he or she does not comprehend the time or sequences required for combed hair, brushed teeth, matching clothes, and timely bathing. From early childhood to old age, ADD individuals are out of step with any culture that values good organization.

ADD Individuals Are Often Late

Persons with ADD are rarely on time. Their lifestyle is that of being late for meetings and appointments. My grandmother, who had no knowledge of ADD, would say in exasperation: "He is always late. He will be late to his own funeral." Because the ADD brain has no internal clock to keep track of time, these individuals are known for being tardy to class, late for scheduled appointments, not there on time for dates, and running behind in job completion. Outside pressure to make them be punctual triggers intense frustration and stress but not improved time habits. Living with ADD places a time-conscious partner in constant conflict with the tardiness of the ADD companion. Teaching tardy ADD learners often challenges an instructor's patience to the breaking point. Supervising ADD workers on the job brings conflicting time standards into confrontation. Yet the passive surface behavior of ADD individuals does not reveal their internal confusion over time. Being on time is as foreign a concept for ADD as sitting still is foreign to ADHD.

ADD Individuals Are Loose

Success in the classroom and the workplace depends on students and workers having tight, concise mental images that stay clearly focused over periods of time. The ADD brain is too loose to achieve this kind of success. Mental images that begin with clear focus soon melt away into fuzzy, poorly formed thought patterns. What the ADD person knows is not stored as precise, well-organized memories. Chapters 1 and 2 reviewed how the brain stores permanent memories in engrams, and how those engrams are activated to call up knowledge in organized images. The ADD brain stem and midbrain are too loose to filter out irrelevant information and pass along to the parietal lobes only what the brain needs to know. ADD individuals pick up bits and pieces of new knowledge but not well-sequenced whole concepts. Memory for details is spotty. Later when engrams are activated to recall specific data, the ADD brain produces partial images and incomplete information. Thought patterns and memories are loose instead of sharply focused. Learning new skills is unsatisfactory because the ADD brain fails to comprehend all of the skill steps in sequence. As the ADD person responds to questions, he or she stumbles over words and delivers only part of the information that is expected. Loose thought patterns cause the ADD brain to stumble every step of the way in learning and remembering.

Loose thought patterns are easily seen in pencil-and-paper assignments over which ADD learners are confused. In spite of drill and practice with basic skills, these students continue to struggle with simple assignments. Figure 3.1 shows how ADD interferes with arithmetic problem solving. The ADD brain often cannot keep track of the many variables that are involved in working homework math assignments.

ADD Individuals Cannot Listen

Listening well requires maturely developed self-discipline. For listening to be successful, the frontal lobes, temporal lobes, and parietal lobes must maintain clear communication between each other and the midbrain. The listener must tune out distractions in order to pay full attention to the flow of oral information. The ADD brain cannot do so. Very soon after the ADD individual starts to listen, his or her plugs quietly fall out and attention drifts elsewhere. As a rule, persons with ADD retain less than 30% of what they hear, unless that oral information is repeated several times. Part of good listening for most individuals is eye contact, except when cultural standards forbid eye contact. The ADD listener does not maintain eye contact. Soon after listening begins, the eyes drift away and attention focus is lost. ADD individuals are known as "star gazers" because of this tendency for the eyes to drift away from the speaker. If an ADD individual is to listen successfully, he or she must be supervised. The ADD brain must be called back frequently to continue to hear. Without supervision and reminding, ADD persons soon drift beyond the voice of the speaker and do not come back.

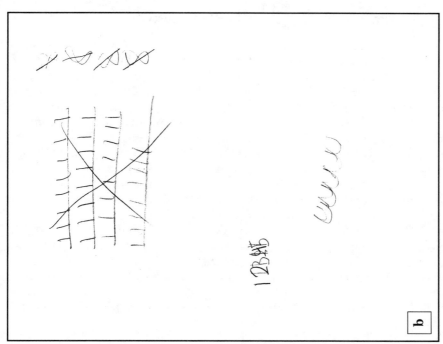

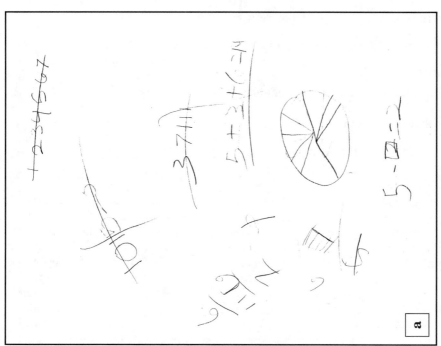

Figure 3.1. Math work of a 14-year-old boy who has ADD. He cannot maintain organized mental images to work problems. He tries to keep track by marking "counters" on his paper or drawing shapes (a). Soon he becomes too confused as he counts marks and practices on scratch paper (b). Then he gives up trying to finish the assignment.

ADD Individuals Are Too Easily Distracted

Paying full attention is a learned behavior. A major goal of wise parents is to teach preschool children how to pay attention. As certain developmental milestones are reached in playing together, sharing with others, and learning to take responsibility, children also are expected to turn attention away from themselves and pay attention to others. A critical part of this developmental sequence is learning how not to pay attention to certain things. Children are taught through a lot of practice how to tune out and ignore irrelevant events nearby. Parents and teachers spend much time coaching youngsters: "Everyone look here, please. Don't let your eyes look away. Is everyone ready? Fold your hands in your lap. Don't let your eyes or hands get busy doing something else. Pay attention now." By age 6 most children learn how to attend to others well enough to fit into a classroom successfully.

The ADD brain does not follow this developmental sequence in paying attention. Loose thought patterns, plugs that fall out too easily, trouble thinking in sequence, and poor listening ability make it impossible for ADD individuals to ignore nearby events. What happens nearby leaks through the midbrain filter into higher brain pathways. On their own, ADD persons do not distinguish between what is necessary and what is irrelevant. This poor filtering creates a state of constant distraction.

ADD Individuals Live in a Make-Believe World

Where does the ADD person's attention go when the plugs fall out and he or she is no longer connected to what is happening? The ADD brain spends a great deal of time in make-believe. Chapter 2 described the high-energy magical thinking of an ADHD teenager daydreaming about owning a fancy truck (see page 34). As attention is lost, ADD individuals slip quietly into a very private world of make-believe. This world of magical thinking is much like writing a play or creating a musical show. Once it disconnects from the outside world, the ADD brain imagines an active scene filled with wished-for objects, pleasant sounds and colors, and perhaps the person's favorite music. On center stage of this magical world is the ADD individual doing whatever he or she dreams secretly of doing well. During childhood, girls often daydream of being a skilled dancer on stage, or riding a special horse, or being a famous movie or television star. Boys often imagine being the champion at martial arts, or flying space ships, or beating everyone else in roller blade hockey. Sometimes the body begins to display the content of the make-believe as pretend dance steps are done or karate chops are delivered. Mostly, however, ADD make-believe remains hidden from the outside world. Those who diagnose attention deficits rarely uncover this silent, invisible world of ADD magical thinking. Individuals who engage in this make-believe are shy or even fearful of revealing where they spend their mental time. It takes a kind, patient adult to establish enough trust with the ADD dreamer to start him or her talking about this private world of make-believe.

ADD Individuals Are Too Quickly Bored

Private World of Make-Believe

Chapter 2 described the rapid boredom of ADHD that is triggered by under-arousal of the prefrontal cortex. The boredom experienced by ADD comes from a somewhat different source. As the ADD brain becomes overwhelmed by confused mental images, the brain stem and limbic system receive danger signals to prepare for "fight or flight" response. Some overly sensitive ADD learners feel too easily threatened by failure or shame as their mental images fall apart. The medulla, pons, and basal ganglia are triggered by the amygdala to stand by for possible flight from danger (see Figure 1.1). If the brain decides that this overwhelming situation poses too much danger, the basal emotions trigger surges of anxiety that may reach the catastrophic level of panic attack or phobia. In most instances, the ADD brain learns in early childhood simply to enter the safety of make-believe. There the mind builds magical scenes in which the ADD individual feels safe. If an ADD child is the victim of repeated abuse, he or she may create a negative fantasy world in which the victim takes revenge on persecutors. In this private world of magical thinking, the hurt child may spend a great deal of time getting even or plotting revenge. Whether the ADD brain chooses to create a pleasant world that surrounds the dreamer with success, or a dreadful world in which the hurt person fashions revenge, the private world of make-believe is the refuge for ADD persons when they cannot cope with the realities of their lives.

Escape Through Doodling

It often is possible to watch the ADD brain engage in make-believe. Many ADD individuals develop the habit of doodling when their plugs fall out and they embark on daydreaming or magical thinking. Figure 3.2 shows how a 10-year-old boy escapes from overwhelming confusion as he does math assignments. Since kindergarten his teachers have been irritated by this habit of doodling on his work pages. Figures 3.3 and 3.4 reveal the daydreaming of an ADD adult. She is a successful classroom teacher when she can set her own pace and follow her own schedule. However, when she must become a passive listener in a meeting or conference, her ADD plugs fall out and she drifts into a private world thinking about other things.

ADD Individuals Are Immature

Compared with others their age, ADD individuals display immature interests and habits. Many ADD persons create inventive private games to entertain themselves when boredom overwhelms the prefrontal cortex. However, these games are similar to those of younger children, such as rolling a pencil up and down the desk top, making paper airplanes, drawing stick figure cartoons, or

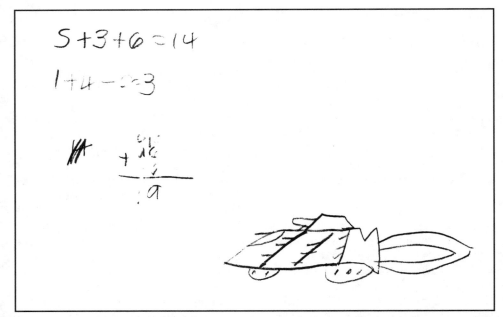

Figure 3.2. Math assignment of a 10-year-old boy with ADD. After working two problems correctly, his plugs fell out and he was engulfed by confusion. After struggling with the third problem unsuccessfully, he drifted into his private world of make-believe and started to doodle. By this time he was unaware of what the rest of his class was doing.

counting buttons on their clothes. When given a choice, ADD individuals tend to choose television programs and movies with shallow themes, silly antics, and a lot of artificial laughter. If an ADD person must view an educational program or drama, he or she soon becomes bored and restless. ADD adults often prefer popular magazines that feature gossipy information about famous people. It is not unusual for ADD adults to develop an obsessive interest in mail-order catalogs that trigger active make-believe: "Oh, what if I could have that? Oh, this would really look good in the bedroom." Lifestyle habits of ADD persons often include rituals and ingrained habits that seem "weird" to others. All of these less mature behaviors are linked to topics of magical thinking and make-believe that occupy so much of the ADD individual's time and mental energy.

ADD Individuals Are Often Depressed

Dark Thoughts of Make-Believe

Active make-believe can be a strongly positive attribute. However, in emotionally sensitive persons with ADD, drifting away from reality into the world of make-believe often involves depression. Hidden beneath the surface of slow

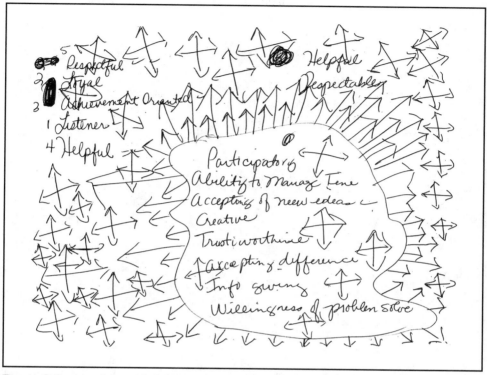

Figure 3.3. An adult with ADD began to take notes during a professional conference. Soon her attention had drifted away from the monotonous presentation by the speaker. Within a few minutes she had filled the page with doodles as her mind was off in her private world thinking of other things.

processing, star gazing, and underachievement is the tendency for brooding and imagining dark possibilities. If the ADD individual is a victim of abuse or overly strict punishment, magical thinking moves toward thoughts of dying. "I would be better off dead," depression whispers. "I wish I could die and get away from all this pain." When the ADD brain sinks into depression, the sorrowful person cannot cheer up. Yet he or she rarely tells others of the heavy emotions that have blanketed the mind and heart. ADD persons in depression begin to brood and cry in private. They withdraw from talking with others, playing games, or attending meetings. They stop eating normally, lose all interest in sexual expression, and become "emotional zombies" with virtually no feedback to others.

ADD children with depression hide from others and find excuses not to join in group activities. They often stop eating but refuse to tell why. Nightmares increase and minor fears become major phobias. ADD adolescents who

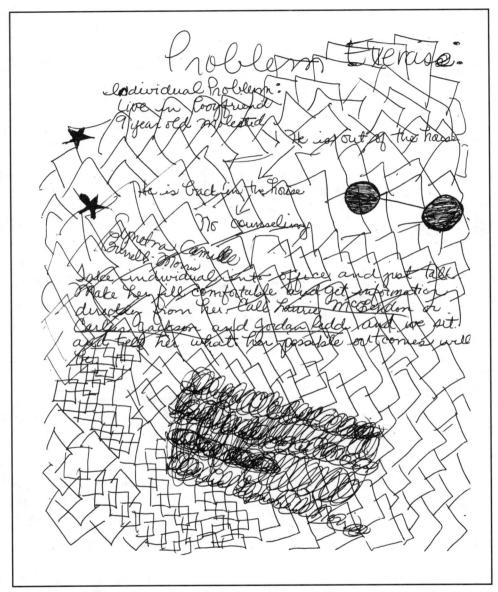

Figure 3.4. After the group returned from midmorning break, the ADD adult tried once more to take notes from the lecture. Soon her attention had drifted away from the oral information. Again she filled the page with doodles while her thoughts were miles away in private thinking.

are depressed often stop caring about personal hygiene and grooming. They withdraw from friends and break off social contacts. Frequently they write morbid poetry or draw black images with heavy strokes. Depressed ADD adolescents become surly when pressed to talk. "Leave me alone!" is their response to adult questions or even to adult kindness. ADD adults who are depressed become mournful and deeply sad for no apparent reason. When they talk to others, they dwell on dark issues such as death and disease.

Risk of Suicide

Many scientists have documented the increased risk of suicide among ADD children and adolescents (Barkley, 1995; Hallowell & Ratey, 1994a; Jordan, 1996a; Ratey & Johnson, 1997; Weiss & Hechtman, 1993). Chapter 2 presented the severity scale from 1 to 10 showing mild, moderate, and severe levels of attention deficit disorder (see page 20–21). If ADD is mild, symptoms of depression come and go with no real problems resulting. If ADD is moderate, cycles of depression are more frequent and intense. If ADD is severe, onset of depression is so frightening that the individual is likely to try to die. For individuals of all ages with severe ADD, dying becomes more appealing than continuing to live under the dark clouds of failure, shame, and acute sadness.

Religious Belief

Religious belief plays a major role in how ADD individuals respond to depression. Those who believe in a better life after death, where pain and sorrow do not exist, are in fact drawn more closely to dying. "After all," their emotions say, "wouldn't I be better off in heaven? Wouldn't my family be better off without having to put up with me?" This "what if" thinking leads the sorrowing person into visions of heavenly peace. On the other hand, individuals who believe that human life ends with death often come to prefer vanishing in death from the universe rather than continuing to live like this. Many ADD persons with depression are afraid to try to die because of fear they would go to hell. Yet they cannot go on living in the state of torment caused by their depression. When ADD symptoms are above level 5 on the severity scale, the risk of suicide becomes a major concern for parents, teachers, and companions.

Checklist of ADD Behaviors

Passive Behavior

_____ Has below-normal level of body activity

_____ Is reluctant to become involved with group activity

_____ Tries not to be involved in group discussion

_____ Avoids answering questions or giving oral responses

_____ Does not volunteer information

_____ Prefers to be alone in play situations and social activities

_____ Avoids being included in games and parties

_____ Spends long periods of time off in own private world of thought

_____ Uses fewest words possible when required to talk

Short Attention

_____ Cannot keep thoughts focused longer than brief periods of time

_____ Is continually off on mental side trails

_____ Must be called back continually to finish the task

_____ Drifts away from task before finishing

Loose Thought Patterns

_____ Cannot maintain organized mental images

_____ Continually loses important details

_____ Cannot do a series of things without starting to make mistakes

_____ Cannot remember a series of events, facts, or details without being prompted

_____ Must have help to tell what has happened

_____ Cannot remember a series of instructions

_____ Cannot remember assignments over time

_____ Cannot remember game rules or game routines

_____ Keeps forgetting names of people, things, places, events

Poor Organization

_____ Must have help to keep life organized

_____ Continually loses things

_____ Must have supervision to stay on schedules

_____ Does not remember simple routines from day to day

_____ Lives and works in a cluttered space

____ Cannot straighten up room or work space without help

____ Vehicle is littered with trash

____ Must have supervision to do homework

Change of First Impressions

____ Continually erases and changes as writing is done

____ Has impression that others are "playing tricks" because things seem to shift and change

____ Word patterns, spelling patterns, math problems seem to change

Poor Listening Comprehension

____ Rarely gets the full meaning of what others say

____ Must have oral instructions repeated and explained again

____ Sits without doing anything instead of asking for information to be repeated

____ Does not keep on listening

____ Attention drifts away before speaker has finished

____ Cannot remember later what speaker said

Time Lag

____ Pauses for long intervals before responding

____ Does not start tasks without being pushed or guided to start

____ Spends long periods of time doing no work

____ Spends long periods of time searching memory for information

____ Whispers softly to self while searching memory or doing written assignments

____ Continually lags behind the schedule set by parents, teachers, or supervisors

Unfinished Tasks

____ Leaves tasks unfinished unless closely supervised

____ Leaves several unfinished tasks scattered around

____ Thinks tasks are finished when they are not

____ Does not realize when more is yet to be done to finish a task

Daydreaming

_____ Spends much time off in a private world of daydreaming and make-believe

_____ Drifts into make-believe to escape stress of learning or performing tasks

_____ Doodles and draws pictures while daydreaming

_____ Refuses to talk when asked about daydreams

Boredom

_____ Becomes bored immediately after starting to do tasks

_____ Begins to play quietly with things instead of working as boredom sets in

_____ Eyes drift away as star gazing replaces boring tasks

_____ Slumps in seat and appears sluggish as boredom starts

_____ Begins to sigh and yawn deeply as boredom sets in

Easily Distracted

_____ Attention drifts to whatever is happening nearby

_____ Cannot ignore nearby events

_____ Stops work to watch what others are doing

_____ Begins quietly to tug at clothes, pick at lint or threads, fiddle with buttons, buckles, or shoelaces

Immaturity

_____ Role-plays imaginary situations like much younger individuals

_____ Does not pay attention to informational programs or drama in movies or television

_____ Chooses shallow or "silly" things to do when others that age choose more serious activities

_____ Sense of humor is like that of much younger persons

_____ Spends time with comic books, mail-order catalogs, or other picture materials instead of reading books

_____ Does not fit in socially with others of same age

_____ Is bored with what others of same age like to do

_____ Cannot carry on small talk at social events

_____ Wanders off alone at social events

Depression

_____ Withdraws into private world of sad make-believe

_____ Stops eating an adequate diet, but refuses to explain why

_____ Stops brushing teeth, combing hair, taking a shower, wearing clean clothes

_____ Hides from others in out-of-the-way places

_____ Becomes irritable or tearful when questioned or pressed to talk

_____ Explodes suddenly in aggressive anger when pressed too hard to share private thoughts

_____ Cries when alone, but refuses to tell why

_____ Writes morbid poetry or draws dark pictures with morbid themes

_____ Becomes obsessed by themes of death or dying

_____ Expresses wish to die, or writes private notes about dying

How ADHD and ADD Disrupt One's Life

4

After 60 years of research, scientists who studied attention deficit disorders concluded that poor attention, whether hyperactive or passive, is a disruptive disorder that upsets life at home, at work, at school, and within personal relationships (DSM-III, American Psychiatric Association, 1980). In Chapter 5 we review other kinds of disruptive behavior that often are attached to ADHD. In spite of a wealth of knowledge about attention deficit disorders, most parents, teachers, diagnosticians, and employers continue to believe that these struggling individuals merely are being stubborn, defiant, or lazy. In this chapter we look at how ADHD and ADD disrupt life in the classroom, at home, and in the workplace.

ADHD and ADD in the Classroom

Regardless of which type of attention deficit a child might have, the basic problem in the classroom is inability to stay plugged into the learning environment. Whether hyperactive or passive, the child does not absorb a steady flow of new information. New facts and skills presented in formal lessons do not enter long-term memory. New experiences within the group do not register fully. Important social skills that help us become friends and good work partners are not learned. Students with ADHD and ADD rarely comprehend more than 30% of what occurs around them unless they receive drill and practice with this information (Jordan, 1992, 1996a). The ADHD or ADD brain fails to add new vocabulary to what the person already knows. The midbrain does not pass on full segments of new data to the higher brain. ADHD and ADD get in the way of mastering new skills, new information, and new steps in social conduct. As time goes by, children who are ADHD or ADD become misfits in mainstream classrooms. The underlying disability of poor attention makes it impossible for them to stay plugged into what occurs outside themselves. Students with ADHD or ADD cannot fit into the regular world of formal education. They bring a cluster of disruptive habits and behaviors into the classroom, creating challenges that few teachers are equipped to meet.

Social–Behavioral Problems

Self-Centeredness

Most youngsters with ADHD or ADD are likable in brief one-to-one relationships. When they are alone for awhile with an adult or playmate, a good relationship usually occurs. These children often are deeply sensitive. They feel the same emotions as other children. They care deeply for pets. They grieve over sorrows that come into the lives of family and friends. They laugh, make jokes, and have lots of fun when they are free to set their own pace in working out mental images. Being hyperactive with a good sense of humor can be an endearing trait for awhile. Being quiet, "loose as a goose," and forgetful can awaken affection and extra concern in a playmate or adult.

When ADHD or ADD youngsters enter a group, a critical difference emerges. When these children must interact with several others for an extended period of time, the successful interaction they achieve in one-to-one relationships breaks down. Individuals with ADHD or ADD spend most of their time dealing with themselves. Inattention makes it impossible for them to focus on the needs of others or to put their own needs aside in order to see the needs of others. However, these persons are not necessarily selfish. Many ADHD and ADD individuals are generous to a fault in letting others share their things. The problem is that the ADHD or ADD brain is preoccupied by personal needs, moments of fear and uncertainty, episodes of magical thinking, figuring out what others are saying, and handling all the impulses that spring from the limbic system. The ADHD or ADD brain is proccupied with itself, usually in some form of make-believe. As we reviewed in Chapter 3, ADD students spend many hours off on private rabbit trails, mentally acting out stories or situations they invent. These quiet ones spend long periods of time drifting through imaginary adventures that would make quite remarkable movies. The body usually is still with no outward sign of activity while the mind is busy creating complicated fanciful scenes. Children with ADHD often act out their inner stories by rocking their chairs, turning furniture upside down to make a fortress, or "marching" and "dancing" with feet drumming the floor. They begin to hum and mumble the dialogues their imagination is creating for magical figures. ADHD daydreamers thrust imaginary swords, do imaginary ballet swirls, or punch out an assailant in a martial arts fantasy. Although the child's attention is turned inward where he or she is the star of a fantastic private world, this overflow of imagination disrupts the class. The teacher must stop the lesson to deal with this noisy disruption, causing classmates to grumble about losing time during these interruptions. As we have seen in Chapter 2, most youngsters with moderate ADHD and ADD youngsters outgrow childhood hyperactivity. As this maturity occurs, much of the invisible magical thinking also disappears. However, during the first several years of formal education, self-centered behaviors are disruptive barriers between children with ADHD and ADD and others in the classroom.

Self-Gratification

During the self-centered years of ADHD and ADD, these children spend most of their mental energy on self-gratification: When do we go to lunch? How much more do I have to do? When can I go home? Did you see my new jeans? I got new roller blades from my grandad. I can't find my pencil. I have to go to the restroom. I don't want to play this game anymore. When can we go outside? You know what I saw last night? These are the concerns of self-centered, less mature individuals who have attention deficits. Whether hyperactive or passive, these kinds of self-centered thoughts occupy most of their time. Formal group learning in the classroom cannot penetrate this thicket of self-concern. Teachers must make extraordinary efforts to break through the self-preoccupation of ADHD and ADD to implant new academic knowledge and skills. The self-centered ADHD or ADD student often is beyond the reach of others except in one-to-one relationships where tight structure can be maintained by the adult.

Boredom

In Chapters 1 and 2, we reviewed the concept of underarousal that triggers boredom in the prefrontal cortex of ADHD persons (see pages 27–28). When students with ADHD or ADD are pressed into group learning, a strong sense of isolation occurs. The ADHD or ADD brain cannot stay plugged into the variety of events happening in the classroom. Loose thought patterns do not develop an organized sense of what the group is doing. Too many loose ends keep the attention deficit child from following conversations and discussions well enough to be a responsive group member. Children with attention deficits cannot deal with a group environment effectively. These struggling learners are isolated from the streams of interaction taking place all around them. Whether hyperactive or passive, these students are alone in the world of formal learning. Oral information from the teacher does not make sense. The purpose of workbook activities does not register. ADHD and ADD learners cannot enter into the spirit of the group as new skills are practiced. Because youngsters with ADHD or ADD cannot compete successfully, they quickly become outsiders in any competitive task. Alone on this island in the stream of learning, the attention deficit child has nothing meaningful to do. Copying from the board or working a page of math problems is risky and boring. Caught in a group activity that gives him or her few rewards and no pleasure, the ADHD or ADD student rapidly becomes bored. Fingers go exploring for something to do. The prefrontal cortex begs for a jolt of excitement. Bored eyes and ears search the room for something interesting going on. Memory drifts or darts away to an experience that was lots of fun. Desire lingers over a wish that has not been fulfilled. Make-believe carries the mind away from the boring classroom into an exciting, active fantasy adventure. As boredom sets in, assigned work stops. Soon the bored child is in conflict with the teacher for not following instructions.

Restlessness

Bored bodies soon become restless. With nothing meaningful to do, the ADHD brain triggers the body to start doing something. One of the first signals of lost attention is restlessness that quickly intrudes on the quietness of neighbors. Squirming wakes up the prefrontal cortex at the same time it makes the furniture rattle and squeak. Restless hands and arms soon knock books to the floor. Restless fingers roll the pencil back and forth on the desk top, irritating nearby classmates. Soon classmates are complaining "Make him stop doing that!" Sighing, yawning, groaning, and explosive breathing add to disruptive body motions. Within a few minutes everyone in the room is distracted and starting to complain. This brings a reprimand from the teacher: "Carl, stop making all that noise!" or "Maria, sit still!" But Carl and Maria, who have attention deficits, have no idea why they are being scolded. Their attention was far away as their bodies became restless and disruptive. ADHD students continually stand up at inappropriate moments, leaving their desks to walk across the room, going too often to the pencil sharpener, lingering at the library table instead of returning to their work, and staying too long in the restroom. These restless students cannot stay put. Overflowing body movement reveals the noisy restlessness of the brain. As we saw in Chapter 2, this noise in the ADHD or ADD brain never stops. The restless brain triggers restless behavior that disrupts the classroom many times each day.

Emotional Sensitivity

Students with ADHD and ADD live on the edge of failure. No classroom task is free from the hovering threat of shame and failure. Loose thought patterns, gaps in knowledge and skills, and plugs that keep falling out are like goblins dancing around the learner's desk, threatening to cause mistakes at any moment. ADHD and ADD persons who live under this never-ending shadow of defeat are understandably sensitive. From their earliest days in school, they have been criticized publicly for "not trying harder." Teachers have said many times: "You did not follow my instructions. Don't you ever listen when I explain?" Parents have said since early childhood: "I've told you a dozen times. Don't you ever hear what I say?" Since kindergarten, adults and classmates have made comments and jokes about how forgetful the ADHD or ADD student is. The statement, "He would lose his head if it weren't fastened on" stopped being funny years ago to the youngster who has attention deficits. Being labeled "lazy" or "just plain careless" is painful and embarrassing. Before the child with attention deficits has been in school very long, he or she has become quite emotional about these accusations that seem very unfair.

Students with ADHD quickly learn to defend themselves. Those with ADD take the pain deep inside instead of showing it. Aggressive ADHD individuals lash out at those who criticize them. They often start fights to avenge their honor. They develop habits of getting even with classmates who tease or make sarcastic remarks. Many schoolbus, playground, and lunchroom scuffles are triggered when ADHD persons fight back. Numerous researchers have documented the fact that most of the antisocial behavior of juvenile delinquency starts with classroom failure (Alexander-Roberts, 1995; Barkley, 1995; Jasuja, 1995; Jordan, 1992, 1996a; Weiss & Hechtman, 1993).

Quiet students with ADD seldom storm out in self-defense. They silently pull back inside themselves, tuning out the classroom atmosphere that inflicts so much pain through failure. For ADD, the most common defense is a quiet decision to pull out all the plugs and become detached. If these overly sensitive students do not hear what others say about them, they will not be hurt by critical words. In choosing this deeply passive retreat into magical thinking, ADD individuals cut themselves off from classroom participation. Formal learning stops while overly sensitive feelings are protected. It is possible for ADD learners to build such thick, tough walls of passive self-protection that it becomes impossible for teachers to reach through the emotional barriers.

Misunderstanding

The lives of ADHD and ADD persons are clouded by misunderstanding. These individuals continually misunderstand what others say or mean. Meanwhile, parents, teachers, siblings, and friends misunderstand ADHD or ADD behavior. Well-organized adults who have no difficulty with their own thought patterns cannot believe that this healthy, bright child cannot do better. Far too often, teachers and parents interpret attention deficit behavior as disobedience, laziness, or lack of effort. Adults often try to force disorganized youngsters to function more efficiently. However, no amount of discipline changes the patterns of ADHD and ADD. If one adult gives too much one-to-one attention to get the child to function, another adult may say that too much coddling is going on: "Jason has to learn to accept responsibility on his own." If adults back away and place all responsibility on the attention deficit child, nothing improves. In fact, when ADHD and ADD students are left alone to carry out responsibility, they are helpless.

Misunderstanding multiplies rapidly in the classroom. Instructions continually are misunderstood and not carried out by ADHD and ADD learners. Friendly comments by classmates often are misinterpreted and blown out of proportion by overly sensitive attention deficit children. Classmates misunderstand the stumbling speech of the ADHD or ADD person who has lost his or her words while trying to tell a story. Diagnosticians who evaluate these strugglers often misunderstand their answers to questions and thus do not see the full extent of attentional problems. ADD and ADHD individuals are among the most seriously misunderstood persons in our culture. They live most of their developmental years being misunderstood and failing to understand the world around them.

Insatiability

Chapter 2 described the problem of insatiability in many persons who are ADD and ADHD (see page 32). Insatiable individuals never get enough. In the classroom, insatiable needs for personal attention and constant approval become highly disruptive. An insatiable person does not leave others alone. This individual cannot study silently or alone. The need for feedback from others is overwhelming. The insatiable student clamors for the teacher's attention regardless of how much time already has been spent in one-to-one contact. Children with insatiable habits cannot stay in a designated space without having someone to share that space. The insatiable individual cannot leave classmates alone during independent study time. He or she must have continual contact through touching, speaking, and being spoken to. This person is overly sensitive, even phobic, about being alone. When frustrated classmates and teachers reach the point of firmly saying: "Stay in your own seat and leave me alone," his or her feelings are shattered. Insatiable individuals burst into emotional pleading, or they loudly blame others for being selfish or not caring. Sometimes the insatiable student retreats into a pout, brooding about how unfair everyone else is. The insatiable person is extremely immature and cannot deal with life issues realistically.

The need for constant company overpowers every other need of the insatiable person. He or she runs extreme risks to gain the attention of others. These individuals expose themselves to great risk of rejection or ridicule in order not to be isolated. An insatiable student is disruptive. He or she places heavy pressure on the emotions of the group. An insatiable person in the classroom demands more than anyone can give. This individual has no concept of privacy or appreciation of the territorial rights of others, as we reviewed in Chapter 2 (see page 28). Inner hunger for response from others overwhelms all other considerations as this individual clamors to be satisfied.

Impact of Failure on Self-Esteem

The most devastating result of ADHD or ADD is loss of self-esteem. As children progress through their developmental years, the normal growth pattern is to accumulate good stories to tell about personal success, prizes won, awards received, and praises earned. Persons with ADHD or ADD are left out of this developmental process for the most part. They do not win prizes for good work.

Their papers are not displayed proudly on the bulletin board. Their progress reports do not earn praise. In fact, most teacher comments to an ADHD or ADD child are negative: "Juan, you didn't follow my instructions again." "Mia, you forgot to put your name on your paper again." "Mark, this is the fourth time I have had to repeat my instructions. Don't you ever listen?" "Shelley, you forgot to give me your homework again." "Robert, your handwriting must be neater." This litany of criticisms and complaints never ends for those who have ADHD or ADD. From the earliest years these struggling students can remember, adults have been saying negative things about their behavior. There is no cumulative memory of praise, compliments, and congratulations for jobs well done. Students with attention deficits have few positive stories to tell. When they do tell stories, they often resort to make-believe to compensate for their history of failure. Then they are accused of "telling lies."

Having no good stories to tell leaves deep scars on a youngster's self-esteem. If everyone else has good stories to tell, but the ADHD or ADD child does not, his or her impression of self becomes negative and inferior. If everyone else wins praise, but the attention deficit person hears only blame or criticism, the impression of self is "I'm not good." In later years, those who outgrow the early problems of ADHD or ADD to become good learners as adults continue to live under the heavy burden of low self-esteem. Being unable to satisfy adult expectations during developmental childhood years implants deeply rooted impressions that the self is bad, inadequate, and of low value. The feeling of low self-worth is an unfortunate legacy when ADHD or ADD is not recognized early so that constructive help can be given.

Problems with Academic Learning

Poor Listening Comprehension

The ability to understand a stream of oral information is very poor with students who have attention deficits. As a rule, the level of comprehension through listening is seldom higher than 30% (Jordan, 1992, 1996a). This means that the ADHD or ADD listener fully understands and retains only one third of what he or she hears in the course of a school day. This deficit in auditory perception has nothing to do with the ability to hear. These struggling learners usually hear well enough. As we reviewed in Chapters 1 and 2, the midbrain fails to filter and organize incoming oral data. The ADHD or ADD midbrain passes only bits and pieces on to the higher brain instead of sending on full messages. Sometimes students with listening deficits try to keep up by interrupting the speaker with "What?" or "Huh?" or "What do you mean?" Often, however, they give no signal that they have not heard everything correctly. When slow mental processing is a factor, the ADHD or ADD student cannot develop a full mental image fast enough to respond to what he or she has just heard. Poor listening is a major obstacle in classroom performance.

Students with listening deficits find it difficult to participate in class discussions. Streams of oral information that are shared rapidly by several classmates do not connect into meaningful mental images for ADHD or ADD listeners. What Jacob says does not connect with what Marcie replies. The teacher's question does not connect with Paula's answer. Again, the student with attention deficit is alone on an island within a stream of flowing talk. This sense of isolation increases rapidly as group discussion continues. Within a short time the attention deficit listener is lost and overwhelmed by boredom. Soon boredom triggers restlessness in ADHD or silent withdrawal in ADD. Conflict disrupts the group as the teacher reprimands Michael, whose plugs have fallen out: "You're star gazing again, Michael. Come on back and join the crowd." Classmates giggle and make fun of Michael, which triggers disruptive behavior as he defends himself.

Teachers face a continual problem in making new information clear to ADHD and ADD listeners. These students do not follow as the teacher explains, gives instructions, and lectures. Bits and pieces of new oral data reach the poor listener's higher brain regions, but the attention deficit person does not develop a full mental image of what was said. This leaves him or her unable to put that oral information to use. As the teacher finishes explaining or giving instructions, she asks: "Does everyone understand?" The student with ADHD or ADD never does. The same individuals raise their hands every time, wanting to know what to do. The same voices interrupt the class: "What are we supposed to do?" If the teacher says, "I just told you what to do," the ADHD learner responds, "No, you didn't. You never told me that" or "I didn't hear you say that." This scene is played again and again, hour after hour, day after day. The attention deficit child's listening skills do not grow no matter how much scolding is done. The midbrain filtering and organizing systems cannot keep up with all of the oral information that swirls around the classroom.

These poor listeners often do quite well in one-to-one relationships where the speaker watches for lost attention, then backs up and helps the person hear it again. One-to-one, an instructor can hold the learner's thought patterns in tight focus to permit full understanding of what is heard. But in group activity where these strugglers are left to do their own structuring, attention span is too short. Without being tightly guided, ADHD and ADD listeners drift or dart away and soon lose the continuity of what they are hearing.

Unpredictable Response

One of the most frustrating characteristics of attention deficit disorder is the tendency to do the first steps of a task well, then begin to make mistakes on later steps in the same task. In Chapter 2, Figures 2.2 and 2.3 (see page 30) show how this breakdown in memory disrupts arithmetic assignments. Memory for math facts and procedures often is good for five or six problems. Then the plugs fall out, causing the attention deficit student to make mistakes on the next several problems. A similar pattern often appears in writing and spelling assignments. Figures 4.1, 4.2, and 4.3 show what happens when an ADD student is pressed to remember quickly in the classroom. In Figure 4.1, a 15-year-old boy with ADD did perfect work in a quiet, one-to-one meeting with his tutor. The quality of his language usage shows that he is well educated in the rules of written expression. However, Figure 4.2 shows the dramatic difference in what he can recall about spelling when he is under pressure to hurry in a group activity. Figure 4.3 further reveals the price an attention deficit student pays when he or she must function without accommodation in a mainstream classroom.

These short-circuit patterns are not caused by carelessness or laziness. As an attention deficit student works through an assignment, memory becomes spotty and unpredictable. Mental images that were clear one moment become cluttered and confused the next moment. Students with these short-circuit patterns seldom maintain fully clear mental images longer than 90 to 100 seconds. They are at constant disadvantage doing assignments that require clear thinking for 15 minutes or longer. No matter how often attention deficit learners

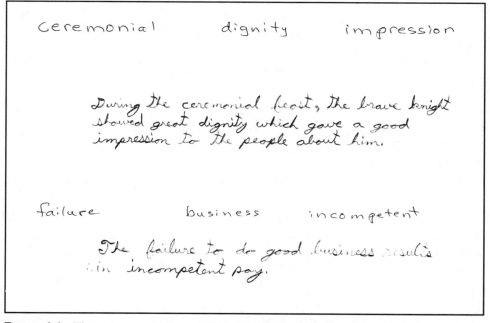

Figure 4.1. This 15-year-old boy is ADD. Working one-to-one with a tutor, he produced excellent writing on this sentence-building activity. He made no mistakes in capitalization, punctuation, or spelling. This work was done in a quiet place. He had all the time he needed to do this task.

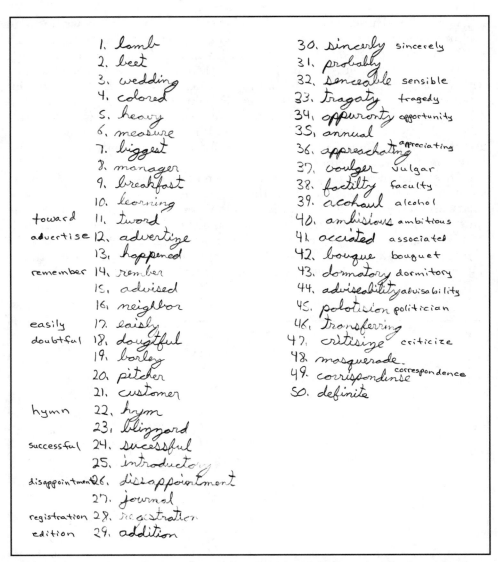

1. lamb
2. beet
3. wedding
4. colored
5. heavy
6. measure
7. biggest
8. manager
9. breakfast
10. learning
toward 11. tword
advertise 12. advertize
13. happened
remember 14. rember
15. advised
16. neighbor
easily 17. easily
doubtful 18. dougtful
19. barley
20. pitcher
21. customer
hymn 22. hym
23. blizzard
successful 24. sucessful
25. introductory
disappointment 26. dissappointmont
27. journal
registration 28. reacstration
edition 29. addition

30. sincerly   sincerely
31. probably
32. senceable   sensible
33. tragaty   tragedy
34. oppuronty   opportunity
35. annual
36. appreachating appreciating
37. voulger   vulgar
38. factilty   faculty
39. acohaul   alcohol
40. ambisious   ambitious
41. acciated   associated
42. bouque   bouquet
43. dormatory dormitory
44. adviseability advisability
45. polotician politician
46. transferring
47. critisize   criticize
48. masquerade.
49. corrispondinse correspondence
50. definite

Figure 4.2. In a 10th grade classroom, the 15-year-old ADD student had to write these words from dictation. The teacher did not slow down to give him extra time. He was continually distracted by noise and movement nearby in the room. It was impossible for him to recall what he obviously knows about spelling.

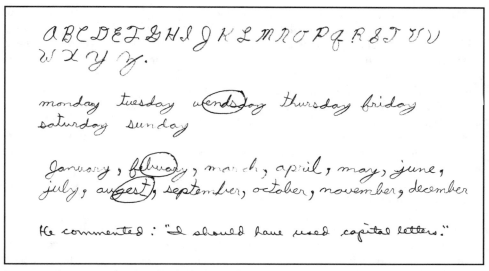

Figure 4.3. The same 15-year-old ADD student was asked to write the alphabet, days of the week, and months of the year as part of a rapid memory activity in the classroom. He started the task with perfect recall of the alphabet, remembering how to write capital letters. Stress from having to hurry interrupted his memory as he wrote the days of the week and months of the year. Later he said to his teacher: "I should have used capital letters."

promise to do better, faulty memory patterns trip them up. Promising to be more careful next time does not change the underlying neurological deficits.

This unpredictability in memory tasks is also seen in oral responses that ADD and ADHD students are asked to make. An attention deficit learner's ability to give complete, quick oral answers is also spotty and unpredictable. In telling what they know, these students continually lose their words. For example, no matter how many times they have named geometric shapes or math signs, they stumble when called on to name a triangle, rectangle, square, "greater than" sign, or "less than" sign. When these short circuits occur, the attention deficit individual is forced to stop, wait for mental images to gather, search his or her memory for the lost word, then try to give the answer the teacher is waiting to hear. If time is limited, as in most intelligence and achievement tests, these frustrated students cannot earn full credit when this memory search takes too long.

Attention deficit students suffer much embarrassment at school when adults and classmates make an issue of their trouble giving answers. "Has the cat got your tongue?" a sarcastic adult might say. "Hey, Joe, spit it out!" an irritated classmate may say loudly. "Old Joe got his tongue tangled again," the most popular student in class says with a laugh. As these put-down remarks encircle the struggling ADHD or ADD student, he or she is once more engulfed by humiliation. These frequent cycles of being unable to answer on command implant deep feelings of helplessness. ADD strugglers take this pain deep inside, where it silently broods and hurts beyond words. ADHD strugglers tend to strike back at their critics, defending themselves or exploding in anger. The result is disruption of the classroom. These built-in cycles of forgetting names, losing one's words, and starting to make mistakes damage sensitive self-esteem. This erosion of self-image begins in early childhood and continues unhealed throughout the school years. It is impossible for ADHD and ADD students who have constant memory loss to develop a strong, positive self-image because they never know what will emerge when they are on the spot to respond quickly before the group.

Poor Organization

Lack of mental organization is a major source of friction in the classroom. The tools of learning are not seen by the ADHD or ADD person as an organized, integrated whole. A book lying on the floor does not seem out of place. A pencil left on the library table is not connected with the writing task that was interrupted when the student went to sharpen the pencil. As these loose, poorly organized students move through the day, there is no cumulative image of where things are or where they ought to be.

In a self-contained class where students stay all day, essential things are continually misplaced. When it is time for math, the math book is missing. When it is time for reading, yesterday's homework cannot be found. When it is time for art, crayons are not in the desk. Students in a curriculum that requires the class to move to a different room each hour are at a serious disadvantage. If attention deficit individuals must go to their lockers for new supplies several times a day, it is impossible for them to be on time to the next class. These students are forever tardy. If they must catch the bus immediately after school, they cannot remember what books to take home to do evening assignments. Parents who pick up children after school continually face problems created when necessary books are lost or left at school, and the building is locked. No amount of scolding or discipline changes these disorganized habits of forgetting. In Chapters 1 and 2, we reviewed the neurological reasons why these attention deficit youngsters cannot maintain organized, long-term memory for duties and responsibilities. If teachers or parents make lists of what the ADHD or ADD student must remember, he or she often loses the list.

Distractibility

When one is a member of a class group, progress depends on being able to concentrate on the main activity while tuning out events that are not related to the task being done. Children with normal neurological processing ability soon learn to ignore anything that is not important at each moment. Youngsters who have attention deficits cannot tune out irrelevant issues. Little events, such as nearby sounds, unexpected activity across the room, movement glimpsed out of the corner of the eye, or a sudden new odor, all clamor for the child's attention. He or she darts or drifts off on each new rabbit trail instead of saying "no" to new impulses. During reading, eyes glance away to see what is happening, and the reader loses the place on the page. While thinking through a problem, the person's attention jumps to something going on nearby, and the mental image of the task is lost. Being unable to ignore distractions leaves these attention deficit students lost and wondering what to do after the distraction has been investigated.

It is impossible for these chronically distracted youngsters to finish a task. They continually leave jobs unfinished or assignments only partly done. They do not get all the way through a work page before attention goes elsewhere. Then they do not manage to come back to finish their work. These restless ones skip portions of most assignments, thinking that all the work was done. Later, as adults scan the unfinished work, conflict is triggered as the student is accused of being careless or not paying attention. ADHD and ADD learners leave holes in their work, not realizing that everything has not been completed. They remember that they were working. In their minds, they stopped because the whole assignment was finished. Persons with ADHD or ADD are not aware when their attention jumps or drifts to a different track.

Burnout

Most individuals with attention deficits begin to lose their mental images within 60 to 90 seconds after starting a task. Those with mild ADHD or ADD may stay mentally focused for 3 to 5 minutes. At a certain time, a type of burnout occurs, causing mental images to fade away or disappear suddenly. This attention burnout happens in several ways. For some persons, the brain goes blank. As a bright ADD girl explained to me: "My brain stops." She described how she starts to do her work with clear images and well-organized information. After 2 or 3 minutes of steady thinking, her "brain stops" and her mind is blank. This always startles her. There is no feeling to warn her that her brain is about to stop.

In a different type of attention burnout, the brain does not go blank. Without warning, the brain jumps to a different thought, much like switching channels on a television set. An adult with ADHD described this to me as "blinking." He said: "I will be thinking clearly about one thing, then my brain blinks and I am fully concentrated on a different thing. I never know when this will happen next." This blinking pattern starts after the man has been reading for 2 or 3 minutes. Once brain blinking begins, he must take a break to let his central nervous system settle down. "My brain really gets wound up if I keep on trying to read after blinking starts," the man explained. Still a different kind of mental burnout involves slow fading away of the original mental image, then a slow fading into focus of a different mental image. This fading cycle comes and goes slowly but steadily in many ADD individuals. Once started, this burnout cycle forces the person to leave the task until the brain has rested. Changing from a passive task to something active recharges the brain, allowing the individual to return to the task until the next cycle of fading occurs.

For the person who has ADHD or ADD, mental burnout will occur after a certain length of time in sustained thinking. To be successful, these individuals must develop work segments that allow them to accomplish what they can before the next burnout episode interrupts their thinking. After burnout is relieved by a short break, the person comes back to do a bit more before the next burnout cycle begins. Parents, teachers, and job supervisors can observe these burnout cycles rather clearly. Quality of work may have been quite good with few errors, then a noticeable change occurs with mistakes popping up and accuracy deteriorating. Good spelling starts to fall apart. Smooth left-to-right sequencing begins to scramble. Accurate math computation becomes filled with "careless" errors. Memory for a routine procedure is suddenly gone, leaving the person fumbling and groping for what to do next. Sentence structure falls apart, with fragments appearing instead of full sentence form. Typing errors suddenly multiply in the middle of smooth keyboard writing. Essay writing falls apart after getting off to a good start. Students with these attention deficit patterns are bewildered, not realizing when burnout cycles begin. Teachers often are puzzled, not understanding what causes such radical fluctuation in a student's performance. Parents who watch these burnout cycles in their children often realize that the youngster is doing his or her best, yet the best efforts fall apart after a certain length of time. Neurological burnout is one of the common causes of disruption in the classroom as irritated adults fuss at helpless students who have no control over these cycles of failure.

Messy Papers

Most attention deficit individuals have trouble writing neatly and producing attractive written work. As we saw in Chapter 1, the motor cortex and frontal lobes in the attention deficit brain cannot maintain well-organized thought patterns during the act of writing. In spite of having a clear mental image of the item to be copied or spelled, a breakdown occurs in the hand motion signals sent by the motor cortex. Without warning, the fingers make incomplete strokes, or the pencil moves the wrong way. Handwriting comes out messy and poorly done. In Chapter 6 we examine a type of learning disability called *dysgraphia* that also produces very poor penmanship. The poor writing of attention deficit disorders is not a learning disability. It is the result of burnout that interrupts fine motor control signals during the act of writing. Figure 4.4 shows this continual fine motor interruption in the copy work of a 13-year-old boy with ADD. Since kindergarten he has been judged harshly by adults who insist that he could learn good penmanship if he just tried harder. By the time he reached third

> Daniel Boone was a courageous
> and vigorous man. Years ago he
> entered the American wilderness
> with visions of all who would
> follow the trail he blazed.
> Westward migration did begin to
> move over his pathways through

Figure 4.4. This copy task was done by a 13-year-old boy with ADD. He had all the time he needed in a quiet place to do this work. It took him 15 minutes to finish this assignment. His plugs kept falling out, and he continually lost the place. He described this kind of work as "very boring." He has no learning disability such as dyslexia. (From Form D, Slingerland Screening Tests for Identifying Children with Specific Language Disability. Permission has been granted to reproduce this example.)

grade, he had become phobic about handwriting. He retreated into his private inner world of make-believe when penmanship tasks were presented.

Erratic Reading Comprehension

Most attention deficit students have adequate skills in phonics. Unless they also are dyslexic, they do not have disability in learning and applying rules of phonics. They tend to stumble over syllables within words, and they cannot always keep sound units in the right sequence. Yet they usually know how to blend sounds together and how to chunk (break words into sound units). Tests of phonics skills often show excellent knowledge of letter/sound relationships. However, reading comprehension tends to be well below grade level and unpredictable.

For example, if teachers study the reading patterns of students who are ADHD and ADD, they often find wide fluctuations in what the reader comprehends from page to page. When the plugs are firmly in and the attention deficit reader is fresh, he or she may score 100% comprehension on the first page. As plugs fall out and burnout begins, the reader's comprehension may drop to 60% on the second page. If the reader takes a break, he or she may score 80%

comprehension on the third page. By this time the ADHD or ADD individual has reached total burnout, and the fourth page score may be 40% or lower. This zigzag pattern in reading comprehension is reflected by the scattered bar graphs shown in Figures 2.5 through 2.8 (see pages 38–39). It is impossible for the ADHD or ADD brain to maintain full attention during sustained reading tasks.

This problem with reading comprehension is similar to that found in listening to oral information. In listening to a stream of speech, the ADHD or ADD brain does not comprehend all that is heard. Only bits and pieces of what the person hears are understood fully. The same pattern occurs as the individual reads. He or she may sound out or correctly recognize every word on the page, but only bits and pieces of the meaning are recorded by the memory. The reader who has ADHD or ADD does not develop a cumulative, ongoing mental image of what the text has said. He or she turns only some of the printed page into inner speech (see pages 14–15 in Chapter 1). The author's written message does not become fluent inner language for the attention deficit brain. The ADHD or ADD brain speaks the inner language of reading in the same broken, choppy way the student listens. This reader leaves a reading task with only partial images of what was on the page. Often it is impossible for the attention deficit person to answer follow-up questions successfully.

The amount of material to be read is critically important for those who have attention deficits. Short attention and rapid burnout sabotage the task of reading large quantities of text material. Within a few minutes, the zigzag pattern of comprehension emerges, making it impossible for the reader to benefit from sustained reading tasks. However, these struggling individuals can be good readers if the assignment is divided into short segments that fit the cycles of burnout. It is not difficult for teachers to break reading tasks into short segments of 2, 3, or 5 minutes that let the reader take short breaks according to each person's burnout patterns.

Avoidance of Work

One of the most difficult problems teachers face with ADHD or ADD students is keeping them at their work. These learners have far more memories of failure in the classroom than moments of success. By the time attention deficit youngsters have entered second grade, they face schoolwork with great dread. If they are overly sensitive to criticism and teasing, they often develop phobias that erupt when a classroom task poses the likelihood of failure. In Chapter 1 we reviewed the issue of emotional memory (see page 15). Recalling events or knowledge always awakens the emotions, pleasant or fearful, that occurred during those moments of learning. Many individuals with ADHD and ADD develop deeply ingrained habits of avoiding situations that threaten to confront the person with failure or emotional pain. These overly sensitive learners cannot tolerate the normal pressure of academic work. They are too easily overwhelmed by emotional surges that accompany classroom failure. These attention deficit individuals spend a great deal of time and energy seeking ways to get out of assignments. They often complain of not feeling well. This complaint can indicate a source of real discomfort, such as eye strain or seasonal allergy attack. When poor vision or allergies exist, the person does indeed have frequent headaches or feels ill. Immaturity of the digestive tract or intolerance for certain foods causes authentic gastric misery. However, most students who make a habit of avoiding schoolwork do not have these kinds of physical problems. Pleading to "go to the restroom" or "I need to call my mother" usually is an effort to avoid tasks that place too much stress on fragile skills.

Youngsters with ADHD actively avoid tasks any way they can. Pencil leads are broken every few minutes, requiring another trip to the pencil sharpener. It is easy to stretch a 45-second pencil sharpening chore into 2 or 3 minutes away from one's desk. Or the student may decide to look up a word in the unabridged dictionary across the room. This simple chore can be extended into a 15-minute search. Or the ADHD person may have left an essential item in his or her locker and must ask the teacher for a hall pass. Once out of the room, it is easy to stretch a locker visit into half an hour. The fact that the student ends up in trouble for this kind of procrastination does not stop the avoidance behavior. To him or her, avoiding threatening work is worth the consequence of being scolded.

Passive students with ADD often develop another type of avoidance. Instead of walking away from the task, they silently drift away into daydreams. Sometimes these star gazers develop cover-up strategies of pretending to work when actually nothing is being accomplished on the assigned task. These dreamers learn how to look busy from across the room while spending time adrift in a world of wishful make-believe. This is when a lot of doodling occurs (see pages 54–56). Later, daydreaming ADD youngsters must face the consequences of work not finished, but their passive mental drifting helps them pass the time without being involved in the dreaded task. It is possible for these silent drifters to float for a year or longer before adults become aware that no skill development is taking place. If the student does just enough to avoid failing the class, he or she might float for several years neither learning new material nor increasing important skills. The avoidance behavior of students with ADD or ADHD is sometimes beyond the reach of the teacher. If avoidance becomes too deep seated, the teacher may not be able to do anything effective to change the learner's negative response to schoolwork.

These are the main characteristics of attention deficit disorders in the classroom. The student's surface behavior appears to be lazy, disinterested, unmotivated, and careless. The individual with ADHD or ADD may drive everyone up the wall by constant clamoring, or he or she may silently drift away, intellectually apart from the mainstream learning taking place in the classroom. Scolding does not change the behavior. Forcing the student to work without help does no good. Poor organization, messy papers, and lost materials continue to frustrate both the teacher and the learner day after day. Punishment does not bring better performance. Unless the underlying neurologically based problem is identified, years of conflict and a lifestyle of chronic failure are set into motion with devastating effects on self-esteem.

ADHD and ADD at Home

As we consider how ADHD and ADD disrupt the lives of parents, siblings, and other close relatives, we must keep in mind the severity scale we saw in Chapter 2:

$$1 \ 2 \ 3 \quad 4 \ 5 \ 6 \ 7 \quad 8 \ 9 \ 10$$

mild   moderate   severe

The impact of ADHD or ADD on the family depends on the level of severity. An aggressive child with ADHD at level 9 will create much more disruption than a passive ADD child at level 5. The clearest way to see the impact of ADHD and ADD at home is to visit two families in which severe attention deficit exists.

James

I first met James when he was 8 years old. He is now 26, finishing a master's degree in counseling psychology. His goal is to become a specialist in treating attention deficit disorders in children. James was born into a deeply religious family that tried hard to live according to biblical teachings. Mr. and Mrs. Able proudly took their son to church when he was 3 weeks old. Partway through the worship service, they were called to the nursery where their infant son was creating a crisis. His screams could be heard all over the church. At 3 weeks of age, he was fighting everyone who touched him or tried to hold him. Thus began years of disruption of the Able family's life as this newborn son brought his frustration and tantrums into their home. James fought his parents, sisters, and all other relatives from the moment he came home from the hospital nursery. No one could reason with him. His demands were insatiable, and his temper often turned violent and destructive. As he learned to move about and handle things, the family lost the privacy they had found so important before his birth. Before he could stand alone or walk, James climbed like a squirrel. In no time, he could be at the top of the bookshelves in the family room. When he was 11 months old, his father caught the tall bookshelf as it was about to topple on top of the baby. After anchoring it to the wall, Mr. Able packed away all of the pictures and crystal objects he and his wife had collected from vacation trips. By the time James was 12 months old, the house had been stripped of anything breakable that he could possibly reach. Before his first birthday, his parents knew that the next several years of their lives would be difficult and hard to bear. They had no idea how they had produced this angry little tiger who demanded everything, gave nothing in return, and seemed bent on destroying the homelife the Ables had worked so hard to establish.

As James grew older, he became the dreaded child of the neighborhood. He hurt several other children and was forbidden by their parents to play with them. He was so aggressive with pets that his parents were forced to give away their beloved cat and middle-aged dog. None of the grandparents or uncles and aunts could handle James's visits. He was so hyperactive and aggressive that none of the older relatives could cope with his strength and disruptiveness. He lived on the very edge of danger with no fear and no display of common sense. In fact, it appeared that he thrived on danger. James took fearful risks that no logical person would take. When he was 4 years old, he climbed to the top of the community water tower that was 200 feet tall. Three firemen finally brought him down after chasing him several times around the catwalk 180 feet above the ground. Like a squirrel, he climbed the tall tree beside the house and leaped to the roof, then slid down the drainpipe to the ground, over and over. It was impossible to take him shopping unless he was in a harness with a leash tied to his father's wrist. If he were not restrained, he would dash off into the shopping mall and disappear.

Mr. and Mrs. Able sought help from many sources. A child psychiatrist attempted psychotherapy with James and his parents. It was suggested that, as parents, the Ables were not doing their best with this child. If they paid more attention to him and less attention to themselves, surely their son would learn to behave normally. The Ables went through several years of heavy guilt believing that it was their failure that produced and kept alive their son's out-of-control behavior. They worked with two clinical psychologists who tried many kinds of management techniques, including biofeedback training to teach the brain how to control muscle stress and reduce impulsivity. Nothing improved James's behavior beyond limited points. After making some improvement, he always returned to his aggressive ways. A series of pediatricians gave different opinions, none of which helped the Ables reduce the disruption in their home. Bedtime was a battle scene, with both parents physically forcing James to take a shower, brush his teeth, get into his pajamas, and turn out the light. Evenings usually ended with his mother in tears, his father furious, and his sisters hiding in their rooms. The only way bedtime was successful was when Mr. Able showered with James, and then lay down with the boy until he finally went to sleep. This procedure got everyone to bed, but it drove a wedge between husband and wife. James seemed to enjoy his power in keeping his parents apart at bedtime. Next morning he was up before sunrise racing about the house. He thrived on less than 5 hours of sleep. The rest of the family members were always exhausted.

James was dismissed from three preschools in town. By the time he was 4 years old, no preschool would accept him. Every child care agency in the community had heard of this uncontrollable little boy. When he was 5, his parents found a private kindergarten that reluctantly agreed to let James attend for 1 week to see if their staff could work with him. After 3 days, he was told not to come back. By this time he had been labeled as emotionally disturbed, severely oppositional, and antisocial. By age 6 he was already beyond the reach of the educational systems of his community.

Meanwhile, the Able family was breaking apart. Mr. Able moved out of the house one night after he and his wife had a verbal battle. Both had become so frustrated over James's incorrigible behavior that each blamed the other for his condition. Words became increasingly bitter. Their anger had been building for several years without being properly channeled or expressed. When it all exploded, the marriage came apart. That night James climbed into his mother's bed and went right to sleep. With his father gone, he had his mother all to himself. His bedtime tantrums stopped and he began to act almost normally once he was in control. Mrs. Able confided to a close friend, "I am finding it very hard to love this child. When I look at my feelings honestly, I sometimes hate him. I'm always angry at him. This makes me feel like a total failure as a mother. This child has cost us our marriage. We have not had a moment's peace since he was born. What am I going to do?"

The Ables were mature enough to patch things together so that the marriage survived, but the home was not a happy place. Finally, the grandparents put together enough money to enroll James in a special day school for emotionally disturbed children. Under the constant supervision of specialists in abnormal behavior, he learned to behave differently enough to remove some pressure from his home.

When he was 8 years old, James's parents brought him to me for an evaluation of his intelligence, learning patterns, and basic academic skills. I spent an entire day with this hyperactive boy who had been disruptive in every situation so far in his life. An amazing bonding occurred that day between James and me. Instead of forcing him to do the tests in traditional fashion, I worked out ways for him to be himself as we did the activities together. Sometimes he lay on the floor with feet bumping the underside of the work table as I asked questions and he answered. At times he rolled back and forth on the large beanbag and chanted responses in rhymes he created on the spot. Sometimes he sat in my lap and snuggled back against my chest. Then he lay flat on the carpet and pounded rhythms with his fists and feet. It was the first time in his life that he had been able to interact with an adult in such a comfortable, positive way. There were no pressures, threats, or fear of failure. The novelty I allowed him to invent ways to communicate brought his thoughts together in multisensory rhythms that let all of his brain pathways function at their best. Eighteen years later, James still talks about that day when he met an adult who did not fight his hyperactivity but accepted him as the intelligent, creative person he really was.

When we met, James was at level 10 on the ADHD severity scale. His presence at home exerted enormous pressure on everyone involved in his life. He was totally disorganized and had no sense of how things should go or be arranged. He was insatiable, never receiving enough to satisfy his cravings for attention. He was completely self-focused, spending his energies on meeting his own needs and desires. He was angry, taking out his frustrations on anyone within reach. He was frightened and experienced awful nightmares that terrified him for days. He was phobic about many things that overloaded his emotions. For example, the sight of an inflated balloon sent him into hysterics. "It might pop!" he would wail, no matter where the family might be. They would have to leave the restaurant, party, or shopping mall where balloons were on display.

James was often vindictive, going out of his way to get even with anyone who offended him or made him angry. He had no friends, playmates, or pets, and no group of peers who would accept him. In all of this, he was bewildered. Why did other kids not like him? Why could he not spend a week at Grandma's house? Why did his family stop going to Sunday School? Why did everyone always yell "No!" and "Stop that, James!" When he and I met, he was a lonely, frightened, stubborn, uneducated boy with underdeveloped social skills. Yet he had enormous potential that lay beyond our reach. What could we do to help this severely handicapped child who showed all of the major signs of ADHD?

Mr. and Mrs. Able were desperate for help with their son, yet they were afraid of medication that had been suggested by several pediatricians. (In Chapter 6, we review medications that often reduce ADHD symptoms in children like James.) The Able family had been counseled by their church leaders that medications like Ritalin and Cylert often turn hyperactive children into zombies with stunted growth. When I realized that it would not be possible to refer these parents to a physician for medication, I urged them to follow a controversial therapy of diet control. (Chapter 6 reviews the opposition to diet therapy that most physicians express.) Yet something had to be done to help this desperate child and his battered family. In our city lived a psychiatrist who was regarded by the professional community as a "maverick." For several years, he had practiced what he called "ecological psychiatry." This method used diet control with extremely hyperactive persons like James who did not respond to other treatments for emotional disturbance or aggressive behavior. I asked the Able family to consider letting this psychiatrist try to help their son.

Because ecological psychiatry involved foods but no medications, Mr. and Mrs. Able agreed to try. The approach was direct and simple. James became a guest in a private clinic for 1 week. He was treated like a very important person, and he was introduced to computers that kept him busy. At the same time, he was systematically tested for food intolerance. The parents were asked not to see their son or call him for the first 4 days. Because of our strong bond, I visited James and spent time watching him work with his computer. He went through withdrawal symptoms for the first 3 days as his body cried out for his old diet. He had tantrums and headaches, but he made it through that difficult time. An amazing difference greeted me when I visited him on the fourth day. James was relaxed and quiet. He was laughing over some jokes he had printed on the computer. He snuggled into my lap with deep affection without any of his old game to control. That morning his attention span was the longest I had ever seen. We began working with phonics skills he never had learned. The old disruptive James was out of the picture when his parents visited that day. Never before had they seen their son able to interact in normal ways that were filled with affection.

James and his family began to follow a careful diet that was developed as his intolerance for specific foods was identified. He was severely allergic (cytotoxic) to white wheat in any form. He could not tolerate milk, which he loved to drink by the quart. He had strong intolerance for several foods in the salicylate group (green pepper, peaches, apples, cucumbers, strawberries, tomatoes). He was highly sensitive to yeast, and he could not tolerate caffeine. Anything containing grape products made him wild. When these culprit food substances were taken out of his diet, James became relatively calm and reachable. On this new diet, James came down to level 6 on the ADHD severity scale. He still was antsy and easily bored, except with computer activities. He lost his temper still and needed a lot of supervision. He continued to balk and be quite stubborn, and he continued to need supervision because of poor organizational ability. Yet as long as he avoided trigger foods and beverages, he was a comfortable member of his family. He learned to function in academic work and eventually became a good student. I cherish the note of thanks I received from Mr. and Mrs. Able a few weeks after James and his family started the diet control program: "We don't have the words to thank you enough, Dr. J. As the Bible says, through you God has 'restored to us the years that the locust hath eaten' [Joel 2:25]. You have given us back our son we thought we had lost forever."

In his natural state, James placed so much stress on his environment, his family broke apart. Without intervention, the home could not cope with his severe ADHD. The combination of hyperactivity and emotional battering was so disruptive that neither the child nor his family could have survived without intervention.

Nate

I met Nate by accident when he was 9 years old. After speaking to a parent group about attention deficit disorders, I was followed to my car by a woman who was crying. She had trouble talking through her sobs. "You have just described my son," she managed to tell me. "All these years I have tried to find out what his problem is. Tonight you have explained it. Everything you said about ADD without hyperactivity fits Nate to a tee." The more the mother talked about her son, the more I wanted to meet him. She was a single parent with two children. By working an extra job on weekends, she provided a modest living for her family. She told me how no one in her family wanted anything to do with her son. "They call him weird," she explained. "His dad has nothing to do with him, and none of the grandparents pay any attention to him. Can you help me with my son?"

Soon after that I met Nate. He is now 22 years old and in college, where he is specializing in computer science. Our first meeting was one of the strangest experiences of my life. Nate was unusually tall for his age. He was thin and awkward with poor motor coordination. He shuffled along in an awkward gait with his arms swinging in stiff jerks instead of being relaxed. I was greatly surprised to notice that he carried a Raggedy Andy doll. Nate introduced me to Roy, his doll. He placed Roy between us on the large round table where I worked with youngsters. He took a piece of gum from the candy dish and unwrapped it for Roy. He fussed with Roy's clothes and made all kinds of little sounds. Nate began speaking in a singsong voice. Then Roy "answered" in a high-pitched, whining response. This conversation between Nate and his doll lasted several minutes. Finally I realized that Nate was telling Roy why they were in my office. He was assuring Roy that everything was fine. As I learned how to interpret this private language, I heard Nate explain, "Mommie thinks something is wrong with me and wants me to talk to this doctor. But nothing is wrong with me, is there, Roy? And nothing is wrong with you, either. This doctor just wants to ask me some questions, Roy. He isn't going to hurt me or give me any shots or any medicine. He's going to tell Mommie that I'm fine and I don't need any shots or medicine. But it's OK, Roy. Don't be afraid. It's OK." This litany continued for more than 10 minutes while I listened with fascination. Here was a 9-year-old boy, as tall as most adolescents, speaking a private language to his doll, making sure that the doll was not afraid. No wonder Nate's relatives called him weird. I knew from the mother's information that Roy did not go to school with Nate. The moment the boy arrived home from after school care, he dashed into his room to be with Roy. They stayed behind the closed door until supper was ready. If Nate had his way, he would spend all of his time alone in his room talking things over with Roy in their private singsong speech.

As I worked with Nate over a period of time, we became close friends. However, it was 6 months before he came to me without bringing Roy. By working slowly and gently with Nate, I discovered that he had severe patterns of ADD. Beneath his quiet, withdrawn surface was a cluster of attention deficits that blocked him in many ways. I finally determined that he was at level 8 on the ADD severity scale. No doubt he had been at level 9 when he first started attending school. Listening comprehension was very poor. Nate understood less than 30% of what he heard unless someone repeated for him. His thought patterns were extremely loose. He rarely went longer than 90 seconds without losing his mental image. He continually experienced the "blink" patterns described in Chapter 4 (see page 75). Without warning, the thought of the moment skipped to a different mental image. Along with this blink pattern were moments of going blank when he lost his thoughts altogether. As I worked with Nate, I remembered a comment made by a bright 8-year-old girl who had ADD: "My brain just stops." So did Nate's brain. No matter how hard he tried to keep on listening, thinking, or doing his work, his brain "just stopped."

On the surface, we might wonder how a passive, intensely private boy who spent most of his time in make-believe with his doll could be disruptive within his family. The more I learned about Nate, the more easily I understood how disruptive his passive ADD patterns were for his mother, sister, and other relatives. Nate had almost no sense of time passing, and he had no sense of organization. His room was a mess, and he never attempted to clean it up. The small house in which the family lived was littered by things he absentmindedly left laying around. His clothing was scattered everywhere. He was extremely slow to start a task, then very slow doing it. He never went from start to finish without being supervised. He could not remember to get home with necessary school materials. After supper, when his mother asked if he had any homework to do, Nate usually could not remember. On those days when he did get home with his stuff, he invariably forgot to take finished assignments and books back to school the next day. Every morning began with his mother nagging him, Nate dawdling and procrastinating, and mother and son having a shouting match because time was running out. Visits to relatives were equally frustrating and discouraging for Nate's mother. He refused to go without his doll Roy. This ritual behavior drove his mother wild. In spite of the snickers and teasing Nate received from relatives, he would not go without his make-believe partner. He sat in his grandmother's living room talking to Roy in their private singsong language even when adults showed irritation. Soon his grandparents, aunts, and uncles were making critical or sarcastic comments that caused Nate to burst into tears from hurt feelings. His mother could not remember a family visit that did not end with Nate crying, relatives criticizing her for not making him throw away that doll and grow up, and her yelling at Nate all the way home. The boy's immaturity, fears, ritualized behaviors, and deep-seated fantasies expressed through his doll were highly disruptive to this single-parent household where the mother exhausted herself earning a living, only to come home each night to this "weird" child who refused to grow up.

Two strategies built a bridge that a gifted tutor used to bring Nate from his world of make-believe into the world of reality. First, Nate was introduced to keyboard writing. Immediately he began to create fantastical stories that were filled with magical characters from his world of make-believe. Soon he had written his first illustrated book about Roy, a mighty warrior who saved his people from an invading tribe of barbarians. Through this medium we guided Nate into doing outstanding work in his language arts and reading programs at school. Second, the tutor introduced Nate to the magical worlds of the *Chronicles of Narnia* by C. S. Lewis and the hobbit tales by J. R. R. Tolkien. As he devoured these make-believe works, Nate's own imagination left behind the fearful immaturity I had seen at first. Soon he was self-confident enough to make some of the best grades in his classroom.

Nate remained a "slob" in his private life. He continued to litter his space with scattered stuff. He continued to be forgetful, forever losing books and clothing. He continued to dawdle and procrastinate at home. Yet the level of disruption within his family quickly dropped as his mother learned not to fret over ADD habits that Nate could not help doing. She agreed to stop taking him to family gatherings, and this removed a major source of heartache for her and her son. His mother learned to close the door to his room so she did not see Nate's mess. He learned to keep his clutter out of the family living area of their home. Nate also learned to keep lists of his responsibilities and school assignments. Each day after school, an older student spent 5 minutes going over these lists with Nate to make sure he had all his things in his bookbag. Instead of engaging in arguments at home, he and his mother learned to review the lists, making sure that Nate was ready for school each day. Part of this routine was the rule that if Nate became stubborn and refused to cooperate with his supervisors, he would face the consequences. This stopped the nagging that had triggered so many morning arguments between mother and son.

As time went by, Nate gradually moved down the ADD severity scale. By age 13, his ADD symptoms were at level 6. By age 16, his attention deficit was down to level 5. By age 19, he was down to level 4. At age 22 his ADD patterns are at level 3. Chapter 5 describes the tag-along Asperger's syndrome that lived in the shadow of Nate's ADD. As an adult, he still is messy in his private space, forgetful enough to lose track of things, and not yet ready for a romantic relationship because he remains self-focused and prefers time with his computer over time with friends. However, he has demonstrated extraordinary talent for computer science that does not require strong social skills for building a successful career.

ADHD and ADD on the Job

During the last two decades of the twentieth century, dramatic changes occurred in the workplace. By the end of the 1980s, it was increasingly difficult for adults with attention deficit disorders to earn a living. Restaurants largely were replaced by fast-food stores that demanded rapid production and strict following of standard procedures. Self-service filling stations no longer needed human beings to clean the windshield, fill the tank, and check the tires. Auto mechanics had to be expert at computer analysis of modern vehicles that are run by computer chips. Working in a warehouse required the skill to create computer printouts and interpret computer-generated codes. Loading trucks no longer was a simple matter of moving crates and boxes. Complex laws governing child care often made it impossible for women to earn extra income by supervising children in their homes. As our culture enters the twenty-first century, the workplace requires computer skills, calm ability to function quickly under pressure, and enough education to qualify for licenses according to government regulations. Adults with residual ADHD or ADD find it very difficult to earn a living. Several million young adults continue to live with their parents because they cannot earn enough to live on their own. Several million parents are caught in the "sandwich generation," having to care for aging parents while still providing for adult children who cannot manage for themselves. Adults with residual ADHD or ADD swell the ranks of unemployed and underemployed workers in our culture.

ADHD on the Job

I met hyperactive, aggressive Jo when she was 13 years old. I became her trusted friend and counselor to whom she turned when her life got out of control. Twenty-one years later, we are still good friends. Jo's parents held their marriage together in spite of the battering experience of rearing a daughter with severe ADHD. Until onset of puberty at age 12, Jo was at level 9 in hyperactivity and lack of self-control. The Barkers survived those difficult years through the help of Ritalin, which is described in Chapter 6. Ritalin brought down Jo's hyperactivity to level 7 for a few hours each day when she was away from her parents. When the Barker family came together again for the evening, the parents endured emotional storms that were unleashed as Jo's pent-up energy and emotions rebounded because Ritalin had disappeared from her brain. By dinner time each evening, she was climbing the walls and driving her parents crazy. Hormone development during puberty gradually reduced the force of her hyperactivity to level 8, then to level 7 by the time she entered ninth grade. With continued treatment through medication, Jo stayed in school with barely passing grades. Outbursts of impulsive, irrational behavior threatened school failure, but private tutoring and frequent counseling enabled her to graduate with her high school class. Mr. and Mrs. Barker wept with relief as they watched their difficult daughter receive her high school diploma. "Surely," they told themselves, "now we will get a break." After 18 traumatic years, they looked forward to the "empty nest" their friends described. Jo was their only child. They dared not have more children when the severity of her ADHD became clear.

Jo received several hundred dollars as graduation gifts. She talked about using that money to rent an apartment with a friend. The Barkers encouraged this plan. They helped Jo and her friend look for an apartment they could afford and shop for household things. Three weeks after high school commencement, the Barkers received a telephone call one evening. It was Jo telling them that she was at a summer resort with several friends. On the spur of the moment, they had decided to party because they were going separate ways in a few weeks. She would be home sometime. Then she hung up without leaving her number or address. Jo was gone for 10 days. Late one night a call came from a sheriff's office in a neighboring state. "I'm in jail," Jo said in her old angry voice. "This bunch of jerks arrested me for drunk driving. Come get me out of this crappy place!" Mr. Barker listened to several minutes of her anger, then he talked with the sheriff's deputy. He learned that Jo and some friends had been stopped going 90 miles per hour in a 45-mph speed zone. Jo, who was driving, started to yell and resist the officer's effort to check things out. The deputy finally determined that she was driving without a license. She registered 0.018 on the breath test for intoxication, twice the legal limit for blood alcohol in that state. Jo faced several hundred dollars in fines. She also needed an attorney to represent her in local court. This postgraduation party cost the Barkers more than $3,000. All of Jo's gift money had been spent with nothing left for the apartment.

For several weeks following this upset, Jo lived in anger toward her parents. "We're back to the days when she was seven before we started Ritalin," Mrs. Barker sobbed one night. Because Jo was 18 years old, her parents could not force her to see a counselor or take medication. "I'm a legal adult!" she yelled. "You can't make me anymore!" Relatives and church friends advised the Barkers to practice "tough love" by forcing Jo to leave their home unless she obeyed their rules. Her parents could not bring themselves to take such a drastic step.

By September, Jo began to calm down and become less angry. Her parents realized that her anger actually was a smoke screen to cover intense anxiety. In reality, she was deeply afraid of stepping out on her own. Jo realized that she had no job skills to offer an employer. "I can't do anything right!" she sobbed one night to her mother. "All my life I've screwed everything up! I can't make it on my own without you and Dad. It makes me so mad at myself! I'm nothing but a _____ failure!"

Jo swallowed her pride and agreed to talk things over with me. In the calm atmosphere of my office, she accepted my encouragement to apply for at least a part-time job. We worked out a list of jobs that would not press her too hard. Her ADHD patterns made it very hard for her to follow oral instructions, especially if there was background noise while she listened. As we saw in Chapter 4 (see page 75), her short attention span caused her to "blink" or "go blank" instead of staying focused on a task. Lack of organization made it hard for her to keep a workspace tidy. Her poor sense of time meant that she must be reminded when and where to be. As Jo and I reviewed all of these patterns, she decided to look for work. She was too bored and restless to stay at home and watch television all day. However, she refused to return to taking Ritalin. "I'm not going back on drugs," she declared. "I'm not a kid anymore."

I warned Jo that being turned down for jobs would be her most difficult challenge. "You are a very sensitive person," I reminded her. "Your first reaction will be to take it as personal rejection if you are turned down when you apply." This prediction was correct. After being turned down three times following job interviews, Jo slipped into a state of depression for several days. Her old fear of failure returned heavily, and her lifelong battle with low self-esteem became acute. She cried, she was angry, and she began sleeping all day. Finally Mr. Barker asked a friend who owned several ice cream shops to give Jo a job to help her build up her courage. The friend agreed. Jo was to begin work at 3:00 p.m. the following Monday.

Jo was late to work that first day. As her parents left the house that morning, they reminded her to watch the clock. Mrs. Barker called at noon to remind her again, but this triggered an argument over the phone. "I'm not a baby!" Jo yelled at her mother. "Stay off my back!" Then she turned on the television and lost track of time. At 2:50, she saw the clock. She dashed to her car and raced off toward work. A few blocks from the house she ran out of gas because she had forgotten to fill the tank when her father reminded her the day before. A neighbor brought gas from his garage and started her car. Then she discovered that she had left her purse and credit cards at home. Back to the house she raced, then rushed to work. She was 20 minutes late and out of breath.

Robb, the manager of the ice cream shop, was irritated by Jo's late arrival. He already was upset because a friend of the boss had gotten his daughter this job. An impressive young man had applied for the position, but Robb was told to hire Jo instead. The new job started on a negative note. Robb was impatient when it was clear that this new worker needed everything repeated. If the manager kept on explaining, Jo interrupted, "What do you mean?" Within a few minutes of on-the-job training, the manager was feeling hostile toward this new employee whom he had not wanted in the first place. Jo began to boil inside, as she always did when anyone in authority told her to listen and stop interrupting. Those words always triggered her anger because it made her feel "dumb" to be told to listen better. She tried to hold her temper under control, but as the work session continued, her old ADHD patterns emerged. Before she had been on the job 2 hours, Jo flared into a shouting match with her new manager. Robb reminded her who was boss. Those words were the last straw. "Well, you can take this rotten job and shove it!" she screamed as she stomped out of the shop.

During the next 4 months, Jo was hired, then fired, from seven jobs. Each time, she promised me and her parents that she would do better. Each time she started a new job, she fully intended to make this one a success. Each time, she soon reached the point of failure. Jo worked a few days selling tie-dyed T-shirts in a boutique. She made so many mistakes at the cash register that the boss finally let her go. She found a job making cinnamon pastries in a shopping mall, but this job required her to work in an open space where shoppers could stand and watch. She could not keep her attention focused on her work. After spoiling several batches of pastry dough, Jo was fired for being "careless." Then she found part-time work that sounded exciting. She was to sell cosmetics by telephone. Like most of her friends, Jo loved talking on the phone. This job lasted half a day. She could not remember the sales message that she was required to say. Besides, she began to feel angry when several people hung up as she introduced herself by phone. Her love of telephone talking did not give her the right skills for this oral communication.

Finally Jo was hired to sell costume jewelry in a department store. All her life she had had a natural talent for fashion. She did well for the first 2 weeks and began to feel confident of her skills. One Friday evening during rush hour, three of her high school friends came by. As they laughed and talked about old times, customers stood in line. Several customers interrupted and asked Jo to help them with purchases. Her old habits of resenting authority emerged, and she said sharply, "Just wait a minute! I'm busy!" Then she returned to gossiping with her friends. A customer complained to the floor manager, who came to see what the problem might be. When the manager told Jo's friends to leave and reminded her that customers were waiting, Jo's lifelong temper flared. She walked off yet another job having a tantrum. Later she rationalized to me and her parents, "I hated that old job anyway. They make you work like a slave and they don't pay anything. I won't waste my time at a place like that!" Three more jobs came and went with similar stories.

As the Christmas season approached, the Barkers realized with heavy hearts how handicapped their daughter was as a young adult with still-active patterns of ADHD. They joined a parent support group called CHADD, which is described in Chapter 6. At CHADD meetings, they shared their sad story with other parents who also were trapped with adult children who had residual ADHD. To their dismay, the Barkers learned that many families still support such children long after high school. Mr. and Mrs. Barker learned that our culture includes many young adults with still-active ADHD. They do not possess job skills that fit today's workplace needs. They do not have the social skills to fit into the adult world successfully. They lack the emotional maturity to absorb normal social pressures without losing self-control. These young adults with active ADHD are restless children in grown-up bodies. They still need the same type of supervision they required during childhood and adolescence, yet they are too proud, insecure, and self-focused to permit parents and other adults to provide supervision. These ADHD adults are demanding in the same selfish ways that spoiled relationships when they were young. They are too shallow to comprehend the principle that it is more blessed to give than to receive. They do not express gratitude to parents who are exhausted from many years of forgiving, providing, and carrying the burden within the family. These residual ADHD adults cannot establish separate lives. They cannot function successfully on jobs. They cannot stay in personal relationships that require give and take. They are locked into lifestyles that are immature, self-centered, and often destructive. And they tend to refuse the help offered by loved ones, friends, and the community. Parents like the Barkers often search in vain for hope that things will soon improve as they wrestle the problems created by their adult children who still have ADHD.

In Chapter 2 we reviewed the question of whether individuals outgrow ADHD or ADD (see pages 36–40). Most specialists in these behavior problems agree that youngsters with moderate or mild ADHD and ADD do outgrow many of the childhood symptoms during adolescence and early adult years. During my 40 years working with individuals like Jo, I have seen an extremely late developmental cycle that seldom is reported by research. Of the young adults with still-active ADHD, some begin to move down the severity scale as they near age 30. Many of the severely ADHD adolescents and young adults I have known began to mellow about age 28 and continued to mellow as they reached their early thirties.

Jo followed this extremely late maturity pattern. During her twenties, her life was a nightmare. At age 21 she became pregnant by an extremely immature ADHD man who paid for an abortion. Like most young adults with these behavior problems, she began using social drugs at parties and soon was habituated to cocaine and marijuana. This self-medication did relieve her churning emotions temporarily. Jo also became a heavy user of alcohol. She lived around the community with friends in low-rent apartments. Her parents were forced to install a security system to keep her from breaking in and stealing valuable things to sell for drug money. Every so often, Jo showed up at my office to spend a little time talking with the only mature friend who had not rejected her. When she reached her 27th birthday, I noticed a change in her attitude. She was using less cocaine and marijuana, and she stopped drinking alcohol altogether. She began staying on part-time jobs for 3 or 4 months instead of for only a few days. As she approached her 29th birthday, Jo came by one afternoon to introduce me to Pete, a new man in her life. He was well groomed, well educated, and appeared to be in love with her. This was the first time she had dated a mature man without destroying the relationship through her temper and sarcasm. Mr. and Mrs. Barker were able to have Jo come home for visits that no longer ended in tantrums and destructive words. On her 30th birthday, Jo and Pete told me that they were getting married. She had stayed successfully on a good job for more than a year. The Barkers could hardly believe this good fortune. Between ages 27 and 30, Jo's ADHD patterns had gone from level 8 on the severity scale to level 4. She was a true "late bloomer," like many others I have known over a period of years.

ADD on the Job

Lee came into my life when he was 9 years old, one of the most depressed children I had ever met. The first time we met, he quietly cried with his chin down on his chest. As we became acquainted that day, he surprised me by climbing into my lap. He wrapped his arms tightly around me and sobbed into my shoulder. From that moment, we were bonded for life. I determined that Lee was at level 8 ADD. This explanation helped his bewildered family come together as his strong support team. Since early childhood, he had been the most forgetful, absentminded person his family had ever seen. Through early childhood, kindergarten, and primary grades, Mr. and Mrs. Hobbs tried every trick they could think of to help Lee remember. They covered the refrigerator with stick-on notes reminding him what to do after school, when to feed and water his dog, and where to be at certain times. Then they had to remind him to look at his notes. Every detail of his young life had to be supervised, or else he forgot. After working at their jobs all day, Lee's parents faced the task of rounding up his schoolbooks for homework. They usually had to dash back to school to get something he had forgotten to bring home. They often had to drive to the bus barn to retrieve something Lee had left on the bus. Mr. and Mrs. Hobbs lost track of how many new jackets, caps, gloves, and even socks their son lost during his years in school.

Without adult supervision, Lee could not finish anything he started. The attic was filled with half-finished models of all kinds. His room was littered with half-finished projects and posters he abandoned. His school locker was stuffed with papers that represented half-finished homework never turned in. After dragging him through assignments at night, Mr. and Mrs. Hobbs exhausted themselves reminding Lee to get all of his schoolwork into his book bag. He usually left something important behind as he ran to catch the bus. The orthodontist complained about Lee's failure to care for his teeth and braces. The optometrist could not believe how many times he replaced eye-glasses Lee needed for school. After what seemed a lifetime of constant super-vision, the weary Hobbs family watched their scatter-brained son receive his high school diploma. Their ray of hope was that Lee's ADD patterns had begun to decline during adolescence. At age 11, he was at level 8 on the severity scale. By age 14, he was down to level 7. At age 18, he was about level 6. But he was still "loose as a goose," as his grandmother expressed it.

In every situation, Lee's good sense of humor saved the day. No one could stay angry with him very long. He never seemed upset. He was glad to see oth-ers even when they scolded him for being so forgetful and inattentive. His kindness made quick friends everywhere he went. The fact that he was always rumpled and needed to comb his hair did not take away from his grin and friendly attitude. When Lee forgot to shower and use deodorant for several days, others overlooked his poor grooming. "Wow! That kid sure is ripe!" his Grandpa said every now and then. But Grandpa still bragged on this grand-son to everyone who would listen.

Lee fully intended to go to college, but high school graduation was over and he had not gotten around to applying for college admission. He had forgotten to show up for the college admission test that was required by all of the state schools. He began looking for a job the week after graduation. Within 2 days, he was hired to deliver floral arrangements for a neighborhood shop. The owner of the floral shop was charmed by this young man's smile and friendly attitude. Part of Lee's responsibility was to take inventory of cut flowers and potted plants every Tuesday and Thursday afternoon. Keeping enough flowers on hand depended on those inventories. Lee could read well and had no trouble handling numbers. But as he hurried from work the first Tuesday to go fishing with his grandfather, he forgot to take the inventory. Two unexpected funerals occurred on Wednesday, and the shop ran out of flowers. The florist listened to Lee's apology. "Well, I will forgive it this time," the manager said, "but don't let it happen again. We just can't stay in business if we don't keep track of our inventory." Two weeks later Lee forgot again. This time the manager fired him. "You're one of the nicest boys I've ever had here," the florist said, "but, Lee, you've cost me five hundred dollars. I have to let you go."

It did not take Lee long to find another job. This time he was hired as night-shift cashier in a prepay self-service filling station. His job was to take money or credit cards before customers filled their tanks. He had to watch all the cars that pulled up to the 16 gasoline pumps. He was to stop any pump immediately if the driver tried to fill his tank before paying in advance at Lee's window. The third night on the job, a lull came in traffic. Ten minutes went by with no customers, so Lee started to read a book. Soon he was lost in the story. He did not see four cars pull up to the pumps farthest from his booth. Those drivers knew how to activate the pumps without paying in advance. They filled their tanks, then slipped away without Lee seeing them. The next day, he was fired and had to pay the filling station owner for the stolen gas.

During the next 2 years, Lee was fired from more than 20 jobs. His mother kept a log of her son's job history. "Someday when I write my book," she said many times, "people won't believe it." Lee lost jobs because he was late too many times. No matter how many alarm clocks went off beside his bed, he could not wake up without a struggle. He lost several more jobs because he forgot to do essential tasks. He was fired for wearing soiled uniforms after being warned to make sure he was fresh and clean. Twice he lost his job because he loaded merchandise on the wrong trucks. He had been watching something down the dock and did not notice what he was doing. Lee could not keep track of work schedules unless he was reminded. He lost several jobs because he failed to notice changes for his shift. Three times he was fined for losing important papers on the job. He was forever being nagged for having too much clutter in his workspace. Managers fussed at him for failing to put equipment away before leaving his shift. Yet every time he was fired, Lee was told, "You're one of the nicest guys we've ever had work here, but I have to let you go." This nice guy who had level 6 ADD could not cope successfully with workplace expectations.

When Lee was 21 years old, he was still living at home with his parents. They continued to help him make car payments and pay his bills. Then he met a girl and fell in love. Mr. and Mrs. Hobbs were delighted with Nancy. "That girl has common sense," said Mr. Hobbs, as they watched her reason with Lee. Nancy was able to give advice in a way that did not offend or embarrass him. She began to help him notice that he needed to improve his appearance. On

Saturdays they went shopping, where Nancy taught Lee how to pay attention to clothes and styles. She suggested that he let her help him keep track of how he spent his money. Then she showed him how to keep track of time by using a folding calendar that fit into his pocket. Nancy coached Lee in watching clocks wherever he happened to be. She helped him understand why it is important not to start reading a book on the job or make too many phone calls while he was at work. By the time Nancy and Lee announced their engagement to be married, he was holding the first steady job he had had since high school. By letting Nancy become his supervisor, Lee learned to compensate for residual ADD. As his mother eventually wrote in her book about rearing a son with ADD, "The key to success for anyone who has ADD is finding a supervisor. Children who have ADD need supervision. Teens must have supervision, although they rebel against it. Adults who still have ADD also need good supervisors. My son became a successful man when he had the good sense to marry the most wonderful supervisor in the world."

Tag-Along Syndromes that Imitate ADHD and ADD

5

In Chapter 1, we reviewed the earliest speculations about disruptive behavior that included poor attention, chronic distraction, and impulsive lifestyles (James, 1890; Still, 1902; Tredgold, 1908). One hundred years ago, scientists had not yet separated true attention deficit disorders from a host of other syndromes that often tag along together. In Chapter 2 we reviewed scientific progress during the twentieth century in learning to recognize differences between attention deficits and other disruptive behaviors that imitate ADHD and ADD. By 1991 Russell Barkley and his colleagues were ready to separate tag-along syndromes from ADHD and ADD. Barkley's research demonstrated that 65% of those who are diagnosed as ADHD also display a look-alike syndrome called *Oppositional Defiant Disorder (ODD)*. Of those diagnosed as ADHD, an additional 30% also display a highly disruptive lifestyle called *Conduct Disorder (CD)* (Barkley, 1990, 1995). Researchers at the University of Massachusetts Medical Center pinpointed an even more complex form of disruptive behavior, *Multiplex Developmental Disorder (MDD)*, which often is linked to ADHD (Barkley, 1990). In their book *Shadow Syndromes*, Ratey and Johnson (1997) separate ADHD/ADD from the overlapping syndromes of monopolar depression, hypomanic personality, rage disorders, mild autism, forms of addiction, anxiety, and attention "surplus" disorders. In Chapter 4 we met James, the angry little ADHD tiger, whose often violent ODD behavior and CD were triggered by cytotoxic reactions to certain foods. This overlap of two or more syndromes is called *comorbidity*. Like shingles on a roof, a variety of disruptive behaviors often hide behind each other to make positive identification of ADHD or ADD rather difficult.

Oppositional Defiant Disorder

Oppositional Defiant Disorder (ODD) is intensely disruptive without being violent or overly aggressive. The surface of ODD presents many of the ADHD patterns described in Chapter 2. However, hiding beneath the attentional deficit overlay is a lifestyle that is negative, hostile, and defiant of authority. No matter how much guidance and counseling parents or teachers might provide, the ADHD/ODD person cannot fit successfully into the family, a classroom, social groups, or the workplace. Yet this disruptive individual does not meet the diagnostic criteria for such mental illness categories as *Antisocial Personality Disorder* or *Psychotic or Mood Disorder.*

Temper Tantrums

The habitual temper tantrums of ODD go far beyond loss of temper that all persons experience from time to time. ODD tantrums are like thunderstorms that explode without warning and blow roofs off buildings or knock down power lines. Once the storm has released its aggressive energy, it moves away quickly. ODD tantrums follow a pattern that my grandmother explained: "That person doesn't lose his temper. He uses his temper." I did not understand what she meant until I became a classroom teacher of ADHD/ODD youngsters. As their tantrums burst on classmates and adults, the exploding anger always had a purpose: to enable the self-focused child to get his or her own way. As soon as everyone gave in and the angry child got what he or she wanted, the tantrum stopped as suddenly as it had begun. My grandmother's wisdom was correct. Individuals with Oppositional Defiant Disorder do not just lose their temper. They use their anger to gain self-satisfaction.

Arguing with Authority

A disruptive characteristic of ADHD is arguing over misunderstandings. However, when the misunderstanding has been corrected, persons with ADHD stop arguing and begin to use the information they first misperceived. Arguing plays a different role in ODD behavior. Persons with ODD "get up in the face" of whomever is in charge, daring that parent, teacher, coach, job supervisor, or police officer to enforce the rules. "You can't make me" and "I don't have to" are the battle cries of those with ODD. This hostile challenge of authority comes as automatically as a sneeze. In Chapter 4 we met Jo, who defied authority all her life until her late blooming occurred after age 30. In one-to-one counseling relationships, frustrated individuals like Jo confess in pleading terms, "I don't know what makes me do this. I don't want to be this way. I just can't help it." Nerve pathway differences in the midbrain (brain stem, medulla, amygdala, hippocampus), as well as differences in how the parietal lobe and prefrontal cortex are made, permit this runaway pattern of challenging authority. No matter how hard the ODD individual tries not to flare under authority, an automatic "in your face" challenge occurs.

Deliberately Annoying Others

Just as iron filings are attracted to a magnet, Oppositional Defiant persons are drawn to others. Being ODD means that the individual cannot leave others alone. It is important to separate normal childhood development from the pervasive patterns of ODD. It is normal for children of preschool age to "pick on" each other. This is due partly to curiosity, partly to relieve boredom, and partly to exert individuality. Children with normal neurological development soon learn to stop picking on others. Oppositional Defiant youngsters do not.

An insatiable need to have the full attention of others is part of the disruptive package of ODD. Persons with ADHD/ODD not only are loose, poorly organized, and overly distracted, they also cannot leave others alone. These disruptive persons spend their time and energy looking around to see what others are doing. Then they move into the private spaces of others, demanding to be part of that activity. If family members want to be quiet or alone for awhile, the ODD individual does not. He or she begins to do things that force others to pay attention. For example, if a parent is reading quietly, the ODD person starts to make noises that he or she knows will irritate the reader. Soon the reader gives the desired attention by saying "Stop that!" or "Leave me alone." Once the other person's attention is engaged, the ODD individual continues the intrusion by triggering still stronger emotions. Soon a battle of wills has begun, which was the ODD intention. In the classroom, if quiet work time has begun, the ODD member starts a subtle campaign to disrupt this group activity. He or she makes small noises that are designed to attract attention. The ODD person may begin to flip bits of paper that hit a classmate's face or workpage. Or the ODD child may start foot games against a classmate's chair or table leg. Soon the quietness is broken, and the ODD individual has attracted the attention he or she craves—no matter that the attention received is negative or even harsh. The point of ODD behavior is to make it impossible for others to ignore this restless, self-centered individual.

Blaming Others

Perhaps the most perplexing part of Oppositional Defiant behavior is the automatic response of blaming others. A dozen witnesses may have watched the ODD person commit a disruptive act. Yet the automatic response when challenged is "I didn't do it" or "He made me do it. It's not my fault." As ODD youngsters enter adolescence, and later reach adulthood, this automatic habit of blaming others brings them into confrontation with civil authority. We who work with adjudicated delinquents and convicted felons find this ODD pattern in a majority of those who are under the jurisdiction of a court. An unfortunate consequence of Oppositional Defiant Disorder is the lifestyle of blaming others instead of admitting the truth. By the time ODD youngsters have entered their teen years, many have become chronic liars who rarely tell the truth about their own responsibility.

Overly Touchy and Irritable

Oppositional Defiant Disorder causes a person to be so touchy and irritable that it is impossible for others to offer constructive criticism or advice. In Chapter 4 we read of Jo's instant irritability. The least hint of advice or criticism triggered her self-defense. To keep from hearing anything that pressed her to improve, she lashed out verbally to stop such comments from her parents, teachers, or job supervisors. My childhood years living on a farm taught me the meaning of the question "How do you pet a porcupine?" Answer: "Very, very carefully." This sums up the problem of getting along with someone who is ADHD/ODD. Their prickly, overly touchy, irritable reactions cause others to draw back and keep a safe distance.

Overly Angry and Resentful

A persistent goal for parents and instructors of young children is to teach the social principle of forgiveness. We want youngsters not to carry grudges beyond a reasonable length of time. Social skills include the habit of turning loose old anger. Oppositional Defiant Disorder does not learn this part of the Golden Rule. ODD persons go through life feeling angry and resentful. These dyslogical emotions are not based on reality. Even when individuals who are ADHD/ODD are treated generously and fairly, they continue to make angry accusations and display active resentment. Parents, teachers, or job supervisors often find it impossible to change these negative feelings in individuals who hang onto old anger, brood about old hurts, and refuse to forgive or be forgiven. This characteristic of ODD quickly disrupts all relationships. Sooner or later, family members, classmates, teachers, and coworkers get enough. Rejection by others is the unfortunate outcome of a lifestyle that harbors grudges without trying to build a more positive outlook.

Being Spiteful and Vindictive

Old anger soon longs for revenge. A major earmark of Oppositional Defiant Disorder is an active effort to get even. ODD individuals do not forgive, neither do they turn loose of old grievances; they yearn to hurt real or imagined enemies. Gaining revenge is a motive that drives the imagination of ADHD/ODD individuals day and night. As these overlapping syndromes live side by side, language habits of the ADHD/ODD person become a weapon against others. These individuals load their conversations with sarcasm and put-down comments designed to hurt feelings and embarrass others. When adults try to correct such abusive verbal behavior, the ADHD/ODD youngster explodes in self-defense: "I don't care! She said it first!" Young adults like Jo go out of their way to say harsh things about others: "I don't care! I won't take that crap off anybody!" This lifestyle of speaking spitefully and seeking revenge isolates the ADHD/ODD person from normal social relationships. No one wants to spend time with someone who speaks hatefully of others and continually wants to get even.

Conduct Disorder

Conduct Disorder (CD) is much more aggressive than ODD. The CD syndrome involves "repetitive and persistent" intrusion into the privacy and basic rights of others. This means that from early childhood, the youngster with CD follows a lifestyle of aggression that invades the lives of others. In Chapter 4 we met James, the hostile, aggressive, and destructive child who was unwelcome everywhere outside his home. Approximately 3 out of 10 persons diagnosed as ADHD also display several of the following symptoms of Conduct Disorder.

Aggression and Violence Toward Animals and People

Children with Conduct Disorder quickly become known as bullies. Everywhere they go, they intimidate others aggressively. They habitually make threats that frighten other children and cause concern in adults. These CD aggressors start fights, both verbally and physically. This lifestyle of bullying others includes threatening physical harm. To get their own way, individuals with Conduct Disorder brandish sticks, baseball bats, broken glass containers, stones or bricks, knives, and even guns.

These aggressors often are physically cruel to animals and people. They go out of their way to kick dogs and cats, cut tails off animals they catch, and slap or kick smaller children. It is not unusual for an aggressive person with CD to tie someone to a tree and abandon him or her for several hours or overnight. Individuals with this lifestyle rarely show remorse or guilt for their aggressive, intrusive behavior. In Chapter 4, James never cried. No matter how severely he hurt or frustrated others, he felt no sorrow or saw any reason to apologize.

Destruction of Property

A major compulsion of Conduct Disorder is the urge to start fires. This should not be confused with normal childhood curiosity about how fires start and why things burn. Many children start one or two fires as they experiment. Children who develop normally learn from those events not to do so again. Conduct Disorder often includes a compulsion to set fire to dry grass, trees, piles of lumber, old buildings, or abandoned tires. Older adolescents and adults with CD frequently commit arson that burns large buildings or acres of forest.

Lying and Stealing

An unfortunate characteristic of Conduct Disorder is the habit of telling lies. This usually occurs in the context of "conning" someone into satisfying a self-focused desire. Individuals with CD rarely tell the truth about money, job performance, what they do privately, or their loyalty in relationships. Along with "conning" others and telling lies, these persons also tend to steal. Stealing from others becomes a type of game that leads to shoplifting, forging checks for quick money, charging purchases to another person's credit card, tricking a telephone operator into placing forbidden calls, or slipping books past the library security system. This compulsion to steal is a "catch me if you can" game. Adolescents and adults who are CD often carry this compulsion to steal to the level of breaking into a neighbor's house or into a local business, just to see if they can do so without being caught. Stealing and lying are not based on need. These behaviors are driven by impulses and compulsions that rarely are linked to actual need.

Disobeying Rules

From early childhood, youngsters with tendencies for Conduct Disorder deliberately break the rules. This behavior is automatic. Whenever a rule is presented, the CD personality balks and rebels. Any restriction on this person's freedom triggers an automatic response: "You can't tell me not to. I'll do it anyway." Habitual disobedience starts early with the child refusing to mind parental time limits. If the child must be home by 4 o'clock, he or she stays out until 7 o'clock. If a 12-year-old child is told to be home by 10:00 p.m., he or she stays out all night, which triggers a neighborhood search by police and worried parents. Running away from home is a major tendency for children with Conduct Disorder. Skipping school enters the picture as soon as the student has places to hide during the day. Escaping from adult confinement becomes a challenge that Conduct Disorder cannot ignore.

Overlap of ADHD and CD

When ADHD overlaps with CD, it is not always easy to separate the two syndromes. One imitates the behavior of the other. The major difference is that ADHD is not a hateful pattern. The ADHD person is loose, poorly organized, forgetful, restless, and accidentally rude and intrusive. Yet he or she does not mean to hurt others. Those with ADHD are sorry when their mistakes come to their attention. On the surface, Conduct Disorder may resemble ADHD because the person is overly active, inattentive, focused on self, and unable to stay on a task from start to finish. However, CD is hateful, aggressive, compulsive, and completely selfish. Whoever stands in the way of an individual with Conduct Disorder is at high risk of being hurt.

Multiplex Developmental Disorder

During the 1980s, scientists who studied ADHD began to see a tag-along syndrome that appeared in approximately 5 out of 100 individuals with ADHD. In 1986 David Cohen introduced the term *Multiplex Developmental Disorder* (MDD) to describe a lifestyle of "odd and peculiar behavior" that creates lifelong difficulties in five areas: thinking, socializing, sensory perception, motor coordination, and connecting emotions and feelings to events (Cohen, Paul, & Volkmer, 1986). Following Cohen's lead, David Dinklage and David Guevremont at the University of Massachussetts Medical Center developed clinical guidelines for separating MDD from ADHD. For the first time, we had a way to distinguish between attention deficits with hyperactivity and a different syndrome that tags along with ADHD in 5% of the population. On the surface, MDD looks like schizophrenia. However, these individuals do not meet diagnostic standards for labeling them as schizophrenic or psychotic because they do not hallucinate, hear voices, or have delusional thinking (Barkley, 1990). The following symptoms separate MDD from ADHD.

Irregular Thinking

When we spend time with individuals who are MDD, it soon becomes apparent that their thought patterns are irregular. They do not think about life, other people, or events the same way most persons do. Those who study MDD often use the terms "odd," "weird," "eccentric," and "bizarre" to describe how MDD individuals think and talk. As in ADHD, thought patterns tend to be loose and disorganized, yet what the MDD person says begins to make sense if one listens carefully. In imitation of ADHD, MDD jumps track in midsentence, skips from an unfinished topic to something else, and leaves out words so that what is told is only "half told." When asked a question, the MDD listener often responds by saying something unrelated to the question. Sense of time is scrambled so that the MDD speaker does not tell events in chronological order. Something that happened 10 years ago may become mixed with what the speaker is saying about yesterday or today. In telling about things, the MDD person begins to speak in symbolic language, using metaphors instead of telling facts. For example, a person with MDD might tell a story this way:

> My grandma came to our house for supper last night. And a year before that I went on a fishing trip with my grandad. We borrowed Uncle Paul's bass boat and I got a new Zebco rod and reel at K-Mart. And I wanted to stay out all night but my brother had to go to Sunday School. What was I talking about? Oh, yeah. We caught twelve big ones, and Grandma fried them last night and I ate two by myself. You know? Like eating half a watermelon by myself. Only it's a lot saltier. Did you know that fish sometimes fly? I heard that on the Discovery channel. But watermelon is better because ten years ago I got real sick eating fried crawdads. When I was a little boy, Grandma used to fry chicken like that. You know. In a big old skillet with a lot of grease. Like putting too much butter on your bread. And five years before that, I caught a big catfish with my bare hands. And in my dream, it meowed like my uncle's old tomcat. You know. Like a mocking bird does. Cats try to catch mocking birds, but they shouldn't because mocking birds eat a lot of bugs. Some fish know how to fly. Or did I say that already? And squirrels can fly, but they don't have feathers. Did you know that Grandma has a feather bed I get to sleep in sometimes? When I was three. My Grandad knows how to fry squirrels, too, but I like watermelon better.

It is easy to understand why terms like "odd" or "weird" are soon applied to individuals who are MDD. Listeners usually lose patience with MDD speakers. Persons who are MDD rarely get to the point of what they are asked to tell. In the middle of telling, they jump track and start to talk about something that fascinates them, or something that occupies much of their imagination but has little or nothing to do with the subject at hand. MDD persons tend to add so much irrelevant detail to their stories that others give up trying to listen.

As MDD individuals interact with others, they often misunderstand what others intend or mean by what they say and do. Persons with MDD read too much meaning into what they see or hear. They overinterpret small details to the point of losing the meaning of what really was said or done. This becomes a kind of perseveration that causes the brain to lock onto a minor issue and not turn it loose. For example, the following chain of misunderstandings is typical of MDD.

MOTHER: "Joan, I want you to get ready to go to town with me. Come in the house and get cleaned up."

JOAN: "Why are we going to town?

MOTHER: "I have to buy some groceries, and we need to pick up the clothes at the cleaners."

JOAN: "Why did you take groceries to the cleaners? Why didn't you take the groceries to the store?"

MOTHER: "Now don't start that with me, Joan. That isn't what I said."

JOAN: "Mom, why did you take the clothes to the grocery store? Did you take my blue dress? Why did you take my blue dress to the grocery store?"

MOTHER: "I didn't take your blue dress anywhere, Joan. It's hanging in your closet."

JOAN: "I don't understand. Why did you take my blue dress to the grocery store? Why didn't you take it to the cleaners?"

MOTHER: "Drop it, Joan. I'm not talking about your blue dress."

JOAN: "Mom, I don't understand. Why take my blue dress to the store? You know I need it to wear to Sunday School."

MOTHER: "Oh, for heaven's sake, Joan! Drop it! Get ready to go to town with me."

JOAN: "But, Mom. I still don't understand. I need my blue dress for Sunday School. Why did you take it to the grocery store? Somebody might steal it, and I won't have it to wear Sunday."

Irregular Social Skills

This kind of sidetracking and perseverating on misperceived ideas also occurs in social situations. For example, Joan came home from a birthday party to tell this story:

MOTHER: "Did you have a good time at the party?"

JOAN: "No. I hated it. I don't know how to make a donkey."

MOTHER: "What are you talking about, Joan? What do you mean, you don't know how to make a donkey?"

JOAN: "That's what I said. I can't make a donkey. And I hated that old party. It was boring. I don't know how to make a donkey. And the other kids started talking about me and laughing. I hate that old party!"

Joan's mother called the mom who had hosted the party. She learned that the children played the game Pin the Tail on the Donkey. Each child was given a paper tail and a pin. A blindfold was put over the child's eyes, and he or she had to guess where the tail should be pinned. Joan had made a big issue of putting on the blindfold. "She kept saying that she couldn't see how to make the donkey if her eyes were covered," the mother explained. "I didn't know what she meant. Finally Joan went off by herself to another room. Then it was time to cut the birthday cake." This misperception of a social event and the belief that others were talking about her are typical of MDD behavior.

Like most youngsters with MDD, Joan does not process social events in a normal way. Her great difficulty with the structure of language and the names of people, places, and things constantly trips her up as she tells about important events in her life. For example, for her 13th birthday, Joan's Uncle Carl took her to the wonderfully funny stage show *Joseph and His Technicolor Dream Coat.* In her own way, Joan had a good time and could not wait to tell her grandmother. "We went to Joseph's many coat of colors," she reported. "And a week after that I'm going to camp." "That will be lot's of fun," her grandmother said. "Do you have your things packed and ready to go?" "Well, I don't know about that," Joan replied. "I just have one duffle bag, and I don't think I can get two quarts of clothes in it."

MDD individuals do not read body language or social signals well enough to keep up with what goes on in social activities. The brain stem and midbrain do not filter and organize incoming data well enough to build accurate mental images. Persons like Joan fail to read facial expression, body language, and gestures that are essential for good communication. MDD individuals fail to pick up subtle tones of voice that signal light-hearted teasing. They do not comprehend *double entendre,* the use of words that have double meanings. MDD persons live by literal, concrete meanings. They do not see or hear subtle variations in language and body posture. This causes them to miss the punch line in jokes and fail to see what is funny when laughter breaks out in the group. In any social event, the MDD person is soon on the outside of the group and wanders off to do his or her own "weird" thing. MDD individuals begin to daydream in the middle of a group activity. They become preoccupied with their own imagination and soon are unplugged from what the group is doing.

MDD individuals do not learn social politeness. They are unaware when they come too close, stand too close, or crowd others too much. Many MDD persons do not maintain eye contact, as most people do during conversation and active listening. Those with MDD look away, glance around, and even turn to one side instead of looking into the speaker's face. An especially disruptive habit of most MDD individuals is their tendency to walk away during a conversation, or to get up and mill around the room during group discussions or classroom listening events. Persons like Joan do not learn how to keep secrets or be discreet about private information. They blurt out embarrassing comments or "news" with no sense that their comments are inappropriate.

A major problem for Joan's mother to handle is her daughter's unrealistic perception that she is popular among her classmates. Joan believes that everyone at school likes her and wants to be her best friend. In fact, her classmates think that she is "goofy" and "strange," and they avoid her whenever they can. This false belief that she is well liked leads Joan to spend much time on the telephone calling classmates in the evening, thinking that they are glad to receive her call. The opposite is actually true. Those who receive her calls go to great lengths not to be available for Joan's rambling, pointless, "goofy" conversations. In reality, individuals with MDD have few friends. A type of "social blindness" keeps them from understanding how to make friends or maintain friendships. Joan has no idea what social skills are required to share interests with others and treat others with respect.

Partly to blame for not having friends is the MDD pattern of poor hygiene. Unless they are closely supervised and "forced" to practice hygiene, MDD individuals like Joan do not brush teeth, shower regularly, shampoo hair often enough, use deodorant, or change socks and underwear. Soon they offend others with bad breath and body odor that adds to their reputation for being "weird." MDD persons rarely have a good sense of choosing what to wear. Without supervision, they come to school or social events dressed in mismatched garments, or wearing things that are completely inappropriate. Many MDD persons develop rituals in how they dress. They lock onto one or two favorite garments and refuse to wear anything else. It is not unusual to find individuals with MDD wearing the same shirt or blouse, the same jeans or sweatpants, or the same socks and underwear every day of the week. These irregular individuals see nothing inappropriate in wearing worn-out sneakers to church or to a wedding. Ritual behavior includes odd or peculiar hairstyles. Many MDD individuals either pay no attention to the condition of their hair, or they stubbornly cling to outdated or bizarre hairstyles that attract teasing and criticism.

Disturbed Sensory Perception

MDD individuals often fail to perceive what goes on around them. Or they may think that one thing occurred when the opposite event actually happened. For example, Joan complains about loud noises when she is in large groups. She often covers her ears and begs for the loud noise to stop. Others around her hear only low-level sounds and are bewildered by Joan's overreaction. Yet when she listens to music, she turns the volume up so high that everyone complains about the loudness of her music. After going shopping at the mall, Joan may complain for several hours about how loud all that noise was. Yet when her parents demand that she turn down the volume of her CD player, she insists that she can barely hear the music. Since infancy, Joan has recoiled from being touched or hugged. "Oh!" she squeals. "You're hurting me!" Yet when she sees an adult cuddling her younger brother, she climbs into the adult's lap, demanding to be hugged for several minutes.

Some MDD individuals have active phobia about having their heads under water during a shower or bath. This overreaction to water touching the hair triggers crying and shouting matches when adults insist that the child must bathe or shampoo. Some MDD youngsters have panic attacks under bright lights, or when they see inflated balloons. It is not unusual for a hysterical emotional reaction to erupt when the MDD child sees large areas in bold, bright color, or overly busy patterns in wallpaper or floor coverings. Yet the same MDD person may use vivid colors when decorating his or her bedroom or create very busy patterns when making drawings. The limbic system of the MDD individual cannot cope with certain types of stimulus from the environment without triggering excessive emotional reactions.

Irregular Motor Coordination

Many MDD individuals walk in a peculiar way that is more a shuffle than a stride. Body posture while sitting or standing often seems "odd." Arms hang stiffly instead of in a normally relaxed way. Legs remain stiff while walking instead of flexing in normal rhythms. MDD persons tend to slouch instead of standing upright, both while walking and standing still. The body moves forward in a series of lurches instead of gliding forward with normal coordination. Most MDD individuals move along with a "weird" gait, more like loping than striding. Many persons with MDD develop eccentric rituals in the way they swing their arms, clasp and unclasp their hands, hunch their shoulders in circular motions, crane their necks again and again, or stamp the feet as toddlers do instead of setting each foot down in a normal walking style.

It is not unusual to see MDD persons constantly looking to each side as they walk, as if expecting an attack from an enemy. This furtive, hunched posture causes them to lunge along in a pattern that attracts much negative attention. At the same time, MDD individuals often make blowing noises with their lips or sucking sounds with teeth and tongue as they move about. They often develop habits of snorting through the nose while moving. These unusual physical habits brand these persons as "odd," "weird," or "peculiar."

Disturbed Emotional Expression

How the emotions are expressed is quite different in most individuals who are MDD. Emotional expression (often called *affect*) follows different cycles than most people exhibit. For example, Joan rarely laughs, cries, or expresses affection when others do so. In family events or in the classroom, she remains outwardly passive and uninvolved in whatever emotions are flowing around her. At her grandmother's death, she did not cry or show any sign of grief. At class parties, she never joins in the robust laughter that often rocks the room. When a classmate is injured on the playground and several children begin to cry,

Joan remains neutral and unemotional. However, at home she explodes emotionally over minor events that no one else thinks are important. "Mom, where is my pink sweater?" Joan calls out. "I don't know, Joan. Where did you put it yesterday?" Mom replies. Suddenly Joan bursts into tears and wails loudly: "You never help me find my stuff. You don't care if I lose my sweater!" Mom must stop what she is doing to take charge of this emotional situation so that Joan can finish getting ready for school. Her pink sweater was lying on her book bag, exactly where she laid it the night before. Not remembering where it was triggered a panic attack accompanied by sobs and excess emotion.

When Joan's grandmother died, she remained calm throughout the funeral proceedings. With dry eyes and no apparent emotion, she demanded answers to many misperceived issues, as we saw above. However, two days after Grandmother's funeral, Joan became grief stricken and inconsolable when she found a dead bird in the backyard. Her mother and father spent several hours guiding Joan through the grief that flared at the sight of a dead bird, but not at the experience of losing a beloved relative. Like many who are MDD, Joan tends to laugh at inappropriate moments. She rarely giggles or laughs when others are doing so, yet she disrupts movies and television shows by giggling and laughing during death scenes on the screen, or when someone is badly injured or abused. This "weird" laughter also erupts inappropriately when others are injured. At school one day, a classmate suffered a broken arm in a playground accident. Joan burst into laughter that escalated out of control. Finally the teacher called her mother to come for her so the class could settle down from the accident.

Mood Swings

Central to the challenge of managing ADHD are cycles of extreme mood changes that disrupt the individual's life. ADD persons tend to present the same passive mood most of the time. Those with ADHD are emotionally all over the place with no predictability from day to day of what moods to expect. Barkley (1995), Ratey and Johnson (1997), Schacter (1996), and Weiss and Hechtman (1993) have documented several tag-along syndromes that imitate ADHD and are frequently found in the shadows of attention deficit with hyperactivity.

Excess Happiness or Sadness

In Chapter 1 we reviewed the balance of emotions that are regulated by right-brain monitoring of negative (pessimistic) feelings and left-brain monitoring of positive (optimistic) feelings (see page 13). We learned of Zaidel's discovery of the right brain "Oops center" that watches for language mistakes as the left brain uses language. We reviewed Ramachandran's research in how lesions, or unidentified bright objects (UBOs), in the right brain cause stroke patients to be overly optimistic as they deny the reality of their physical disabilities. In their book *Shadow Syndromes,* Ratey and Johnson (1997) describe how the right brain uses its negative/pessimistic point of view to balance the positive optimism of the left brain. When right-brain emotional control is disturbed by lesions (UBOs), the person loses balance between positive and negative feelings. UBOs along axon pathways in the right brain trigger excessive optimism that is not balanced with reality. Conversely, when left-brain emotional control is disturbed by lesions along axon pathways, the individual becomes overly pessimistic and cannot blend positive and negative feelings realistically.

Bipolar II Manic/Depressive Illness

Many individuals live on an emotional roller coaster that swings them unwillingly from normally balanced emotions to soaring, frightening heights of elation, then downward to dark, sorrowful depths of depression. This chronic swing of moods from depression to elation is called *Bipolar II Manic/Depressive Illness.* At one pole is the dark cavern of sorrow and grief that makes the person want to die. At the opposite pole is giddy elation that makes the person want to jump over tall buildings or fly to the moon. Life at either extreme is out of control. During deep depression, the individual is so withdrawn into a private emotional world that he or she cannot function as a member of the family, the workplace, or the classroom. At this level of emotion, death becomes a very attractive option that would stop the tortures of these enormous mood swings. During manic elation, the individual reaches a state of mind often called madness. The out-of-control individual cannot function on the job, at home, in learning situations, or in personal relationships. Accidental suicide or violent death frequently mark the early end of life for manic individuals who lose all sense of danger and engage in high-risk behaviors that dangle them over the edge of safety. When ADHD is part of the Bipolar II equation, life often becomes so out of control that the individual must be hospitalized for his or her own protection.

Bipolar I Manic/Depressive Illness

A moderate form of Manic/Depressive Illness often tags along with ADHD. In Bipolar I, the poles of depression and elation are not as far apart as they are with Bipolar II illness. Manic highs do not reach the level of self-destructive madness, and depressive lows do not reach the level of wanting to die. Mood swings occur in cycles, but the differences between depression and elation do not make a productive life impossible. Barkley (1995) has estimated that 45% of ADHD individuals and their blood relatives display symptoms of the Bipolar I tag-along syndrome.

Hypomanic Personality

In her book *An Unquiet Mind,* Kay Jamison (1995) describes two levels of manic behavior: the *black mania* of Bipolar II and the *white mania* of Bipolar I. She describes her own experience with black mania:

> Both my manias and depression had violent sides to them. . . . Being wildly out of control—physically assaultive, screaming insanely at the top of (my) lungs, running frenetically with no purpose or limit, or impulsively trying to leap from cars. . . . I have, in my black, agitated manias destroyed things I cherish, pushed to the utter edge people I love, and survived to think I could never recover from the shame. . . . (page 120)

White mania (hypomania), the milder Bipolar I version of true manic elation, has enough positive characteristics that these individuals often refuse medication or other treatments that would eliminate their manic patterns. Jamison describes her personal refusal to give up white mania:

> I simply did not want to believe that I needed to take medication. I had become addicted to my high moods; I had become dependent upon their intensity, euphoria, assuredness, and their infectious ability to induce high moods and enthusiasms in other people. . . . I found my milder manic states powerfully inebriating and very conducive to productivity. I couldn't give them up. (pp. 98–99)

Ratey and Johnson (1997) point out that white mania, or hypomania, allows individuals to be "better than normal." During hypomanic cycles, persons think more rapidly than those who are in the normal range of emotional balance. In this state, also called *soft manic-depression* or *soft bipolarity,* individuals are more creative, and they score higher on IQ tests. During their white mania cycles, persons are friendlier, more fun to be with, and more productive. As Kay Jamison revealed about herself, it is very hard for anyone to give up these positive qualities in order to become "normal." In fact, those who experience soft bipolar cycles rationalize why they do not need to change. They correctly argue that even though they are somewhat giddy and even silly, they do not become paranoid, as Bipolar II persons often do. They are never delusional, as Bipolar II individuals often are. They never need to be hospitalized for dangerous mood swings, and their white mania never destroys life or property through high-risk behavior. When ADHD comes with tag-along hypomania, it is often impossible to convince the individual that anything should be changed in his or her lifestyle.

In separating hypomania from ADHD, diagnosticians look for seven major patterns that set white mania apart:

1. *Exaggerated self-esteem (grandiosity)*. The hypomanic personality struts and prances with inflated ego and self-importance. This is self-advertisement on a grand scale. Outsiders see a person who is vain and arrogant, but who nonetheless is successful and worthy of respect. The hypomanic personality is self-centered. He or she uses others without respecting the worth of others. In describing themselves in autobiographical sketches or during public presentations, persons in white mania cycles exalt themselves with grandiose phrases and exaggerated terms. They take credit for accomplishments that were achieved by others. Yet this self-centered individual displays a charismatic aura that attracts the loyalty of others. Hypomanic persons inspire followers to overlook the arrogant, self-focused lifestyle of the person who has placed self on an egotistical pedestal.

2. *Reduced need for sleep*. Individuals in white mania cycles have little need for sleep. It is not unusual for these high-energy persons to be wide awake again after 3 or 4 hours of rest. During these charged-up cycles, hypomanic individuals make phone calls at inappropriate times, waking others during normal hours of sleep or calling too early in the morning. In the early part of the twentieth century, Jimmy Durante, a famous comedian who rarely slept, rationalized to friends for his middle-of-the-night intrusions: "When Durante is awake, no bird sleeps." This hypomanic disregard for sleep often becomes a disruptive factor that strains relationships to the breaking point.

3. *Nonstop talking*. The impulse to keep on talking is often called *hyperlexia*. Individuals with hypomanic personality are dreaded because of their habit of talking nonstop. Every thought the brain develops, no matter how trivial, is uttered in spoken words. Hyperlexic persons cannot stop conversing, commenting, lecturing, or explaining. Even when they have nothing important to say, they say something to fill every moment of silence. This hyperlexic tendency exerts verbal pressure in all situations. The manic speech flow interrupts sermons, classroom lectures, movies, and television shows. Hypermanic persons constantly are on the telephone. They purchase mobile phones for their vehicles, portable pager units to receive all calls, and cordless phones they carry around at home. They cannot refrain from making and receiving phone calls during restaurant meals. Hypermanic individuals tend to become addicted to chat room communication on the Internet. They talk to the computer screen and argue with Internet bulletin board comments coming across their screen. They replace speech with keyboarding as they interact with chat room activities for hours at a time. Nonstop talking from hypomanic individuals drives everyone "nuts." This characteristic of white mania is highly disruptive and soon triggers resentment and rejection from others.

4. *Racing thoughts and mental images*. Hypomanic individuals cannot keep their thoughts and mental images from racing. They often have the feeling that their brains are like a stock car race that never stops. This mental racing goes on and on, even during sleep. During white mania cycles, these persons find themselves pacing the floor rapidly, trying to keep up with racing mental

images. Speech soon lags behind ideas that are speeding in the brain. Successful hypomanic persons develop a type of shorthand writing that lets them scribble chunks of ideas before the racing brain leaves important thoughts behind. It is not unusual to see these individuals whisper rapidly into cassette recorders to preserve the good ideas their churning brains create.

5. *Distractibility.* It is impossible for hypomanic individuals to ignore what goes on around them. Eyes dart everywhere to see what is happening or who is going by. Ears pick up every sound. The nose whiffs every odor. Internally, the racing brain hums to itself, talks to itself, and darts off on mental rabbit trails as memories are triggered by nearby events. The hypomanic brain cannot go from start to finish. Too many side trails beckon with interesting things to be explored. Eye contact is lost, even when the person earnestly wants to listen. Sentences are left unfinished as the voice shifts to another topic. Tasks are left incomplete as cascades of new interests take the hypomanic attention elsewhere.

6. *Fixation on goal-directed activity.* In spite of being easily distracted, a major social problem of hypomania is the intensity of going after specific objectives. The hypomanic person is highly goal directed, but these goals tend to be very narrow in focus. This goal-directed intensity quickly becomes obsessive. For example, at 4:30 p.m. the hypomanic boss decides that everyone in the office must go to dinner together tonight. With that single goal in mind, he or she starts an obsessive string of activities that must be handled now: Where should we go for dinner? Can we all get there by 6:30 p.m.? Everyone make arrangements to be part of the dinner group. Marge, get a babysitter. Joe, cancel your committee meeting on the church board. Jeanne, postpone the Wilson sales conference to another night. Dave and Flo, hurry the last office appointments so everyone is gone by 5:30. This flurry of unexpected activity places heavy pressure on the office staff who had other plans for the evening, especially Marge, a single parent with two preschool children in daycare. The hypomanic boss pays no attention to this intrusion into the private lives of his or her staff. The goal of everyone going to dinner tonight is the only issue of importance, regardless of inconvenience to others.

7. *Compulsive high-pleasure activities regardless of consequences.* Hypomanic persons tend to forget responsibility and they indulge themselves in activities that yield high pleasure, regardless of consequences. The individual may go on an exciting shopping spree that adds thousands of dollars to credit card debt. It makes no difference that the person's financial position is close to bankrupcy. A hypomanic businessperson might go ahead with a high-risk investment in spite of urgent warnings from financial advisors. Or a married individual might become caught up in a thrilling spur-of-the-moment sexual affair with the spouse of a close friend because hormones are running high during this white mania episode. This is often called the "Scarlett O'Hara syndrome" after the famous moment in *Gone With The Wind* when the impulsive/compulsive Scarlett says: "I'll think about that tomorrow. After all, tomorrow is another day."

Hypomanic personality imitates ADHD in several important ways: impulsivity, distractibility, racing thoughts, self-focus, short attention span, and hyperlexia. When ADHD overlaps white mania, it is often impossible to separate the syndromes completely. By itself, ADHD is not arrogant or grandiose. ADHD seldom devises schemes to use others. In fact, when persons with ADHD focus on the needs of others, they tend to be overly generous, truly wanting to help. Those with ADHD tend to be open to guidance on how to do better. When all the plugs stay in, the intelligence behind ADHD allows persons to achieve surprising goals. ADHD does not come and go in cycles. It is a constant factor, although attention deficits tend to diminish in severity as physical maturity takes place.

Chronic Depression

A different kind of excessive emotion frequently tags along with ADD. Chronic monopolar depression often hides in the shadow of passive attention deficit disorder. In Chapter 2 we reviewed the levels of severity of ADD (see pages 20–21). When ADD is mild, depression also tends to be mild. ADD persons toward the low end of the severity scale tend to live with sadness that does not escalate to more intense levels. This quiet sadness is like fog over the landscape. It feels somewhat heavy inside the chest. It is expressed almost silently by sighing and sad, wishful thinking that often appears in drawings or sorrow-tinged poetry and stories. This mild depression that lingers in the shadow of ADD is not dangerous. There is little thought of death or dying. This form of depression centers more on unfilfilled desires. Fantasy images surrounding mild depression are of sad events or sad imaginary characters whose wishes never come true. Nighttime dreams center around themes of loneliness or being abandoned, but not of frightful events. This level of depression seldom expresses itself in crying. UBOs often appear in left-brain scans of these mildly depressed ADD persons. These lesions in the brain's information highway create an imbalance between left-brain optimism and right-brain pessimism that the sad ADD individual cannot correct. Instead of having a normal balance between optimism and pessimism, these persons live with an excess of sadness, which causes them to interpret life pessimistically.

As ADD moves up the severity scale, the level of depression tends to increase. A moderately ADD person at level 5 to 7 on the severity scale tends to live with moderate depression. In the way that moderate ADD interferes with academic learning, this level of sadness interferes with emotional well-being. Moderate depression involves vivid daydreams of a sad, pessimistic nature. This individual seeps tears that often surprise outsiders. Why is Allen crying? In this state of moderate depression, Allen does not sob, yet tears often stream down his face during class time, family events, and especially when he is alone. As he stays alone for long periods of time, Allen wonders about the blessings of death he has heard adults describe for older ones who have "gone to heaven." Wouldn't it be better if he could go to heaven, too? In heaven he would not be lonely or sad. He could be with his grandparents who used to love him so much. As Allen's thoughts shift to school, his sadness is heavy inside his chest because he feels left out. He is never chosen for playground teams. Teachers rarely select him to do popular things like carry a note to the office or lead the class to lunch. When Allen thinks of his family, he focuses on the many moments when adults reprimand him for being forgetful, or for losing his things, or for not making better grades. As these sorrowful daydream images capture his attention, Allen begins to weep silently. "Life is so sad," he thinks with a deep sigh as tears drip down his cheeks. Children who grow up with these invisible feelings rarely attract enough adult attention to receive intervening help. It is not unusual for youngsters like Allen to pass through childhood, adolescence, and into adulthood without the underlying chronic depression being recognized or healed. Adults focus on the ADD patterns reflected in the ADD checklist in Chapter 3 (see pages 57-61). Attention deficit children with lifelong depression keep their chronic sadness a secret.

Severe ADD also tends to come with its shadow syndrome of severe depression. When ADD is above level 7 on the severity scale, depression tends to be severe. This excess of negative, pessimistic feeling robs the individual of hope. There is no hope of making good grades, or of being happy like everyone else. There is no hope of having friends, being elected team captain, or being a popular leader of the class. There is no hope that parents will stop nagging and scolding about forgetfulness, laziness, and other shortcomings. At this point of hopelessness, the ADD person with severe depression wants to die. Thoughts of death permeate daydreams, imagination, fantasy thinking, and nighttime dreams. ADD persons with severe depression speculate how they might die. Daydreams are filled with detailed plans for how death might be accomplished. Fantasy thinking builds imaginary scenarios in which the person who has died watches relatives at the funeral and overhears what they say. When this level of sorrowful emotion is reached, suicide becomes increasingly likely. Feelings of sadness and grief become intense. Individuals at this level of depression live with a frightening tightness of the chest, as if hands were squeezing the heart and lungs. They become short of breath with heart racing and blood pressure soaring. Yet these depressed individuals rarely reach out to anyone for help. They suffer in silence, victimized by daydreams of dying and nightmares of death. Alone, they sob into the pillow, or muffle sounds of weeping under a blanket. This extremely private suffering is commonly described by ADD individuals who survive suicide attempts and at last find a compassionate counselor who understands.

High Functioning Autism

Several scientists have researched the relationship between ADHD, ADD, and high functioning autism (Denckla, 1985, 1991; Jordan, 1996a; Ratey & Johnson,

1997; Weiss & Hechtman, 1993). Autism is a catastrophic neurological condition in which the brain regions we reviewed in Chapter 1 do not integrate. Too many nerve pathways are incomplete, and too many bridges are out along information highways. The limbic system cannot communicate with the higher brain regions, and higher brain lobes do not communicate with each other. Each brain region is like a separate community that does not seem to know that the others exist. Like all syndromes, autism exists in varying degrees of severity. At the low end of the severity scale, mild autism permits the person to develop limited literacy skills, often to the ninth grade level. In certain instances, autistic persons demonstrate extraordinary talent in one area while remaining severely disabled in most other areas of talent. For example, the movie *Rain Man* told the story of an autistic adult who had astonishing mental arithmetic skills. At the same time, he required supervision for daily living. Often he could not interact verbally with others, and he could not tolerate being touched. This extraordinary display of mathematical talent wrapped inside the isolation of autism is called *autistic savant*.

Asperger's Syndrome

During the 1980s, Martha Denckla at the Johns Hopkins University School of Medicine called attention to a shadow syndrome that often tags along with ADD (Denckla, 1985, 1991). Denckla's brain imaging research linked a form of high functioning autism to ADD. This tag-along behavior pattern, called *Asperger's syndrome,* often imitates ADD. In Chapter 4 we met Nate and his surrogate Roy (see pages 84–87). Hiding behind Nate's severe ADD was a form of very high functioning autism that caused outsiders to call the boy "weird." In childhood, Nate was indeed eccentric with bizarre behaviors that baffled his mother and other relatives. He has become a successful computer scientist, a specialist in designing ingenious computer programs. Yet he continues to have appallingly inadequate social skills. As an adult, Nate is "weird" in virtually every social sense. In a university classroom, he sets the curve for high grades in computer science courses. On the job, he amazes his supervisors and colleagues with his ingenious skills in devising new computer programs. Yet he lives alone, a contented recluse who still talks to Roy at night. His apartment is a mess, littered with piles of soiled clothes and scattered books and papers. His kitchen area is offensive. Yet the work space around his three computers is immaculate. With his computers, Nate lives a highly ordered, ritualized life that gives him great satisfaction. Even though he forgets to change his socks and underwear for days at a time, this eccentric man copes with ADD at a level of success that brings respectful praise from satisfied clients and employers.

Asperger's syndrome is distinctive as we separate it from ADD. The following behaviors trigger comments that label persons like Nate as "weird," "eccentric," "strange," and sometimes "obnoxious."

1. *Awkward gross motor coordination.* From early childhood, individuals with Asperger's syndrome are awkward as they stand, walk, run, hop, skip, or play ball. This poor motor coordination produces a stiff, awkward body posture that keeps the individual from relaxing in normal ways. For example, as Nate stands around at a social event, his body seems stiff. His arms hang at odd angles instead of relaxing down the sides of his body. His legs do not bend and flex in normal ways. When he sits, Nate's body continues to appear stiff and awkward. His body joints do not bend to fit the contour of the chair or sofa. At table for a meal, his arms and legs cannot find a relaxed position. Even when Nate goes to bed, his body does not fall into a typically relaxed position. During sleep his arms, legs, and torso remain stiffly awkward.

2. *Flat tone of voice.* Individuals with Asperger's syndrome do not speak in normally fluent ways. The voice tends to be flat and monotone without the usual rising and falling tonal inflections. When persons like Nate enter a stream of conversation, they take on a pedantic tone of voice that sounds like a stilted lecture. Speech is slow and deliberate rather than flowing and spontaneous. Very quickly this monotonous, flat vocal pattern becomes boring to listeners. Others soon find excuses to move away from this "lecturing" voice that drones on and on.

3. *Failure to read social signals.* A major problem of Asperger's syndrome is the person's failure to notice or read the social signals others give. All of his life, Nate has stood too close to others. From early childhood his mother tried to teach him not to stand so close when he talked or listened. "Don't get up in people's faces," his mother said a thousand times. But Nate has never learned this simple social skill. Those with Asperger's syndrome do not have a built-in sense of distance in social situations. As he interacts with others, Nate is blind to social signals that mean "Back off" or "Give me a break" or "Not now." Persons like Nate barge into private space without recognizing the rudeness of such behavior. This blindness to personal space becomes offensive when Nate develops body odor because he failed to shower, or when his socks begin to smell after the fourth day of being worn, or his breath is bad because he does not brush his teeth.

4. *Awkward at small talk.* In spite of a high IQ and an excellent academic record, Nate has never learned how to make small talk in social interactions. When he and I meet for one of our cherished visits, he cannot think of little things to say. At work, at parties, or at church events, he hangs around awkwardly, not knowing how to enter the flow of conversation. By the time he thinks of an appropriate comment, the conversation has moved on to another topic. Nate tried to date girls a few times after he entered college, but he could think of nothing to say on a date. Soon word spread on campus that girls should avoid this weird man. "He gives me the creeps, staring at me that way without saying anything," his dates reported to their friends. This quickly closed the door to dating during his college years.

5. *Slow thinking and responding.* A major characteristic of Asperger's syndrome is slow mental processing. It is impossible for Nate to hurry as he

thinks. When he has all the time he needs, his brain produces brilliant thoughts, but if he must hurry, he is lost. As Nate talks with me, he has all the time he needs. In this context, he amazes me with his intelligent thinking and problem solving. Slow thinking is a handicap for Nate when he is under pressure to respond rapidly.

6. *Excellent recall of trivial detail.* Individuals with Asperger's syndrome have extraordinary recall of detail. Nate astounds his friends and colleagues by his knowledge of trivial details related to computer science. He knows bits and pieces of information about computers that others have never heard before. His idea of a good time is to tell all he knows about computer science. Soon he has lost his audience, even those who are also gifted at telecommunication. As Nate takes center stage reciting his immense store of trivial detail, his monotone voice drones on and on as if he is delivering a lecture. Listeners slip away, leaving one or two captive persons who have not managed to escape this boring experience. Unfortunately, Nate does not recognize the strong signals this departure represents. His habit is to follow the last person, trying to corner him or her into hearing the rest of his pedantic recital. Yet Nate is respected for having such an astonishing fund of knowledge. He is the one to ask when anyone needs obscure information about computer science.

7. *Limited sense of humor.* Individuals with Asperger's syndrome think in literal, concrete terms. Their brains handle facts but their thought patterns do not respond to humor. It is very difficult for Nate to catch the meaning of a joke. He is baffled by friendly teasing. When others laugh, he wonders why. Sometimes he tries to memorize a joke so he can join in storytelling in the coffee lounge. Yet his effort to tell a joke or funny story is embarrassing. It takes too long for him to find his words, he adds too many trivial details, and he forgets the punch line. Before he finishes telling the joke, others have moved away and stopped listening. Nate tries to analyze humor the way he analyzes a computer problem. He does not understand how humor works.

8. *Narrow range of interests.* Because the Asperger's brain deals with trivial details in a literal fashion, individuals like Nate lock onto only a few topics of interest. As Nate passed through adolescence, his talks with me guided him toward the specialized logical thinking that is required for understanding computer science. Once he discovered his talent for this narrow field, he became a specialist. As he entered early adulthood, Nate also developed an obsessive interest in creating crossword puzzles. Now his only interests are computer programming and how words interface in visual patterns. His only reading relates to these two interests. His only conversation is about these two areas of expertise.

9. *Obsessive splitting.* An earmark of Asperger's syndrome is the obsessive impulse to split hairs. The Asperger's brain deals in details that must be perfectly aligned. Any detail that is incorrect or out of place drives Nate crazy. Oddly, this obsession with detail does not connect to his living space or personal hygiene. The obsession to split, then split the splits, is an unfortunate

social problem. Nate cannot refrain from correcting others as they make mistakes. During a lecture, he interrupts to correct the speaker, regardless of how this disrupts the class process. After church, he shows the minister a list of errors the preacher made in quoting scripture or in grammatical usage. I witnessed this Asperger's pattern when Nate invited me to attend a conference at which he presented a new computer program. I sat by him as another person made a presentation. The speaker showed a cartoon to illustrate the issue of stress in overcrowded situations. In the cartoon, a little man was squeezed into an elevator that was packed with passengers. The point of the presentation was to stimulate group discussion on the topic of social crowding. As the group began to respond, Nate stood up. "There are too many people in that elevator," he said in a loud voice that interrupted the group activity. "I beg your pardon?" said the startled presenter. "The law says that only twelve people may get on an elevator," Nate declared in his monotone pedantic voice. "There are thirteen people in that picture." A growl of irritation swept the room. "Oh, shut up!" I heard someone say. "Sit down, you jerk," another voice muttered. Nate had no idea why his interruption was inappropriate, or why so many people were upset at what he had done.

10. *Triggers dread in others.* Soon after Nate is hired for a new job, enrolls in a university class, or joins a single adult church group, he triggers dread in others. His habits of poor hygiene, obsessive splitting, boring style of talking, and awkward social skills quickly mark him as someone to avoid. Nate has no idea why this happens. When he and I discuss this issue, I draw diagrams showing him in a room with others. I write a list of Asperger's tendencies that others find objectionable. With these visual aids, he sometimes recognizes his behavior, yet he does not understand why others pull away from him socially. He cannot perceive why no one returns his phone calls or why others leave him alone when he talks about computers and word puzzles. This blindness to social interaction baffles and discourages him. The Asperger's brain does not understand these subjective issues.

11. *Inappropriate social habits.* Persons with Asperger's syndrome do not develop appropriate social habits. Awkward body coordination, poor conversational skills, narrow range of interests, absent sense of humor, and blindness toward social signals keep Nate from learning how to "dance the tribal dance." He has no idea how to dress appropriately, or how to handle food and beverages in social situations. His eating habits are sloppy as food spills from the corners of his mouth, and he smacks and slurps loudly while eating. He talks with his mouth filled with food. Nate thinks nothing of blowing his nose on a napkin or picking food from his teeth with his fingernail. When gas builds up, he belches loudly or offends those nearby by discharging intestinal gas. He shows up at social events wearing soiled sweatpants, old athletic shoes, and a grungy T-shirt with an inappropriate message front and back. No matter how often we discuss these issues, his Asperger's brain does not learn new social habits.

12. *Ritualized behavior.* The Asperger's brain must be highly structured to make sense of the world and to survive in society. This requires rituals that do not change. As a child, Nate invented Roy, the doll who became his ritual companion. As he grew older, Nate drove his mother to distraction by obsessive rituals in how he dressed, ate meals, and kept his room. As an adult, he is highly ritualized in the clothing he wears. Nate's dress ritual is to wear T-shirts with messages for others to read. In his closet, 31 T-shirts hang in alphabetical order according to the first word of the shirt's message. He wears these shirts in alphabetical order, starting with A on the first day of the month, then progressing through the alphabet until the end of the month. For shoes, Nate wears a certain brand of running shoes. He has seven pairs of shoes that he wears in numerical sequence each day of the week. His trousers are a certain brand of jeans, all green in color. He eats meals one food at a time. As he finishes one food, he turns his plate to eat the next item, then turns again to eat the next serving, until his meal is finished. If anyone intrudes into Nate's rituals, he becomes so confused and upset that his anger erupts in tantrums. Immediately he puts everything back in its ritual order. It is impossible for him to share space with a roommate or coworker because of this obsessive need to keep his life strictly ordered.

13. *Stubbornness.* All his life, Nate has been a quietly stubborn person. His behavior is called *passive/aggressive.* On the surface, it appears that he does nothing when others press him to act, to hurry, or to respond. Inwardly, his emotions and feelings become quite active as his Asperger's brain chooses not to cooperate. Individuals with passive/aggressive tendencies absorb a great deal of pressure and insult. At first glance, it appears that they pay no attention to outside pressure. However, persons like Nate begin a slow-burning resentment toward whoever is applying pressure. The Asperger's brain decides to ignore the intrusion, yet invisible emotions begin to churn. Low-level anger begins to surge toward an outburst. At a certain point, this surge of anger explodes in a shouting match, flinging things around the room, or sometimes pushing or shoving the intruder away.

14. *Controlling others.* Outsiders often are surprised to hear Asperger's individuals described as controllers. Their passive behavior hides a personality trait that compels them to control every situation, if possible. When I first met Nate and his mother, I quickly recognized his success in controlling the household. Every time Nate's ADD/Asperger's behavior brought his mother to tears, he was in control. Each time his stubbornness triggered a shouting match, he was in control. Every family reunion he disrupted placed him in control as his mother left the event early to take him home. As an adult, Nate strives to control others one-by-one through his expert knowledge of trivial detail. He guards information that others need, sharing it only when it becomes clear that they need his help. The habit of standing too close to others is a control technique. Even when this triggers negative reactions, Nate has gained control of where others stand or when they move away. Having control is a major source of emotional satisfaction for the Asperger's brain.

15. *Boring personality*. At a national conference on learning disabilities, Martha Denckla presented information about Asperger's syndrome. Someone asked: "Dr. Denckla, how would you best describe Asperger's." Without hesitation, Denckla replied: "Boring! Boring! Boring!" At first this seemed a rude response, insensitive to the struggles of persons like Nate. Yet Denckla was candidly accurate. A major characteristic of Asperger's syndrome is the quality of being boring. The slow-paced, monotone speech patterns are boring. Listening to an endless recital of trivial detail about an obscure topic is boring. Tolerating hair-splitting interruptions of group discussions is boring. Spending an evening with an Asperger's individual is boring. Without question, Denckla's description was accurate. Regardless of my affection for Nate, he is boring. Following one of Nate's boring presentations, a weary colleague commented: "A little Asperger's goes a long way."

16. *Rationalizing*. One of the most annoying characteristics of Asperger's syndrome is the person's automatic habit of rationalizing. I have never seen Nate admit being wrong unless he first goes through an elaborate explanation of why it was not his fault, why someone else was to blame, and why his own behavior was not the problem. If I wait long enough, he eventually confesses that his behavior might not have been perfect. Yet he never fully acknowledges his responsibility without listing reasons why someone else should not take the blame. This tendency to rationalize is part of the narrow range of logic that drives the Asperger's brain. Rationalizing is a form of splitting hairs. Persons like Nate cannot face life without this support system of rationalization. To say simply "It was my fault" denies Nate the satisfaction of analyzing every possible detail, like creating a new computer program or developing a new crossword puzzle.

17. *Creativity within a narrow range of talent*. Nate is one of the most creative persons I know within the narrow landscapes of computer science and crossword puzzles. Within these boundaries, he has few equals. This intensely focused talent has produced ingenious computer programs that greatly improve literacy skills for adults with learning disabilities. During his lifetime, Nate's creativity with computers will change many lives. He will leave a beneficial mark on the world. Unfortunately, there is no flexibility to permit him to expand his horizons socially or intellectually.

18. *Works best alone*. Asperger's individuals are rarely effective team members. Asperger's syndrome results in too many social limitations to permit persons like Nate to fit into work groups, committees, or leadership teams. Fortunately, Nate's unique talents with computer science make him a valued employee on projects that he can do alone. Working by himself in his ritualized private space is the only way he can be productive.

19. *Poor leadership ability*. A sad reality of Asperger's syndrome is the fact that individuals like Nate cannot be effective leaders. No matter how hard they try, their eccentric ways alienate others too quickly to permit leadership qualities to emerge. When an Asperger's individual is named to a leadership

position, he or she becomes an autocratic, dictatorial ruler rather than a leader. The first thing such a person does is to develop a rule book. Then the Asperger's supervisor enforces the rules in a literal fashion. Soon the work-force or staff are upset by arbitrary decisions that are based on picky adher-ence to rules rather than personal merit. When persons like Nate are assigned to supervisory roles, group morale deteriorates quickly. Asperger's leaders can-not generate loyalty. Their type of leadership is arbitrary and inflexible to the point of being offensive. The habits of rationalizing, splitting hairs, and liv-ing by rituals are demeaning to personal dignity and threatening to personal freedom.

Attention Surplus Disorders

During the 1970s, Howard Wishnie at Massachusetts Mental Health Center developed a model of human personality based on his work with drug addicts and prisoners who were prone to violent anger (Wishnie, 1977). Wishnie sug-gested that each of us has two selves: the internal self we keep hidden from society, and the external self we put on public display. As effective members of society, we create a "false self," which we present to the outside world. This external self often is partly a product of our fantasy or make-believe. From early childhood, each of us carefully practices certain public behaviors that help us identify with groups to whom we want to belong. Through a type of role-play, we rehearse these external behaviors until we get them right. This false self attracts others in whom we are interested. The external self is our passport into the areas of society we hold in high esteem. Beneath the false self is the "true self" that may be quite different from the version of ourselves we place on public display. The true self harbors all the self-doubts, fears, anx-ieties, and shame that play out in our dreams. The internal self knows the truth about our weaknesses and shortcomings. This true self is brutally hon-est to the point of inflicting emotional pain when we try to kid ourselves about who and what we really are.

Wishnie's model recognized that most individuals maintain a realistic bal-ance between who we know ourselves to be and how we present ourselves to the world. As we role-play through the external self, we do not deny the other side of the story that we tell to the world. However, certain persons do not have a healthy balance between their internal and external selves. For example, individuals with mental health problems, such as paranoia or schizophrenia, live with a split between the outside and inside selves. Those persons cannot reconcile or blend what their internal perception believes with what their external experience sees and hears. This personality split results in inner emo-tional states that are out of step with external reality. Brain imaging science has documented the presence of lesions (UBOs) in the axon pathways of many persons who cannot reconcile their internal and external selves. Certain indi-viduals are biologically unable to maintain a healthy balance between the true inner self and the false outer self. When this imbalance reaches a certain point of disproportion, strong emotions from the midbrain (amygdala) overwhelm logic in the higher brain (prefrontal cortex). A mental state of overfocus emerges in which the limbic system takes charge. This is often referred to as *Attention Surplus Disorder.*

Intermittent Rage Disorder

In the shadow of ADHD, we often find an overfocused syndrome that frequently explodes in rage. In Chapter 1 we reviewed the role of the prefrontal cortex in controlling strong emotions that start in the limbic system (amygdala). Like a logical parent, the prefrontal cortex is responsible for keeping child-like impulses of the midbrain under control. Chapter 1 explained the neurological rhythms and cell firing patterns that allow the brain to think clearly, pause before acting, and maintain socially acceptable behavior. When lesions occur along certain axon pathways, the prefrontal cortex loses its logical control over destructive emotions that erupt from lower brain regions. Instead of maintaining wide focus on all important issues, the brain becomes overfocused on strong emotions and feelings. When the internal self feels threatened or overly ashamed, anger explodes in torrents that intimidate anyone who is nearby.

According to Wishnie's model of personality, something external happens that "pierces through" the tough false self and penetrates the tender, vulnerable internal self. This invasion of the true self is so threatening that the person's emotional control disintegrates. In a state of shock, the individual faces certain choices. He or she can die (in a figurative sense) under the glare of truth, or strike back in a violent act of denial. This is a version of the "fight or flight" dilemma we reviewed in Chapter 1. Wishnie concluded that tantrums (intermittent rage episodes) occur when the inner self chooses to turn the threat back on the intruder through violent anger that forces the intruder to back away.

Intermittent Rage Disorder imitates the quick irritation of ADHD, yet it is distinctly different. After 25 years of treating violent criminals, James Gilligan (1996) at Harvard School of Medicine concluded that rage and violent anger stem from overwhelming feelings of shame within the internal self. Ratey and Johnson (1997) explain that rage disorder originates in inadequate neurological development that does not let the prefrontal cortex stay in command. Whatever is the underlying cause for Intermittent Rage Disorder, the external behavior is the same. This person becomes enraged when another driver cuts him or her off in traffic. A tantrum explodes when someone in authority criticizes his or her work. An eruption of anger occurs if a spouse says a wrong word when the volatile person is not feeling well. Abusive anger boils over when a crying child will not shut up. Temper tantrums erupt under any stress that reminds the inner self that it is incompetent, unworthy, shameful, or helpless.

In his book *Emotional Intelligence,* Daniel Goleman (1995) describes these rage episodes as "emotional highjacking." Partly because of UBOs that interrupt thought transmissions down axon pathways, the limbic system highjacks the logical prefrontal cortex and holds it hostage. In biological terms, surges of rage that highjack higher brain centers fill the brain with so much static and noise that normal brain processing "short circuits." Normal cell firing rhythms are disrupted, and the brain suddenly is out of sequence. The brain becomes overfocused on single issues that are taken out of context by the limbic system that is momentarily cut off from the logical prefrontal cortex.

Anxiety Disorder

Another type of overfocus is chronic fretting and worrying that never stops. Earlier in this chapter we reviewed chronic depression that often tags along with ADD. UBOs along axon pathways create an imbalance between right-brain pessimism and left-brain optimism. In many ADD individuals, anxiety also hides in the shadows. Anxiety is a state of constant worry and fretting. This emotional state is based almost entirely on a type of make-believe thinking. The right brain and limbic system lock onto negative possibilities and spend their time asking "What if?" What if I fail the next test? What if we don't have enough money to pay our bills? What if my mother gets breast cancer? What if the stock market crashes and we all go broke? In this state of mind, the brain is overfocused on negative possibilities and cannot stop wondering "What if?" Anxiety Disorder squanders the fretting person's mental, emotional, and spiritual energy. Intelligence is beyond use because of constant fretting. Individuals who are caught in this web of anxiety are helpless to stop this waste of emotional power.

Visual Perception Disorder

Approximately half of those who are diagnosed as ADHD or ADD also have a brain-based disorder with visual perception (Irlen, 1993; Jordan, 1996a; Payne, 1994; Pollan & Williams, 1992; Weisel, 1992). This problem in clearly perceiving visual images is called by two names: *word blindness* and *Irlen syndrome.* Toward the end of the 1880s, scientists and educators in Europe were perplexed by the fact that certain individuals with normal vision (20/20 acuity) became "word blind" when they looked at black print on white paper under bright light. In spite of having 20/20 visual acuity, those persons declared that they saw black print begin to swirl, move sideways, move up and down, and fall off the edge of the page. In every other way, those word blind persons had normal eyesight. Separate classrooms were established in Scandinavian countries, Germany, England, and Scotland where word blind students learned to compensate for this visual perception disability (Broadbent, 1872; Hinshelwood, 1900).

The phenomenon of word blindness was first studied in the United States by Samuel T. Orton (1925) following World War I. However, it was not until the 1970s that the first solution for word blindness was discovered. Helen Irlen, a psychologist working with dyslexic adult readers at Long Beach Community College in California, discovered that if struggling readers placed sheets of colored spotlight filters on their book pages, the print often stopped moving and distortions of the printed page frequently disappeared. During the 1980s Irlen perfected a standard method for identifying word blindness, then applying the right color or combination of colors to printed pages. This technique became known as the Irlen procedure. In 1991, Irlen's book *Reading by the Colors* renamed her procedure as the Irlen syndrome.

Still, no one knew why adding color to reading corrected the visual misperceptions of word blindness. In the early 1990s, Margaret Livingstone and her colleagues at Harvard Medical School discovered a missing link in the brain pathway that connects the retina of each eye to the visual cortex (Livingstone, Rosen, Drislane, & Galaburda, 1991). In 1993, Stephen Lehmkuhle and his associates at the University of Missouri School of Optometry corroborated the Harvard information (Lehmkuhle, Garzia, Turner, Hash, & Baro, 1993). Figure 5.1 shows the magnicellular pathway that carries visual information from the retina to the midbrain. The magnicellular pathway is composed of two types of transmission cells. Large *magno cells* rapidly transfer part of each visual image to the brain stem, where that data waits until small *parvo cells* more slowly deliver the rest of the visual information. When the magno cells are fully developed, the brain stem blends these batches of visual data and sends that information to the parietal lobe, which fires it on to the visual cortex. In word blind individuals, the magno cells are incomplete. A missing chunk, much like a bite out of a cookie, exists on the edge of the magno cells. This missing section causes magno cells to deliver only part of what the eyes see. The visual cortex receives distorted images that move about and fail to blend into focused images. If the word blind person glances quickly at fixed objects or printed information, then looks away, he or she is not aware of the distortions shown in Figures 5.2 through 5.7. However, if the individual with Irlen syndrome stares at something for several seconds, as must be done to read, a variety of visual distortions occur. Figures 5.2 through 5.7 show what most word blind individuals see when they keep looking at black print on white paper, especially under a bright flourescent light. Livingstone's research also has demonstrated that adding the right color (or colors) to the printed page and adjusting the level of light "fills in" the missing segments of magno cells. This stops the print distortions shown in Figures 5.2 through 5.7. PET scan and MRI images of the magnicellular pathway change from abnormal to normal when appropriate light levels and colors are added to a word blind person's visual processing (Livingstone, 1993).

Word blindness, or Irlen syndrome, triggers a cascade of behaviors that often imitate ADHD or ADD. Soon after the word blind individual starts to read under

(*text continues on page 130*)

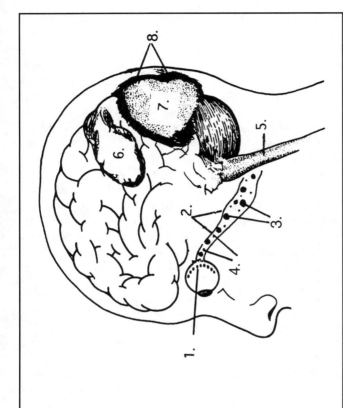

1. Photoreceptors in the retina
2. Magnicellular visual pathway that connects the retina and brain stem
3. Magno cells
4. Parvo cells
5. Brain stem
6. Parietal lobe
7. Visual cortex
8. Occipital lobe

Figure 5.1. Between the retina and brain stem is the magnicellular "visual highway" made of two kinds of cells that work together in pairs to carry visual impressions to the limbic system. Large cells called *magno cells* rapidly transfer portions of what the eyes see to the brain stem, where this first information waits. The small cells called *parvo cells* more slowly transfer the rest of the visual image. The brain stem filters out unnecessary details and starts to blend necessary data into complete visual images. This filtered, partly organized data is then sent to the parietal lobe, which fires it on to the visual cortex in the occipital lobe. Irlen syndrome is caused by incomplete development of the magno cells. This deficit in cell development triggers the distorted, moving images shown in Figures 5.2 through 5.7 Adding color "fills in" the missing segments in the magno cells. This permits the brain stem to develop complete images of what the eyes see on the printed page. [From *Overcoming Dyslexia in Children, Adolescents, and Adults* (2nd ed.), by D. R. Jordan, 1996, Austin, TX: PRO-ED, Inc. Copyright 1996 by PRO-ED, Inc. Reprinted with permission.]

Luis squeezed Maria's hand as they felt the airplane dip downward for the last time. Together they held their breath waiting for the squeal of tires against the runway. Suddenly they felt the landing bump. Then the engines roared with a mighty backward push. The airplane slowed its race down the runway. Through their tears of joy Luis and Maria heard the voice of the cabin attendant saying: "Welcome to Dallas/Fort Worth. Please remain seated until the aircraft has come to a complete stop at the terminal. Have a good day in the Dallas area, or wherever your travel may take you."

Figure 5.2. Without warning the page blurs out of focus, then comes back into focus. This pulsing effect places great strain on the eyes. The reader can make the print clear for a moment by widening the eyes, or by squinting the eyes almost closed.

Luis squeezed Maria's hand as they felt the airplane dip downward for the last time. Together they held their breath waiting for the squeal of tires against the runway. Suddenly they felt the landing bump. Then the engines roared with a mighty backward push. The airplane slowed its race down the runway. Through their tears of joy Luis and Maria heard the voice of the cabin attendant saying: "Welcome to Dallas/Fort Worth. Please remain seated until the aircraft has come to a complete stop at the terminal. Have a good day in the Dallas area, or wherever your travel may take you."

Figure 5.3. Lines begin to swirl, like a wheel rotating, as the eyes focus on a particular word.

Luis squeezed Maria's hand as they felt the airplane dip downward for the last time. Together they held their breath waiting for the squeal of tires against the runway. Suddenly they felt the landing bump. Then the engines roared with a mighty backward push. The airplane slowed its race down the runway. Through their tears of joy Luis and Maria heard the voice of the cabin attendant saying: "Welcome to Dallas/Fort Worth. Please remain seated until the aircraft has come to a complete stop at the terminal. Have a good day in the Dallas area, or wherever your travel may take you."

Figure 5.4. Letters move sideways to stack on top of each other, or whole words stack, then move apart. This produces a smudged effect that makes reading impossible.

Luis squeezed   Maria'shandasthey   felttheairplanedip
downwardfor   thelasttime.Together   theyheldtheir
breathwait   ingforthesqueal of tir   esagainstthe   runw
Suddenlythey   feltthelandingbump.   Thentheengi   nes
roaredwithamig   htybackward push.   Theairplaneslow
itsracedowntherun   way.Throughthe   irtearsofjoy   Luis
andMariaheard   thevoiceofthecabin   attendantsaying
"WelcometoDal   las/Fort Worth.Plea   seremainseated
untiltheaircr   afthascometoacom   pletestopatthe   ga
Haveagood   dayintheDallasarea,or   whereveryour   trav
maytake   you."

Figure 5.5. Words move sideways, creating a "river" effect, as if small rivers are cascading down the page. These rivers change rapidly as words continue to move back and forth.

Luis squeezed Maria's hand as they felt the airplane dip downward for the last time. Together they held their breath waiting for the squeal of tires against the runway. Suddenly they felt the landing bump. Then the engines roared with a mighty backward push. The airplane slowed its race down the runway. Through their tears of joy Luis and Maria heard the voice of the cabin attendant saying: "Welcome to Dallas/Fort Worth. Please remain seated until the aircraft has come to a complete stop at the terminal. Have a good day in the Dallas area, or wherever your travel may take you."

Figure 5.6. Inside portions of words slowly fade away, then come back. This "washout" effect greatly increases reading difficulty for word blind individuals.

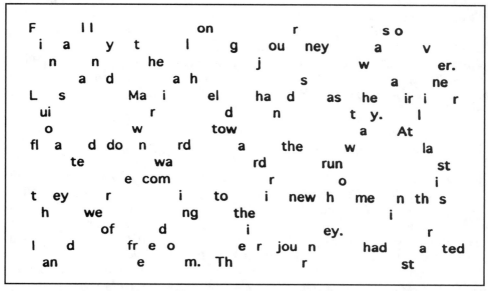

Figure 5.7. Some Irlen syndrome readers see lines ripple up and down, like a flag in the wind. Laying a marker below each line often stops this ripple effect.

bright light, both eyes begin to sting or burn. The reader squints the eyes to shut out bright light. After a few minutes, both eyes begin to hurt or feel uncomfortable. Many readers with Irlen syndrome lean over their work to shade pages from overhead light, or they hold a hand up to the forehead to shade the eyes. Word blind individuals often want to wear a baseball cap into the classroom and let the bill shade the eyes. Print begins to blur in and out of focus in a pulsing pattern (see Figure 5.2). Many word blind readers see a swirling pattern like a wheel turning over the page (see Figure 5.3). Words and lines of print often stack on top of each other, then separate (see Figure 5.4). Rivers of space start to run down the page as words slide sideways, then come back together (see Figure 5.5). Letters begin to flicker or blink on and off. The inside portions of words often fade away, then return (see Figure 5.6). Sometimes the reader sees words sliding off the edge of the page. At a certain point of visual stress, whole lines ripple up and down like a flag waving (see Figure 5.7).

Many word blind students lean down close with the nose almost touching the page, then they lean back away from the page. Or the reader might lift the book up close to the face, then put it back on the desktop. The body starts to shift and turn in different directions that lets the person view the page from different angles. After a few minutes, a headache develops across the forehead (frontal headache), then moves over the temple regions (temporal headache). When Irlen syndrome individuals keep on trying to read, they often develop headache at the back of the head and down the neck (occipital headache). As these word blind patterns set in, the reader begins to fidget, squirm, glance away, and appear to be ADHD. When Irlen syndrome is corrected, symptoms of ADHD disappear. The tag-along syndrome of poor visual perception often is mistaken for ADHD.

Learning Disabilities

In the book *Overcoming Dyslexia in Children, Adolescents, and Adults,* I have documented close links between ADHD, ADD, and learning disabilities (LDs), especially various forms of dyslexia. My research through 40 years of diagnosing and remediating dyslexia indicates that 65% of those who are dyslexic also have ADHD or ADD (Jordan, 1972, 1988a, 1988b, 1996a). In looking at LD patterns in attention deficit disorder patients, Russell Barkley (1995) estimates that 20 to 30% of those with ADHD also have LD in math, reading, or spelling. During 20 years of research with dyslexic adults, Laura Weisel (1992) has found ADHD or ADD symptoms in 45% of her clients. Research by Carolyn Pollan and Dorothy Williams (1992) with adjudicated delinquents and persons receiving public assistance in the state of Arkansas has shown that 46% of those with LD also have significant symptoms of ADHD or ADD. Learning disabilities often tag along in the shadow of attention deficits.

Of the LD patterns that imitate ADHD and ADD, the most commonly seen are types of dyslexia. In the book *Overcoming Dyslexia in Children, Adolescents, and Adults,* I have documented the two types of dyslexia that usually hide in the shadows of attention deficit disorders (Jordan, 1996a). The concept of dyslexia was first presented in 1884 by the German ophthalmologist Reinhold Berlin, who was perplexed by the struggle to read that he saw in intelligent individuals with normal eyesight (Berlin, 1884). Until the 1960s, most people followed Berlin's view that dyslexia consists of reversed letters, words read backwards (mirror image), and inability to develop normal reading skills. In the early 1970s a much broader understanding of dyslexia emerged. In 1972 the book *Dyslexia in the Classroom* documented the broad scope of dyslexic patterns in reading, spelling, listening comprehension, written language usage, handwriting, and arithmetic computation (Jordan, 1972). Neurological research by such pioneers as Norman Geschwind (1984) and Albert Galaburda (1983) discovered brain pathway differences that are linked to dyslexia. Brain imaging studies of dyslexic individuals by Frank Wood (1991) at the Bowman-Gray School of Medicine documented slow blood flow and irregular glucose metabolism in dyslexic brains. We now recognize two subtypes of dyslexia that often tag along with ADHD and ADD.

Auditory Dyslexia, or Tone Deafness to Spoken Language

Since Berlin's studies of dyslexia in 1884, teachers have wondered why certain students never learn phonics. Regardless of how much drill and tutoring is done, some learners never connect sounds to letters in spelling or reading. These "tone deaf" individuals have normal hearing, yet they never learn to "hear" vowels and soft consonants that are the building blocks of words. In 1993 Paula Tallal, a neurobiologist at Rutgers University, and her colleagues discovered a missing link in the auditory pathway between the limbic system and higher brain regions that process oral language (Tallal, Miller, & Fitch, 1993). Figure 5.8 is a diagram of the auditory pathway from the middle ear, where speech sounds are converted into electrical codes, through the medial geniculate nucleus, where coded speech is filtered and organized, and finally to the higher brain where those codes are turned into "brain language." Tallal's research discovered a chain of auditory nerve cells between the medial geniculate nucleus and the parietal lobe. These auditory cells work in pairs. Some of these cells process soft/slow language sounds (vowels and soft consonants). The other cells process hard/fast language sounds (hard consonants). Auditory dyslexia (tone deafness) occurs when the soft/slow auditory cells do not "hear" the soft, slow sounds of our language.

For example, all spoken words are made of sound chunks in a certain sequence, such as the word *cut* (hard-fast sound /k/, soft-slow sound /u/, hard-fast sound /t/). Persons with auditory dyslexia are "tone deaf" to the soft, slow middle sound /u/. Individuals who are tone deaf cannot develop good spelling from memory because they do not hear all of the speech sounds in sequence. As these dyslexic individuals listen to speech, they fail to hear chunks of sound

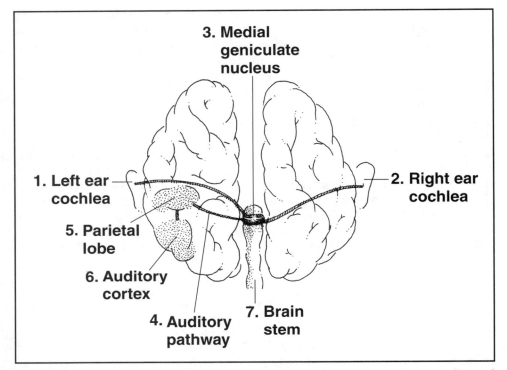

Figure 5.8. The cochlea in each middle ear gathers speech sounds that are changed into electrical codes. These sound codes are sent to the medial geniculate nucleus in the brain stem. The medial geniculate nucleus organizes the soft/slow and hard/fast sound chunks into word patterns, then fires that data to the parietal lobe, which sends it on to the auditory cortex. The auditory pathway between the brain stem and parietal lobe has two types of cells that work as a team. Larger cells process the soft/slow sounds of vowels and soft consonants. Smaller cells process the hard/fast sounds of hard consonants. Auditory dyslexia occurs when underdeveloped larger cells do not transfer the soft/slow speech sounds in the right sequence. The auditory cortex receives only part of the original oral speech. This makes it impossible for the dyslexic person to connect sounds to letters in listening, reading, and spelling.

inside many words. Figure 5.9 shows how auditory dyslexia appears in writing. On a dictated writing test a 13-year-old girl with tone deafness wrote what she thought she heard the teacher say. Figure 5.10 shows the work of a dyslexic student in high school trying to write phrases and sentences from dictation. He cannot write all the sounds because he does not hear them. Yet this individual has excellent hearing for nonlanguage listening. All his life he has stumbled over similar words because he cannot hear differences in speech sounds. For instance, he cannot tell the difference between "idea" and "ideal." To him, "furnace" and "thermos" are the same. He fixes the furnace to get heat, and he puts hot coffee in a furnace to take to a ball game. When someone says "olive," he hears "olly." All his life, his grandmother has cooked chicken in "olly oil." He thinks that nails and bolts are made of "medal."

Tone deaf individuals have the habit of saying "What?" or "Huh?" or "What do you mean?" as they listen. Persons with ADHD also interrupt this way, demanding to hear it again. The difference is that tone deaf individuals cannot hear these differences, while ADHD persons are too distracted to pay full attention while listening.

Visual Dyslexia

Visual dyslexia is not a problem with eyesight. Most persons with visual dyslexia have normal vision (20/20 acuity). The problem arises from confused orientation with left to right, and top to bottom. The dyslexic brain wants to interpret the outside world backwards and upside down. Normal visual perception in our culture is to scan in a certain sequence: left to right. In the written languages of Western cultures, alphabetic sequence and reading from printed pages are done left to right. At the same time, printed symbols must be interpreted top to bottom. From early childhood, youngsters are drilled in this left-to-right, top-to-bottom brain orientation. Cultures in the Middle East and Far East follow an opposite or partly opposite orientation, often reading bottom to top and right to left. Regardless of cultural orientation, the dyslexic brain wants to do it backwards or upside down. For example, several English language letters never become automatically recognized: *d-b p-q M-W u-n.*

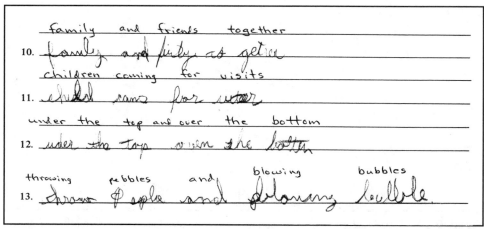

Figure 5.9. Tone deafness is clearly seen in this work of a 13-year-old girl who is dyslexic. She cannot hear all of the soft/slow, hard/fast speech chunks in the right sequence. She fails to connect correct sounds to letters, and she loses letter sequences as her pencil touches the paper.

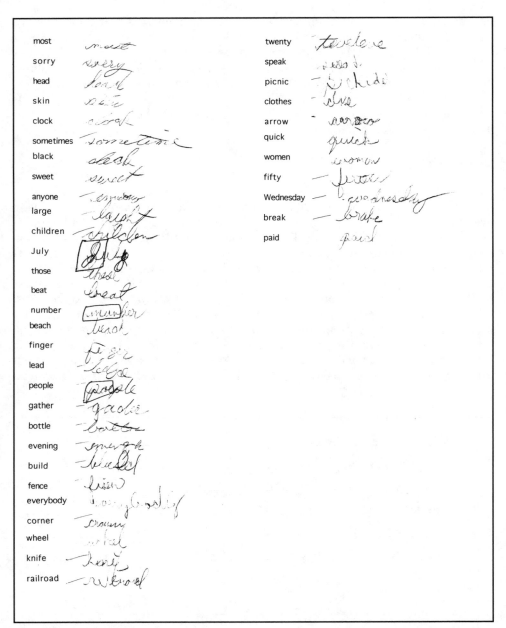

Figure 5.10. A high school student with auditory dyslexia tried to write a list of words from dictation. Tone deafness to speech sounds keeps him from hearing individual speech sounds in the right sequence. He often cannot connect sounds to letters from memory. Occasionally he remembers a spelling pattern correctly because he has memorized it.

Mirror image causes many words to be read backwards: *stop-post won-now tub-but on-no.* Visual dyslexia creates backward spelling inside words: *form-from Apirl-April bran-barn.* Persons with visual dyslexia continually misread words they see in print: *Tulsa* for *Altus exist* for *exit hummingbird* for *hamburger.* Outdoors, dyslexic individuals reverse left and right, as well as up and down. Top and bottom often are reversed in dyslexic thinking. Remembering north, east, south, west is frequently impossible for these struggling learners. Figure 5.11 shows how visual dyslexia creates confusion in reading and word matching. It is not unusual to find these kinds of errors in the work of ADHD persons who are too distracted to think about keeping details in correct sequence. These patterns disappear as ADHD diminishes during puberty and early adult years. In dyslexia, these backward or scrambled mental images remain for life.

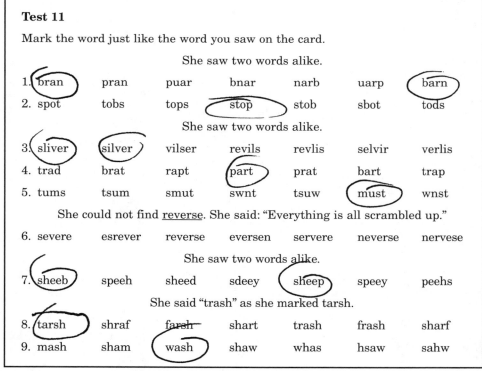

Test 11

Mark the word just like the word you saw on the card.

She saw two words alike.

| 1. | bran | pran | puar | bnar | narb | uarp | barn |
| 2. | spot | tobs | tops | stop | stob | sbot | tods |

She saw two words alike.

3.	sliver	silver	vilser	revils	revlis	selvir	verlis
4.	trad	brat	rapt	part	prat	bart	trap
5.	tums	tsum	smut	swnt	tsuw	must	wnst

She could not find <u>reverse</u>. She said: "Everything is all scrambled up."

| 6. | severe | esrever | reverse | eversen | servere | neverse | nervese |

She saw two words alike.

| 7. | sheeb | speeh | sheed | sdeey | sheep | speey | peehs |

She said "trash" as she marked tarsh.

| 8. | tarsh | shraf | farsh | shart | trash | frash | sharf |
| 9. | mash | sham | wash | shaw | whas | hsaw | sahw |

Figure 5.11. This 21-year-old dyslexic woman worked hard to match words. She whispered and touched each word, spelling it to herself. Finally she circled her choice of what matched the word she had seen on a card. She continually said: "Oops! That's not right. Uh-uh. I got it backwards. Let's see. It had d. Wait, was it b?" Even with this practice, her memory would not maintain left-to-right, top-to-bottom orientation. This activity is part of the *Jordan Written Screening Test.*

How To Help People with ADHD and ADD

6

· **👫👫**

Legal Status of LD, ADHD, and ADD

Eligibility Through Score Discrepancy

The year 1984 was a watershed one for special education in the United States. Before 1984, struggling learners received special help at school when parents, tutors, physicians, counselors, and classroom teachers put together enough testimonial evidence to build a profile of special need. This testimony included such observations as playground behavior, how the child functioned as a team player, disruptive behavior on family holidays, level of struggle in the classroom, inability to keep up with assignments, and standard scores from achievement tests. When this wide point of view convinced school leaders that a child needed help, the struggling learner was assigned to a resource room or learning lab outside the mainstream classroom. This method of determining eligibility used such labels as "learning disability," "dyslexia," or "attention deficit" to admit struggling learners into special remedial programs.

In 1984 all states except California adopted a new standard for determining legal placement of students in special help programs. This new approach to identifying special learning need (LD) was controlled by arbitrary differences between standard test scores. To earn the legal designation of LD, a student must earn an IQ score of 90 or higher on an intelligence test, usually a form of the *Wechsler Intelligence Scale*. The student also must take a standard achievement test, such as the *Woodcock–Johnson Psycho-educational Battery*. Standard scores in reading, math, and language usage were subtracted from the IQ score. If a certain cutoff discrepancy score was reached by this subtraction, the student was labeled LD (learning disabled). Each state established its own cutoff discrepancy score to control how many special-need students could qualify for remedial help at school. Some states set a 15-point discrepancy as the entry level for LD special education. Other states required a 20-point discrepancy. Still others required as much as a 22-point difference between IQ and standard achievement scores. This score-based determination of special need replaced the former method of gathering reports from adults who observed the child in different situations. A major part of the change in identifying LD was to omit ADHD and ADD from the definition of learning disabilities. Some types of learning disabilities (dyslexia, dysgraphia, dyscalculia) continued to be acknowledged legally as LD. Attention deficit disorders were not.

For example, at age 10, Joe struggles very hard in fourth grade. After repeating kindergarten, he entered first grade at age 7. For 3 years he received intensive tutoring after school and during summer vacations. In spite of this extra help, his reading, writing, spelling, and math skills remain far below his grade level. Joe was promoted to fourth grade in hopes that he would "outgrow" his learning difficulties. In October of fourth grade the school psychologist administered a diagnostic test battery to see if Joe might be LD. The following standard scores were obtained:

Wechsler Intelligence Scale for Children (WISC–III)	Full scale IQ	98
Woodcock–Johnson Psycho-educational Battery, Revised	Reading	82
	Math	84
	Language	81

When the achievement scores are subtracted from IQ 98, Joe shows a 16-point discrepancy in reading skills, a 14-point discrepancy in math, and a 17-point discrepancy in language skills. In October of fourth grade, Joe's family lived in a state where a 15-point score discrepancy was required for LD recognition. He was diagnosed as "showing indications of having specific learning disability," and he was immediately placed in an intensive remedial program outside his mainstream classroom.

In February of fourth grade, Joe's father was transferred to another state that required a 20-point score discrepancy before a child could receive assistance for LD. In this new school, Joe no longer qualifies as having learning disability. Midway through fourth grade, he was "dumped" back into a mainstream classroom in spite of the fact that his literacy skills are far below his grade level. The only option for recertifying Joe's need for special help is for his parents to go through due process. This requires the family to hire private counselors and legal advisors to build a case of Joe's special need. This costly due process effort will be considered by the school, but there is no guarantee that this appeal will reinstate Joe's placement in a special education program. By the mid-1980s, thousands of struggling learners like Joe had fallen through the cracks of the score-discrepancy model for determining LD.

Full Inclusion

As the impact of the 1984 shift to standard score criteria became apparent, many parents, educators, and other professionals became alarmed. In 1985 the U.S. Department of Education proposed the *Regular Education Initiative (REI)*, which would begin to phase out much of traditional special education (Will, 1986). A new model called *full inclusion* would place students with "mild disabilities" in mainstream classrooms where teachers would be assisted by aides trained to work with special-need learners. Adoption of the score-discrepancy standard and the move toward full inclusion created an uproar among influential leaders. James Kauffman and Daniel Hallahan (1995), Larry Silver (1991), Martha Denckla (1991), and others "declared war" on these efforts to limit access to specialized help for struggling learners.

IQ Is "Irrelevant" to LD

From this debate over meeting the needs of struggling learners came a new concept of how to define learning disabilities. In 1993 Jack Naglieri and Sean Reardon published a strong challenge to the notion that LD should be determined by standard scores. Their article "Traditional IQ Is Irrelevant to Learning Disabilities—Intelligence Is Not" set off a vigorous debate in educational circles. Somewhat earlier in 1991, Martha Denckla drew an ovation at a national conference when she declared that it is ridiculous to require an arbitrary IQ score for those who struggle to take IQ tests: "If (the proponents of score-discrepancy) need an IQ, then let's give them a universal IQ 90. Now, let's get on with the business of finding out why otherwise bright kids have trouble with learning." Denckla went on to propose the concept of *executive function*. She declared that in finding out why certain learners struggle, she wants to know how the prefrontal cortex and the limbic system get along together, or fail to get along. "The prefrontal is our executive," she explained. "It gives logical orders that the rest of the brain is supposed to follow. I contend that a breakdown occurs in executive function when we find attention deficits and learning disabilities" (Denckla, 1991).

Executive Function

Following Denckla's lead, in 1992 I developed the *Jordan Executive Function Index for Children* and the *Jordan Executive Function Index for Adults* (see Appendixes A and B). This survey pinpoints specific habits of paying attention, organizing one's life, and saying no to impulses. As teachers and parents prepare to intervene, offer help, or develop self-monitoring systems for ADHD and ADD individuals, it is important to determine whether symptoms are mild, moderate, or severe. It is also important to determine individual strengths and weaknesses in maintaining attention, being organized, and coping with impulse.

Medication

The issue of whether to prescribe medication for ADHD or ADD is somewhat controversial. In Chapter 4 we met James, whose behavior was out of control. His parents were torn between personal conviction that it was somehow "wrong" to control children through medication and their desperation to have a normal family life. James suffered from overlapping behavior patterns. In the shadow of severe ADHD lurked Oppositional Defiant Disorder (ODD) and intermittent episodes of Conduct Disorder (CD). In Chapter 4 we also met Jo whom I knew as a difficult child, a rebellious adolescent, and a dysfunctional young adult. During her school years, Ritalin reduced disruptive behavior enough to let her stay in the public school stream. On her 18th birthday, Jo rebelled against medication, and her parents helplessly watched her life fall apart. Those who object to stimulant medication for youngsters do so out of fear of possible side effects. Yet the side effects of unrelieved ADHD and ADD can be far worse than the mild side effects of medication that some individuals experience.

Barkley (1995) has estimated that 65% of those diagnosed as ADHD also have ODD. One in three (30%) of ADHD individuals also have CD. My clinical experience with struggling learners indicates that as many as 65% of those with dyslexia also have ADHD or ADD (Jordan, 1996a). In Chapter 5 we saw that Weisel (1992), Pollan and Williams (1992), and Payne (1994) have documented approximately 45% overlap of LD, ADHD or ADD with behavior disorders. Part of the confusion over whether to medicate ADHD and ADD lies in the difficulty of separating tag-along syndromes from true ADHD and ADD. If we do not correctly diagnose various types of tag-along disorders, then medication can indeed "backfire" and create unacceptable side effects.

Cortical Stimulants

When ADHD and ADD stand alone, a highly useful treatment is cortical stimulant medication that increases levels of dopamine in the prefrontal cortex. This awakens the underaroused frontal brain so that it can work normally. Barkley and his colleagues at the University of Massachusetts Medical Center have reported a wide range of effectiveness in treating ADHD with stimulant medication. Their success rate ranges from 50% to 95%, depending on how well tag-along syndromes are separated from ADHD. If no overlapping behavior disorders are taken into account, 50% of their ADHD patients improve with cortical stimulant treatment. When behavior disorders or mood disorders are treated with antidepressants or other medications at the same time ADHD is treated with stimulants, 95% percent of their patients improve.

Treatment for ADD follows a similar range of success. If an ADD individual is treated with cortical stimulant with no recognition of underlying depression, the success rate with medication is about 30%. When tag-along depression is treated along with stimulant medication for ADD, the success rate rises to 55% (Barkley, 1995).

Correcting Underarousal

In Chapter 1 we reviewed the problem of underarousal of the prefrontal cortex (see pages 26–28). In certain individuals, this executive portion of the brain is too sluggish to stay in charge of other brain functions. The "executive" in charge of the brain is too lethargic to do its job. Cortical stimulant medication "wakes up" the executive prefrontal cortex. As the prefrontal brain becomes alert, the neurotransmitters dopamine and norepinephrine increase along the axon pathways. This renewed balance in brain chemistry puts the brakes on impulses that want to escape from the limbic system. With cortical stimulants, there is noticeable decrease in aggression, disruptive behavior, noncompliance (refusal to cooperate), and noisiness. Fine motor coordination improves (handwriting, handling small objects). Memory for details becomes faster and more accurate, and short-term memory for new data improves. Social behavior shows marked improvement as the individual earns more praise, finishes more tasks, and gets along better with others.

The most important benefit from cortical stimulant medication is that the person's intelligence is more usable in organized, productive ways. Figure 6.1 shows the benefit of Ritalin for a 19-year-old man who had been an underachiever all his life. With cortical stimulant, his intelligence became much more usable and productive. The most commonly prescribed cortical stimulant medications are Ritalin, Cylert, Dexedrine, and Adderall (several forms of Dexedrine combined into one medication).

Low Dosage Strength

The key to success in using cortical stimulant medication is to keep dosage strength as low as possible. In 1989 Harvey Parker developed the Standard Ritalin Dosage Chart that continues to guide physicians in prescribing cortical stimulants: *low dosage*—0.3 mg per kilogram (2.2 pounds) of body weight; *medium dosage*—0.6 mg per kilogram (2.2 pounds) of body weight; *high dosage*—1.0 mg per kilogram (2.2 pounds) of body weight. For example, a child who weighs 44 pounds (20 kilograms) would be given 6 mg for low dosage, 12 mg for medium dosage, or 20 mg for high dosage. A rule of thumb is that cortical stimulant should not make the person feel different. As the prefrontal cortex becomes aroused, it silently takes charge of the limbic system, allowing outsiders to see decreased ADHD or ADD. The person taking medication should not feel strange or weird. If hyperactivity is toned down to a calm behavior level, the brain has been overmedicated and cannot learn effectively.

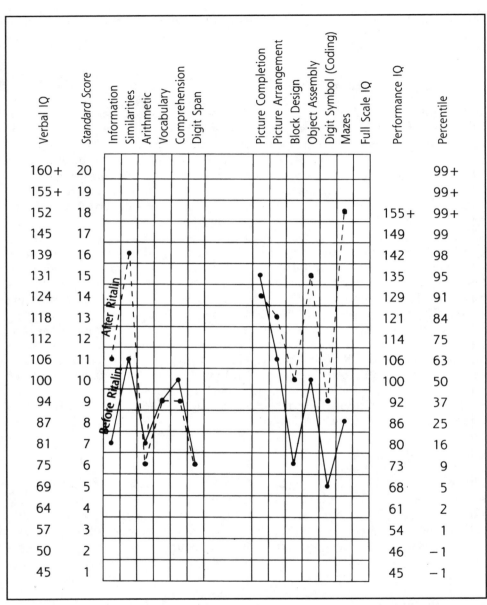

Figure 6.1. *Wechsler Adult Intelligence Scale–Revised* scores of a college student taking Ritalin for ADHD control. Solid line shows his IQ test performance without medication. Dotted line shows his improved mental ability 1 year after he started taking Ritalin.

Rebound from Medication

Many ADHD youngsters spend a reasonably quiet day at school while taking stimulant medication, then explode with an energetic release of pent-up energy as the school day ends. Parents often suffer through frantic evenings as rebound energy turns the child into an erupting volcano. Rebound tends to run its course by bedtime, although some rebounders do not calm down until midnight. Some families decide to live with uncontrolled hyperactivity rather than endure the rebound effect every evening after school. Many youngsters who rebound from stimulant medication also have a tag-along syndrome of food intolerance. When trigger foods are removed from the diet, rebound from medication often diminishes or disappears. Three types of stimulant medication generally are prescribed to arouse the sluggish prefrontal cortex.

1. *Ritalin (methylphenidate).* For half a century, Ritalin has been used worldwide with attention deficit individuals. When prescribed sensibly at low dosage strength, it is one of the safest medications ever used. Ritalin is non-addictive and non-habit-forming. Correctly prescribed, it does not stunt growth or delay puberty. Approximately 3 out of 100 individuals cannot take Ritalin because of biochemical intolerance. This medication rapidly enters the brain and reaches its peak effect in 1 to 3 hours, then remains active in the brain for 3 to 6 hours. In most individuals, a morning dose will be out of the brain by noon. A second dose at noon will be out of the brain by late afternoon. Approximately 30% of those who take Ritalin have mild side effects, such as decreased appetite (especially at noon), trouble falling asleep, feelings of anxiousness or nervousness, increased irritability, or the tendency to cry easily. Some individuals complain of stomachache or mild headache. These side effects usually disappear after 2 or 3 weeks on medication. Sometimes tic behavior (odd muscle movements) appears until the brain adjusts to the medication. If side effects are too disturbing, stopping medication clears the brain of all traces of Ritalin within 24 hours.

2. *Cylert (pemoline).* Cylert is often prescribed when Ritalin is not effective. Cylert is much slower than Ritalin to enter the brain and arouse the prefrontal cortex to full executive function level. This medication requires 1 to 2 hours to enter the brain and does not reach its peak effectiveness for an additional 2 to 4 hours. Once Cylert is active, it continues to stimulate the prefrontal cortex for 7 to 9 hours. In addition to stimulating the prefrontal regions of the brain, pemoline may also affect liver functions. Approximately 3% of patients have a hepatitis-like reaction to Cylert. This is why a liver function medical test must be done every 3 to 6 months. Occasionally skin rash develops as a side effect. Otherwise, most individuals can take this medication safely and comfortably.

3. *Dexedrine (dextroamphetamine).* Dexedrine was the first type of cortical stimulant used for ADHD (see page 2). Like Cylert, this stimulant is slow to enter the brain and take effect. Dexedrine does not begin to stimulate the prefrontal regions for 2 to 3 hours after it is taken. It does not reach peak effectiveness for 3 to 5 hours, but it lasts 7 to 9 hours once it starts to work in

the brain. Dexedrine has few side effects for most individuals. Occasionally it triggers strong side effects, like those described for Ritalin. A new form of Dexedrine is called Adderall. This is a long-lasting (time release) medication that combines several forms of dextroamphetamine. When Dexedrine was first used during the 1940s and 1950s, high dosage strength often was prescribed to calm down hyperactive behavior. At high dosage level, Dexedrine often delayed the start of puberty. When this stimulant is used at low or moderate dosage strengths, there is no evidence that puberty is delayed.

Antidepressant Medication

Because of the high rate of mood disorders and depression in the shadow of ADHD and ADD, it now is common practice to combine stimulant medication for arousal of the prefrontal cortex with antidepressant medication for the limbic system. As Barkley's research has demonstrated, using antidepressants for tag-along mood disorders almost doubles the effectiveness of medication for ADHD and ADD (Barkley, 1995).

Antidepressants increase levels of the neurotransmitters dopamine and norepinephrine. As brain chemistry comes into normal balance through this medication, a wide range of improvements is seen. Attention span increases while the body becomes less restless or hyperactive. The person is noticeably less irritable and not so angry. A positive mood emerges with more open happiness, less anxiety, and less worry or fretting. Social relationships improve, along with happier times at home, at school, and at work. Antidepressants are slow to enter the brain and reach their peak effectiveness. Once the brain is fully medicated, the effect lasts around the clock until the next dose is taken. These medications must be taken consistently. Missed doses trigger headaches, nausea, muscle ache, stomachache, poor sleep, and emotional overflow with bouts of crying, sadness, and nervousness. Withdrawal from antidepressants must be gradual and done under a doctor's supervision. Side effects often appear, such as slower heart rate, dry mouth, constipation, moments of blurred vision, and some trouble urinating. Persons who have a history of seizure disorder tend to have increased seizures while taking antidepressants. Because the brain builds up tolerance for these medications, a wide variety of antidepressants is now available. After a year or two, each medication loses its effectiveness and a different antidepressant must be started. These include Aventyl and Pamelor (nortriptyline), Petrofrane and Norpramin (desipramine), Welbutrin (bupropion hydrochloride), BuSpar (buspirone HCl), Tofranil (imipramine), Tryptonal (amitryptilline), and Elavil (amitriptyline).

Antiobsessive Medications

In earlier chapters we reviewed the disruptive behaviors of obsessive/compulsive disorders. Several medications are available to increase the presence of serotonin. Increased serotonin helps to reduce obsessive or compulsive habits. These medications are called selective serotonin reuptake inhibitors (SRRIs). This group of antiobsessive/compulsive medications includes Anafranil (clomitramine), Prozac (fluoxetane), Paxil (paroxetine HCl), Zoloft (certraline HCl), Luvox (fluoxamine maleate), Effexor (venlafaxine HCl), and Serzone (nefazodone HCl). Persons taking these medications must have frequent medical supervision to make sure that side effects do not develop. A frequent side effect for SSRI medications, especially Luvox, is that emotions become "bottled up" and cease to flow normally. While moods become more stable, the individual keeps emotions inside. When SSRI medication is changed or discontinued, tears flow like a river until the bottled-up emotions have been released. The brain builds up tolerance to each of these SSRI medications, requiring change to a new antiobsessive medication after 1 to 2 years.

Antiaggression Medication

In Chapter 4 we saw the aggressive behavior of James and Jo, who often exploded in tantrum behaviors that destroyed relationships. Several medications have been designed to put the brakes on the limbic system's outbursts of aggression, violence, tantrums, and automatic refusal to obey authority. These medications increase cooperation while reducing excessive frustration. Antiaggression medications work rapidly, entering the brain within 30 to 60 minutes, and remain active from 3 to 6 hours. Side effects sometimes occur, including lethargy, drowsiness, headache, dizziness, dry mouth, constipation, nausea, or stomachache. These side effects usually go away after 2 to 3 weeks. Because these medications can increase blood pressure, reduce heart rate, and slow down physical growth, it is essential that persons taking antiaggression medication be monitored by a physician. The most commonly prescribed medications are Catepres (clonodine), Tenex (guanfacine), and Inderal (propanolol hydrochloride). Catepres can be administered through a skin patch that is worn around the clock. A newer medication, Aurorix (moclobemide), is now available to reduce restless, disruptive behavior. However, Aurorix cannot be administered along with Ritalin, Cylert, or Dexedrine. Aurorix is considered a "third line" of treatment for disruptive behaviors when cortical stimulants and antidepressants have not been effective.

Diet Control

For two reasons, 1973 was a memorable year in my life. That year I left university-based clinical work with struggling learners to join my wife in private practice with LD, ADHD, and ADD persons of all ages. Immediately we plunged into the world of frustrated parents, struggling youngsters, disruptive adolescents, and discouraged adults who could not get their lives in order. Also in 1973, Ben Feingold in San Francisco became a national media sensation with his proposal that hyperactivity and attention deficits are related to food allergies, as well as to chemical additives and sugar. Through national talk shows and other media, the public heard Feingold claim that 50% of ADHD behavior could be reduced or eliminated by taking trigger foods, sugar, and chemicals out of the child's diet. Like a thunderstorm breaking over the city, our diagnostic center was deluged by excited parents who wanted Dr. Feingold's kind of help with their disruptive youngsters. Soon hundreds of Feingold diet chapters had formed across the country with parents exchanging recipes they insisted had reduced hyperactivity in themselves and their offspring. Our staff became sharply focused on behaviors that might be related to food and beverage intake. As we saw in Chapter 4 James became a new person when trigger foods were removed from his diet.

Feingold K-P Diet

In 1975 Feingold published his widely read book *Why Your Child Is Hyperactive*. For the first time we could separate media hype from what Feingold actually proposed. The book revealed that Feingold's concepts of diet control for ADHD and ADD had been misrepresented. Unfortunately, initial publicity that reduced the Feingold diet to inaccurate "sound bytes" had left an indelibly bad impression in the minds of many professionals. To this day, Ben Feingold's contribution to managing ADHD behaviors through diet is severely underestimated. The Feingold K-P diet divides foods into two groups. Group 1 consists of foods that contain natural salicylic acid (salicylate foods). In nature, this family of plant chemicals appears in many foods. Among fruits containing salicylic acid are apples, apricots, blackberries, strawberries, oranges, cherries, raspberries, gooseberries, peaches, plums, and grapes. Any food product that contains grape extract, such as grape juice, wine, sweeteners, flavors, or coloring agents processed from grapes brings salicylic salts into the body. Salicylate vegetables include tomatoes, cucumbers, and bell peppers. Today's popular fast foods include many items containing tomato sauce and tomato catsup. All types of cucumber pickle products appear in fast-food menus. Feingold contended that hyperactive, disruptive behavior is often triggered by eating or drinking salicylate foods and beverages.

Group 2 in the Feingold K-P diet consists of chemical additives that saturate prepared foods in grocery stores and on restaurant menus. Since 1975, the Food and Drug Administration has removed several chemical dyes, preservatives, and flavoring agents from food processing. However, one must read labels very carefully to find food products that do not contain chemical additives. Prepared foods continue to contain such chemical additives as sorbates, sulphites, benzoates, nitrates, nitrites, antioxidants, and propionates. In addition, artificial coloring agents are added to virtually every kind of prepared food product, including freshly ground meats.

Feingold's aggressive presentation of his diet control concepts triggered a wave of opposition among physicians and other scientists. Many controlled studies have been done to challenge (or verify) Feingold's contention that hyperactivity is caused by reactions to foods and beverages. The medical community has concluded that no evidence exists to support Feingold's claims (Barkley, 1995; Green & Chee, 1994).

Intolerance to Food

Lost in the public debate over the Feingold diet is a critical distinction between allergic response to certain food substances and body chemistry intolerance for certain foods. Careful reading of Feingold's work discloses that he did not claim that allergies to group 1 and group 2 foods cause hyperactivity and disruptive behavior. Nor did Feingold contend that sugar by itself is a major culprit, as many parents believed. The Feingold model was based on a body chemistry reaction to certain food substances called *food intolerance*. The clinical term for this reaction is *cytotoxic*. Many children, adolescents, and adults have dramatic intolerance for certain foods or beverages. This is similar to being poisoned by something that enters the bloodstream. Being intolerant (cytotoxic) is not the same as being allergic. An allergy triggers a chain of defensive body chemistry responses to rid the bloodstream of the irritating substance (mold, dust, food substance). A rash may appear, nasal passages may become congested, eyes may water, or the person may sneeze and cough. Yet an allergic condition seldom makes the central nervous system ill. In contrast, intolerance to food or food substances poisons nerve pathways and causes swelling of brain tissues. Ironically, many individuals become "addicted" to foods or beverages their bodies cannot tolerate. When cytotoxic substances are denied, the body cries out for more. This chain reaction of eating or drinking a culprit food, becoming "ill," then wanting more is typical of true addiction to alcohol, nicotine, caffeine, or other drugs.

During our years in private practice with thousands of ADHD and ADD individuals and their families, my staff and I witnessed countless episodes of food or beverage intolerance that triggered outbursts of tantrums, aggression, violence, rebellion, hyperactivity, mood swings, and depression. In tracking these events in our client families, we learned to advise parents and teachers to avoid certain kinds of food substances that escalated disruptive behavior. Whole milk proved to be a major trigger for many ADHD individuals. Removing or strictly limiting milk intake frequently reduced hyperactivity, irritability, and rebellion while increasing attention span, improving sleep, and fostering better social relationships. We found many individuals who could not tolerate products made from grapes or tomatoes. No more pizza, spaghetti dinners, catsup on French fries, or beverages containing grape extracts. Many of our clients were intolerant of refined white wheat products because wheat glutin is concentrated in these foods. Whole grain or multigrain products solved the problem. Numerous ADHD or ADD individuals could not tolerate chocolate, although they craved it. By itself, sugar seldom triggered intolerance in our clients. The cytotoxic trigger was what surrounded sugar in pastries, candies, and beverages. We taught parents how to change family habits in grocery buying and food consumption to avoid foods that triggered behavior outbursts. As Feingold pointed out, the entire family must agree to follow the new eating plan. Most families who made those dietary changes found that everyone felt better, following a period of grouchy withdrawal from trigger foods and beverages. In spite of the controversy surrounding the Feingold diet and other dietary proposals, many ADHD and ADD individuals are intolerant to certain foods and beverages. The quality of their lives improves significantly when culprit substances are removed from the diet.

Tight Structure

The basic problem of ADHD and ADD is that these individuals have no internal structure to guide them dependably. Thought patterns are too loose to stay on a constructive course very long. Memory is too spotty and unreliable to let rules and regulations guide behavior from day to day. It is impossible for persons with attention deficits to live a consistently regular or orderly life without outside help.

Help with Organization

The greatest need faced by anyone with ADHD or ADD is for someone else to help keep things organized and on schedule. Parents must become the source of the child's organization, or a companion must help an ADD or ADHD partner stay on track. Teachers must provide consistent classroom guidelines that tell students what to do. When attention deficit symptoms are at level 5 or higher in severity, adult leaders must be the eyes and ears of colleagues who have ADD or ADHD. This requires extraordinary patience on the part of parents, teachers, companions, and workplace leaders. New mercies must be extended again and again without punishing forgetful individuals who are poorly organized. Outsiders must remember that attention deficit persons cannot help being forgetful, disorganized, overly active, overly passive, or too loose to stay plugged into their world. Certain basic strategies must be maintained by "supervisors" if loose thinkers are to get safely through childhood and adolescence before they begin to outgrow the syndrome.

Help with Listening

Chapters 2 and 3 described the poor listening comprehension we find in most individuals who have ADHD or ADD. They seldom retain more than 30% of what they hear, unless it is repeated and reinforced. The most effective way to guide an attention deficit individual is to follow all oral information with written lists and outlines. If the person is expected to do three things, the supervisor must make a list of those specific tasks. Each task should be numbered so the ADHD or ADD individual has a brief visible outline:

1. Make your bed.
2. Empty the trash.
3. Feed the dog.

This kind of task outline should be posted where the person will see it several times during the day: on the refrigerator, on the bedroom door, on the bathroom mirror, on the family bulletin board, or on the dashboard in front of the steering wheel. Then the supervisor reminds frequently by asking "Have you done everything on your list?" This brief verbal reminder sends the ADHD or ADD person back to the list to check his or her progress. At school, teachers make lists of assignments, projects that will be due on certain dates, and material the student should take home. These brief lists are taped to the student's desktop or bookbag where they will be seen several times during the day. The teacher must continually remind the attention deficit youngster: "Joe, have you done everything on your list? Do you have all your books ready to take home?" This kind of monitoring usually is required until the middle teens. About age 14, most youngsters with attention deficits begin to remember better on their own. Some individuals continue to need this kind of help into their late teens or early twenties. As we saw earlier, one in five ADHD or ADD children will become attention deficit adults. On the job, they must continue to receive lists of tasks the supervisor requires them to finish each day.

Help Keeping Personal Space Clean

Regardless of age, persons who are moderately or severely ADHD or ADD cannot stay organized without help because mental images are too loose. The brain does not perceive when a room is messy, a work space is cluttered, or a vehicle is littered with trash. These individuals do not notice when personal stuff is scattered all over their space. They cannot maintain an orderly living space or work space unless they are supervised. Outsiders who supervise must remember what attention deficit disorder is. ADHD and ADD create a brain-based inability to keep mental images focused longer than brief periods of time. Attention continually is distracted away from the main point of focus to whatever occurs on the edges of the person's life. Supervision must be provided anytime moderately or severely ADHD or ADD persons are expected to carry out responsibility. For attention deficit youngsters, this includes doing homework, taking a bath, shampooing hair, mowing the yard, picking up dad's tools, getting home from school with all necessary materials, getting to places on time, and remembering instructions from parents and teachers. For older adolescents and young adults with ADHD or ADD, this means frequent reminding to look at written schedules and other lists of responsibilities. Anytime a supervisor or companion expects an ADHD or ADD individual to follow through from start to finish, the person with attention deficits must be reminded in order to succeed.

Guidebooks for ADHD and ADD

An hour of browsing in a large bookstore will lead parents, teachers, companions, and supervisors to a variety of easy-to-read guidebooks for helping individuals with ADHD and ADD. For example, Colleen Alexander-Roberts (1995) has published *A Parent's Guide to Making It Through the Tough Years: ADHD and Teens.* This excellent book offers guidelines for positive discipline, developing social skills, sexuality and dating, getting along at school, and coping with tag-along syndromes that hide behind ADHD. This book does not address ADD, the nonhyperactive form of attention deficit disorder. Russell Barkley's (1995) comprehensive overview *Taking Charge of ADHD: The Complete, Authoritative Guide for Parents* is filled with information about family patterns of ADHD, lifestyle problems of ADHD, medications for ADHD, and practical suggestions for guiding children through difficult school years. Christopher Green and Kit Chee (1994) present a wealth of good information in *Understanding ADD.* Green and Chee use the label ADD to discuss attention deficit with hyperactivity (ADHD). This book is unusually easy to read. At a glance, the reader can find answers to many questions about attention deficits without having to read a lot of text. Edward Hallowell and John Ratey's (1994b) book *Answers to Distraction* presents answers to hundreds of questions frequently asked by parents and teachers. This book covers the range of ADHD problems at home, in society, at school, and in the workplace. An especially helpful guide for parents is John Taylor's (1994) book *Helping Your Hyperactive/Attention Deficit Child.* Taylor discusses only the hyperactive form of attention deficit disorder, but his book covers such critical issues as marital stress, understanding one's own feelings, counteracting misbehavior, and providing positive play experiences to release ADHD stress.

Several excellent books discuss ADHD and ADD in adults. For example, James Thomas and Christine Adamec (1996) present *Do You Have Attention Deficit Disorder?* This book uses the label ADD to describe both hyperactive and nonhyperactive attention deficits in adults. Simple guidelines are given to help individuals discover if they have unidentified ADD. Many useful suggestions are offered for learning how to stay organized, be punctual, and compensate for attention deficits at home and in the workplace. Lynn Weiss (1992) offers *Attention Deficit Disorder in Adults: Practical Help for Sufferers and Their Spouses.* This book deals candidly with intensely personal issues such as abuse, inner pain, sexual problems in ADD marriages, and how to let go of old memories of abuse, anger, loss, and grief. This book is filled with hope and encouragement.

Kate Kelly and Peggy Ramundo (1993), themselves nurse practitioners who are ADD, have published the delightful book *You Mean I'm Not Lazy, Stupid or Crazy?!* This personal account of adults coping with ADD offers practical guidelines for others who struggle with attention deficits. Edward Hallowell and John Ratey (1994a), who are ADD, present an excellent book about ADD in adults: *Driven to Distraction*. These authors tell many victory stories about individuals who have learned to live successfully with attention deficits.

John Ratey and Catherine Johnson's book *Shadow Syndromes* (1997) is an outstanding, easy-to-read review of mood disorders and behavioral problems that often hide behind ADHD and ADD. This book describes helpful medications that reduce or eliminate much of the struggle for individuals who have attention deficits that overlap depression, anxiety, or other mood disorders. Sanjay Jasuja (1995) has developed a helpful guidebook for parents and teachers, *Out of Chaos! Understanding and Managing A.D.D. and Its Relationship to Modern Stress*. Jasuja provides many commonsense tips for reducing stress in personal relationships, on the job, and in the classroom. This book does not differentiate between hyperactive (ADHD) and nonhyperactive (ADD) forms of attention deficit.

Allowing for Immaturity

One of the most obvious problems of attention deficit disorder is immaturity. Most individuals with ADHD or ADD are bright. In fact, a majority of these strugglers demonstrate average to superior intelligence on IQ tests, if the person administering the test knows how to work with attention deficits. Most students with ADD or ADHD excel in one or two academic areas when they have enough supervision to finish assignments. Many of them are highly creative, yet they behave like much younger individuals.

For example, Jose is at level 7 in ADD symptoms. He is bright with IQ 117 (mental age: 11 years, 9 months). He is good at spelling (5th grade, 4th month level), and he is enrolled in the third month of 4th grade (grade 4.3). Reading comprehension is excellent (7th grade, 3rd month level) when he is settled down enough to concentrate. Math skills are average at early 4th grade level. Yet Jose tends to act like an immature 6-year-old when it comes to fitting into his class, taking his turn, sharing with others, and accepting responsibility. He fidgets, squirms, irritates classmates, complains about having too much work to do, interrupts, and cannot stay on task without constant reminding. His maturity profile would look like this:

Reading age	12	Beginning 7th grade
Mental age	11½	Middle 6th grade
Spelling age	10½	Middle 5th grade
Chronological age	9½	Middle 4th grade
Math age	9	Beginning 4th grade
Attention span age	7	Beginning 2nd grade
Emotional maturity age	6½	Middle 1st grade

Most adults work backwards in trying to help these "upside down" struggling learners. Traditionally, adults see how old the child is, his or her grade level in school, how well the child reads, and how high the intelligence is. Then adults expect the child to behave and achieve at those higher score levels. This approach does not work with persons like Jose. The only way to have a successful relationship with such a child is to deal with him or her the opposite way. If this bright youngster has the attention span of a child in second grade, and if this 9-year-old boy has the emotional maturity of one in first grade, then adults must begin at that point. Children like Jose must be guided, nurtured, sheltered, structured, and disciplined the way adults expect to deal with a bright 6-year-old boy.

Regardless of age, persons with ADHD or ADD always show this kind of spread between their highest levels of abilities and their lowest levels of maturity. If they are to find success, these individuals must not be judged by their highest areas alone. They must be guided as if they were much younger. Jose's parents must structure his life the way they would if he actually were 6 years old. They must keep him out of situations that demand the emotional maturity of older children. They must not let him become involved in activities in which he will surely fail, become overly frustrated, or be regarded as a nuisance by leaders and peers. To place a bright, sensitive, but immature child in activities designed for more mature older persons is to guarantee that he or she will be humiliated and overstressed. Adults invite heartache and trouble when they ignore the maturity level of youngsters who have ADD or ADHD.

The critical factor for Jose is the extreme difference between his ability to read and think, and his ability to control emotions and maintain good attention. Individuals with this much developmental delay usually are devastated in team sports. They cannot follow coaches' instructions or remember what to do on the playing field. They cannot handle the emotional pressures of winning and losing, nor can they be good partners in sharing and taking turns. Parents and teachers of children with attention deficits must allow for immaturity. Most youngsters with ADD or ADHD begin to catch up in emotional maturity as puberty brings the body forward in physical development. Yet few are as mature as their age-mates until late teen years or early adulthood. When youngsters like Jose do not outgrow these upside-down patterns, they become adults still performing and behaving on the level of a child.

Help with Schoolwork

A cardinal rule for working successfully with ADHD or ADD is this: *A student with attention deficit disorder must have help doing assignments.* These individuals are too loose, too poorly organized, and too easily distracted to study by themselves. Parents and teachers must keep the factor of immaturity in mind. How well can a 6-year-old child study alone? How much schoolwork can a 7-year-old do without help and supervision? Until physical development is finished in late teens or early twenties, persons with ADHD or ADD must have help to study, learn new information, prepare for tests, and finish projects. They cannot function academically by themselves. It is counterproductive for parents to send an ADD or ADHD child to his or her room with orders to study for an hour.

If they are alone, few students with attention deficits manage 10 good minutes of productive study out of an hour. Like all ADHD and ADD learners, Jose must have someone nearby to answer questions, interpret instructions, and bring him back to task when his attention is distracted. This study partner or monitor must be within touching distance to keep Jose focused on his work. Even if no words are exchanged, the physical presence of someone nearby helps immensely to keep the student's attention focused on the task. If Jose is alone, almost nothing is accomplished except daydreaming, wandering off on mental rabbit trails, and losing time in his private world of make-believe.

Consistent Discipline

Children with ADHD or ADD must have discipline. This does not mean spankings or rough scoldings. Discipline for these youngsters means that supervisors maintain consistent rules and limits. A list is made of whatever the limits must be:

1. Do not go into your sister's room without permission.
2. Do not play with Mom's or Dad's things without permission.
3. Do not ride your bike down the street without permission.

Whatever parents feel are necessary rules must be explained carefully and discussed clearly until the child understands what the limits are. Then certain consequences must be invoked whenever rules are broken. If Jose continues to bother his sister's things without permission, certain discipline will follow. If he rides his bike to forbidden areas, then certain consequences will occur. It is essential that adults maintain discipline for ADHD or ADD youngsters who have a poor sense of organization and order. Each family must establish its own form of discipline. Ideally, a child should never be punished when the parent is angry. Of course, adults cannot always do what is ideal. The goal should be for adults to be ready to invoke whatever consequences were announced ahead of time. Sometimes children like Jose respond best to being isolated from the rest of the family or class group until they calm down enough to think things through. Sometimes they should be grounded from doing favorite things when rules have been broken. Sometimes they respond to having to do extra chores. Whatever the rules are, the child must be disciplined when he or she deliberately steps over the line.

Adults always must be careful to make sure that the forgetful, loose, poorly organized child actually disobeyed rather than simply forgot. Children with ADHD or ADD accidentally trespass into forbidden territory because they are too immature to read the "Keep Out" signs. Yet they must have enough consistent discipline to keep them out of danger and to help them learn that limits must be observed.

Professional Help

Parents of children with ADHD or ADD often must have help, especially when tag-along syndromes complicate life for individuals and families. Persons at severe levels of ADHD or ADD place enormous stress on marriages and all relationships within the home and at school. At times, coping with severe ADD or ADHD and shadow syndromes is more than parents can accomplish alone. It is very important for parents to investigate potential professional help before becoming involved with a counselor or specialist. The least effective procedure for finding the right help is to judge a professional person by his or her credentials, which tell nothing about that individual's effectiveness in dealing with ADHD or ADD. The best way for parents to find good professional help is to ask other parents. ADD and ADHD are common problems. In any community, other families are struggling in similar ways. The most obvious problems are posed by aggressive, hyperactive persons like James and Jo, whom we met in Chapter 4, because they attract attention wherever they are. The most difficult ones to help are passive individuals like Nate, whom we also met in Chapter 4, because they live detached from society in private worlds of silent make-believe.

It does not take long to discover other parents who have found help from specific agencies or private practitioners. Public reputation often is the most reliable way for parents to locate help. When several families have been helped to manage ADD or ADHD problems successfully, word spreads quickly within the community. Traditional psychotherapy that relies on talking through troubling events has virtually no effect in changing attention deficit disorders. Parents must remember what we have seen in earlier chapters: that ADHD and ADD are brain-based disorders, not issues of laziness, wilfullness, or stubbornness. The most effective professionals (counselors, physicians, mental health therapists) are those who regard ADHD and ADD from the point of view that the brain is behind schedule reaching expected maturity. This point of view teaches parents how to guide and discipline "late bloomers" more effectively. Parents need to look for professionals who can help them nurture the struggling child's strengths while providing special care for his or her weaknesses.

Parent Organizations

Where do parents turn to find understanding support when things at home or at school are falling apart? Fortunately, two large parent organizations offer much hope and help for ADHD and ADD. The largest support association is Children with Attention Deficit Disorders (CHADD), with more than 500 local chapters in almost every state. National headquarters for CHADD is in Plantation, Florida (Phone: 305-587-3700 or 1-800-233-4050). CHADD sponsors an on-line computer bulletin board for those who wish to chat about ADHD and ADD: alt.support.attn-deficit. CHADD also has an Internet web site that lists support chapters: www.chadd.org. CHADD maintains a national registry of effective professionals and support groups everywhere in the United States. A smaller support association is National Attention Deficit Disorder Association (ADDA), headquartered in Mentor, Ohio (Phone: 1-800-487-2282). This group also keeps a national list of helpful professionals and support groups. A support association for adults with ADHD and ADD is the Adult Attention Deficit Foundation (AADF), located in Birmingham, Michigan (Phone: 810-540-6335).

When children or adults are dyslexic, many communities have chapters of two excellent support associations for learning disabilities. The Association for Children and Adults with Learning Disabilities (LDA) is headquartered in Pittsburgh, Pennsylvania (Phone: 412-341-1515). The LDA office maintains a national registry of communities where LDA chapters are active, along with names of helpful professionals who specialize in treating dyslexia. The Orton Dyslexia Society is headquartered in Baltimore, Maryland (Phone: 410-825-2881). This support association includes physicians, neurologists, and other scientists who specialize in issues related to dyslexia. Parents can receive names of dyslexia specialists throughout the United States, as well as chapters where parents and professionals meet for mutual support. CHADD, LDA, and the Orton Dyslexia Society hold annual national and regional conferences that are rich sources of new information for parents, teachers, and other interested persons. These seminars bring professionals and laypersons together for exciting interaction that sends families home with new hope and confidence. Great strength comes through knowing that parents are not alone in facing the challenges of ADHD or ADD.

Appendix A
Jordan Executive Function Index
for Children

This appendix presents the *Jordan Executive Function Index for Children.* Parents are asked to fill out the Parent Response, background information, three pages of items titled Attention, Organization, and Inhibition, the Summary of Behaviors, and the Rating Scale. A teacher who knows the child is asked to fill out the background information, the three-page questionnaire, the Summary of Behaviors, and the Rating Scale. Scoring instructions are given at the bottom of each page of questions. When all three total scores have been tallied, each total score is transferred to the appropriate place on the Summary of Behaviors. For example, total score from the Attention page goes in the Attention section of Summary of Behaviors. Total score from the Organization page goes in the Organization section of Summary of Behaviors. Total score from the Inhibition page goes in the Inhibition section of Summary of Behaviors. Finally, the three total scores are marked on the Rating Scale graph. The Rating Scale shows at a glance the range of differences between the child's attention, organization, and inhibition behaviors.

Parent response scores should not be combined with teacher response scores. Teachers and parents often see different patterns of attention, organization, and inhibition. Many ADHD or ADD children function at a higher level at school because the day is more highly structured than homelife tends to be. On the other hand, some ADHD or ADD children function better at home when parents provide more structure and one-to-one attention than the child receives at school. A child's strengths are seen in the items marked Usually or Always. Weaknesses are noted by the items marked Sometimes or Never.

Parent Response Section

Identifying Information & Background

Name _____   Date ____ ____ ____
                                                year month day

Grade _____ Retained? ____ ____   Birthdate ____ ____ ____
                              yes   no   year month day

If retained, what year? _____   Age ____ ____ ____
                                                    year month day

Adopted? ____ ____
         yes   no

Speech Development ____ ____ ____   Tooth Development ____ ____ ____
                  early on time late   early on time late

Allergies _____ _____ _____ _____   Otitis Media ____ ____
          none   mild   moderate severe   yes   no

Mother's Pregnancy _____ _____ _____
                     normal   difficult   some problems off and on

Birth Length _____   Birth Weight _____ _____
             inches   pounds   ounces

Born Early? ____ ____   If early, how early? _____
            yes   no

Diagnosed as ADHD? ____ ____   If so, at what age? _____
                   yes   no

Diagnosed as ADD? ____ ____   If so, at what age? _____
                  yes   no

Medication for ADHD or ADD? ____ ____   At what age? _____
                            yes   no

What medication? _____   What dosage? _____

How long taken?

On the next three pages, please mark the item before each statement that is MOST like this student MOST of the time.

Behavior Rating Items

Attention

Never 0	Sometimes 1	Usually 2	Always 3	BEHAVIOR
				Keeps attention focused on the task without darting/drifting off on mental rabbit trails.
				Tunes out (ignores) what goes on nearby in order to keep on doing necessary tasks.
				Keeps on listening to oral information without darting/drifting off on mental rabbit trails.
				Listens to new information, understands it without saying, "Huh?" or "What?" or "What do you mean?"
				Finishes tasks without wandering off on rabbit trails before work is completed.
				Does necessary tasks without needing continual reminding and supervision.
				Can be part of a team or play group without wandering off on mental rabbit trails during the game.
				Follows the rules of games without having to be reminded over and over.
				Can take part in group activities without being called back to attention over and over.
				Remembers what to do after school without being reminded/supervised.
				Remembers phone messages and messages from teachers to parents.
				Cleans up own room/workspace without supervision.
				Does routine chores without being reminded and supervised.
				Pays attention to TV shows/movies without wandering off on mental rabbit trails.
				Notices how others respond to his/her behavior. Picks up cues as to how own behavior should be changed.
				Notices details (how things are alike/different) without being told to notice.
				Notices how/where objects are placed and tries not to bump/knock them over.
				Notices how work pages are organized (how lines are numbered, how details are spaced, where written responses should go).
				Follows conversations without losing it or jumping to a different subject before others finish speaking.

Add all of the scores: 0 for Never, 1 for Sometimes, 2 for Usually, 3 for Always

Attention Behavior Total Score _____

159

Organization

Never 0	Sometimes 1	Usually 2	Always 3	BEHAVIOR
				Keeps track of own things without losing them.
				Gathers up things and gets them back to school without having to be reminded/supervised.
				Keeps track of assignments/school projects without having to be reminded/supervised.
				Keeps room/desk/locker clean and orderly without supervision.
				Keeps clothes/personal belongings organized without being told/supervised.
				Keeps work space orderly while doing tasks.
				Hears or reads instructions, then does the task in an orderly way without supervision.
				Plays with things, then puts them away without being supervised.
				Works with tools/materials, then cleans up/puts them away without being supervised.
				Spaces written work well on page without having to do it again.
				Plans ahead/budgets time realistically without needing supervision.
				Has realistic sense of time without needing reminding/supervision.
				Manages own money realistically without supervision.
				Plans activities, then explains plans to others without help.
				Plans ahead for gifts at Christmas/Hanukkah/birthdays without help.
				Notices sequence patterns (how things should be arranged) without being told.
				Keeps things together in appropriate groups (books on shelves, school papers together, shoes in pairs, tools in sets, knives/forks/spoons in correct place) without being reminded/supervised.
				Keeps schoolwork organized in notebooks, folders, files, stacks without supervision.
				Plays by the rules. Wants playmates/teammates to follow the rules.
				Does tasks in order from start to finish without skipping around.

Add all of the scores: 0 for Never, 1 for Sometimes, 2 for Usually, 3 for Always

Organization Behavior Total Score _____

Inhibition

Never 0	Sometimes 1	Usually 2	Always 3	BEHAVIOR
				Thinks of consequences before doing what comes to mind.
				Puts off pleasure in order to finish necessary work.
				Follows own sense of right and wrong instead of being influenced by others.
				Puts needs and welfare of others ahead of own wishes/desires.
				Says "no" to own impulses when responsibilities must be carried out.
				Makes an effort to grow up instead of remaining immature or impulsive.
				Tries to change habits/mannerisms that bother/offend others.
				Learns from experience. Thinks about lessons learned the hard way.
				Lives by rules/spiritual principles instead of by whim/impulse.
				Accepts responsibility instead of making excuses/blaming others.
				Asks for help/advice instead of being stubborn.
				Apologizes/asks forgiveness when behavior has hurt/offended others.
				Is recognized by peers and leaders as being mature, unselfish, dependable, teachable, cooperative.
				Stops inappropriate impulses/desires before they emerge so that others will not be bothered/offended.
				Sticks to promises/agreements without being reminded or supervised.
				Goes the extra mile for others without complaining or feeling self-pity.
				Sets long-term goals and works toward them without complaining or quitting.
				Absorbs teasing/rudeness without flaring or becoming defensive.
				Is kind toward others. Avoids sarcasm/hateful remarks/putdowns.
				Resists urge to take things apart, tear structures down, rip things apart, pick at things with fingers.
				Is flexible and creative instead of being ritualized and rigid.

Add all of the scores: 0 for Never, 1 for Sometimes, 2 for Usually, 3 for Always

Inhibition Behavior Total Score _____

Summary of Behaviors
Rating Scale

0 to 11	12 to 25	26 to 40	41 to 55	56 to 60
severe	moderately severe	moderate	mild	none

Attention Behavior
Total Score (Transfer from bottom of Attention behavior rating page)

_____ 0–11 **Severe Attention Deficit**
Cannot function in mainstream classroom or group. Must have constant supervision to succeed. Cannot do sustained tasks without one-to-one monitoring. Cannot follow instructions without step-by-step supervision. Very short work time. Loses the task (off on rabbit trails) after 40 to 90 seconds.

Medication and diet control will probably be required before this student can function in academic and social situations.

_____ 12–25 **Moderately Severe Attention Deficit**
Can function part-time in nonacademic classrooms and groups (activity classes, art, music, crafts) if level of stimulus is controlled. Must have continual supervision to succeed. Can work briefly (2 to 4 minutes) in sustained tasks, but reaches rapid burnout. Can follow simple one-step instructions with continual reminding and supervision. Must have one-to-one instruction to fill in gaps in skills and new information. Must be told and reminded to notice.

Medication and diet control should be considered to help this student succeed and earn praise.

_____ 26–40 **Moderate Attention Deficit**
Can function in mainstream classroom and groups with frequent reminding/supervision. Easily distracted. Wanders off on rabbit trails and must be called back to the task. Must have frequent one-to-one help to fill gaps in skills and new information. Must be guided in following through on instructions. Notices now and then, but needs a lot of reminding to notice and pay attention.

_____ 41–55 **Mild Attention Deficit**
Can function effectively in most situations. Occasionally becomes overly distracted by nearby events. Needs frequent monitoring to finish tasks and stay on schedules. Can be taught to monitor self and bring attention back to task.

_____ 56–60 **No Attention Deficit**

Organization Behavior
Total Score (Transfer from bottom of Organization behavior rating page)

_____ 0–11 **Severe Organizational Deficit**

Cannot manage own things without help and supervision. Cannot remember where things are, what things are needed for certain tasks, where things were put when last used. Cannot gather up own things without supervision. Cannot remember what to take home or what to bring back to school. Loses things on school bus, at home, in the classroom, in lunchroom, on playground. Loses clothes, books, bookbag, shoes, jackets, wraps. Cannot recall where they were left. Leaves tools and playthings in yard overnight. Cannot clean up own room without direct supervision.

Must be guided/supervised/monitored in order to finish any task. Often called "lazy" and "careless." In continual conflict with adults who do not understand organizational deficits.

_____ 12–25 **Moderately Severe Organizational Deficit**

Must have supervision and help to organize. Can do better if steps are written on notes. Must be reminded to go back to notes/outlines to make sure everything has been finished. Cannot clean up room or do chores without supervision. Cannot manage school things without being reminded. Can learn to follow checklists and outlines if adults maintain supervision and continue to remind.

Must not be expected to organize or stay on schedule without help.

_____ 26–40 **Moderate Organizational Deficit**

Ability to organize is spotty and unpredictable. Needs a lot of reminding and supervision. Responds well to written reminders (notes, outlines). Must be reminded to refer back to notes and outlines to make sure each step has been followed. Tends to be absentminded. Tends to mislay things. Keeps things in loose piles or stacks that often become mixed together. Must have help cleaning out desk/locker/work space. Has cycles of better organization/poorer organization.

_____ 41–55 **Mild Organizational Deficit**

Can develop effective strategies for staying organized and on schedule. Responds well to keeping calendars, outlines of tasks, schedules on paper. Needs to be reminded frequently. Tends to wander off on rabbit trails and forget. Appears to be absentminded and careless.

_____ 56–60 **No Organizational Deficit**

Inhibition Behavior
Total Score (Transfer from bottom of Inhibition behavior rating page)

_____ 0–11 **Severe Problems with Self-Control**
Cannot function successfully in relationships. Severely self-focused and self-centered. Does not notice the needs or wishes of others. Places self first. Thinks mostly of satisfying own desires. All of personal energy goes toward fulfilling own self-needs. Does not extend affection without demanding something in return. Cannot respond normally to the give-and-take of friendships/family relationships/social relationships. Is irritable, quick tempered, judgmental when pressed to pay attention to others. Attitude is demanding, short tempered, critical of others. Refuses to share. Demands to be first. Wants biggest piece or share for self. Makes insatiable demands on others. Burns others out. Is often rejected by others. Moves from one friend to the next after short term of friendship. Cannot share space peacefully. Usually creates conflict with others. Cannot fit into groups. Tends to be unhappy much of the time. Complains, gripes, finds faults when others see no problem.

This person creates continual conflicts for leaders. Must be handled firmly. Cannot respond to normal suggestions that depend upon noticing others. Continually argues, challenges authority, blames others, indulges in self-pity. Uses others without showing regret or concern.

_____ 12–26 **Moderately Severe Problems with Self-Control**
Has trouble functioning in relationships, but can do so if others are patient and forgiving enough. Must be closely supervised in groups. Triggers frequent arguments/conflicts with peers. Is disliked by certain leaders. Is often rejected by peers and/or adults. Can respond to coaching in how to treat others more kindly, but such lessons do not last. Does not have a natural bent for extending kindness and attention to others.

Leaders must intervene frequently to stop conflict or restore peace. This student requires extra effort from leaders to keep things going smoothly. This person triggers a lot of dislike from peers. A lot of his/her time is spent planning revenge and trying to get even.

_____ 27–41 **Moderate Problems with Self-Control**
Responds to reminding about manners and appropriate behavior. Requires frequent one-to-one guidance in how to behave more appropriately and less selfishly. Can respond well to reminder cues. Responds to guidance/counseling strategies that teach this person how to notice others. Triggers some conflict within group. Has good days/bad days in relationships. Argues a lot over trivial issues. Tends to split hairs over things others take in stride. Is seldom a fully cooperative member of group. Seeks subtle ways to get even with others.

_____ 42–55 **Mild Problems with Self-Control**
Needs frequent reminding about how to interact with others. Responds to guidance about noticing needs/wishes of others. Can learn to put own needs last or postpone wishes until later. Has good day/bad day cycles in relationships. Needs a lot of forgiveness and forgiving.

_____ 56–61 **No Problems with Self-Control**

164

Jordan Executive Function Index for Children
Parent Response Section

Rating Scale

Mark each of the three total scores on this scale to see the difference between the child's attention, organization, and inhibition behaviors.

Severe			Moderately Severe			Moderate
10	9	8	7	6	5	
0 1 2 3	4 5 6 7	8 9 10 11	12 13 14 15 16 17 18	19 20 21 22 23 24 25	26 27 28 29 30 31 32	

Moderate		Mild		None
4	3	2	1	0
33 34 35 36 37 38 39 40	41 42 43 44 45	46 47 48 49 50	51 52 53 54 55	56 57 58 59 60

Teacher Response Section

Identifying Information & Background

Name _____

Grade _____ Retained? _____ _____
                                  yes   no

If retained, what year? _____

Date _____ _____ _____
     year month day

Birthdate _____ _____ _____
          year month day

Age _____ _____ _____
    year month day

Classroom Performance

High Achiever	Average Achiever	Low Achiever
No Struggle	Moderate Struggle	Severe Struggle
High Motivation (always motivated)	Average Motivation (comes and goes)	Low Motivation (seldom motivated)
Fits in well. Likes by peers. Little or no peer conflict.	Some conflict. Not always liked by peers. Usually fits in with adult guidance.	Continual conflict. Disliked by peers. Can't fit in even with adult guidance.
Usually cheerful and happy.	Often moody, touch, grouchy, irritable.	Seldom cheerful. Usually unhappy. Overly sensitive and touchy.
Outgoing. Active. Eager to cooperate. Ready to lead.	Quiet, passive. Willing to follow and cooperate.	Withdrawn. Does not want to cooperate or participate. Unconnected from group.

On the next three pages, please mark the item before each statement that is MOST like this student MOST of the time.

Behavior Rating Items

Attention

Never 0	Sometimes 1	Usually 2	Always 3	BEHAVIOR
				Keeps attention focused on the task without darting/drifting off on mental rabbit trails.
				Tunes out (ignores) what goes on nearby in order to keep on doing necessary tasks.
				Keeps on listening to oral information without darting/drifting off on mental rabbit trails.
				Listens to new information, understands it without saying, "Huh?" or "What?" or "What do you mean?"
				Finishes tasks without wandering off on rabbit trails before work is completed.
				Does necessary tasks without needing continual reminding and supervision.
				Can be part of a team or play group without wandering off on mental rabbit trails during the game.
				Follows the rules of games without having to be reminded over and over.
				Can take part in group activities without being called back to attention over and over.
				Remembers what to do after school without being reminded/supervised.
				Remembers phone messages and messages from teachers to parents.
				Cleans up own room/workspace without supervision.
				Does routine chores without being reminded and supervised.
				Pays attention to TV shows/movies without wandering off on mental rabbit trails.
				Notices how others respond to his/her behavior. Picks up cues as to how own behavior should be changed.
				Notices details (how things are alike/different) without being told to notice.
				Notices how/where objects are placed and tries not to bump/knock them over.
				Notices how work pages are organized (how lines are numbered, how details are spaced, where written responses should go).
				Follows conversations without losing it or jumping to a different subject before others finish speaking.

Add all of the scores: 0 for Never, 1 for Sometimes, 2 for Usually, 3 for Always

Attention Behavior Total Score _____

Organization

Never 0	Sometimes 1	Usually 2	Always 3	BEHAVIOR
				Keeps track of own things without losing them.
				Gathers up things and gets them back to school without having to be reminded/ supervised.
				Keeps track of assignments/school projects without having to be reminded/supervised.
				Keeps room/desk/locker clean and orderly without supervision.
				Keeps clothes/personal belongings organized without being told/supervised.
				Keeps work space orderly while doing tasks.
				Hears or reads instructions, then does the task in an orderly way without supervision.
				Plays with things, then puts them away without being supervised.
				Works with tools/materials, then cleans up/puts them away without being supervised.
				Spaces written work well on page without having to do it again.
				Plans ahead/budgets time realistically without needing supervision.
				Has realistic sense of time without needing reminding/supervision.
				Manages own money realistically without supervision.
				Plans activities, then explains plans to others without help.
				Plans ahead for gifts at Christmas/Hanukkah/ birthdays without help.
				Notices sequence patterns (how things should be arranged) without being told.
				Keeps things together in appropriate groups (books on shelves, school papers together, shoes in pairs, tools in sets, knives/forks/spoons in correct place) without being reminded/supervised.
				Keeps schoolwork organized in notebooks, folders, files, stacks without supervision.
				Plays by the rules. Wants playmates/teammates to follow the rules.
				Does tasks in order from start to finish without skipping around.

Add all of the scores: 0 for Never, 1 for Sometimes, 2 for Usually, 3 for Always

Organization Behavior Total Score _____

Inhibition

Never 0	Sometimes 1	Usually 2	Always 3	BEHAVIOR
				Thinks of consequences before doing what comes to mind.
				Puts off pleasure in order to finish necessary work.
				Follows own sense of right and wrong instead of being influenced by others.
				Puts needs and welfare of others ahead of own wishes/desires.
				Says "no" to own impulses when responsibilities must be carried out.
				Makes an effort to grow up instead of remaining immature or impulsive.
				Tries to change habits/mannerisms that bother/offend others.
				Learns from experience. Thinks about lessons learned the hard way.
				Lives by rules/spiritual principles instead of by whim/impulse.
				Accepts responsibility instead of making excuses/blaming others.
				Asks for help/advice instead of being stubborn.
				Apologizes/asks forgiveness when behavior has hurt/offended others.
				Is recognized by peers and leaders as being mature, unselfish, dependable, teachable, cooperative.
				Stops inappropriate impulses/desires before they emerge so that others will not be bothered/offended.
				Sticks to promises/agreements without being reminded or supervised.
				Goes the extra mile for others without complaining or feeling self-pity.
				Sets long-term goals and works toward them without complaining or quitting.
				Absorbs teasing/rudeness without flaring or becoming defensive.
				Is kind toward others. Avoids sarcasm/hateful remarks/putdowns.
				Resists urge to take things apart, tear structures down, rip things apart, pick at things with fingers.
				Is flexible and creative instead of being ritualized and rigid.

Add all of the scores: 0 for Never, 1 for Sometimes, 2 for Usually, 3 for Always

Inhibition Behavior Total Score _____

Summary of Behaviors

Rating Scale

0 to 11	12 to 25	26 to 40	41 to 55	56 to 60
severe	moderately severe	moderate	mild	none

Attention Behavior
Total Score (Transfer from bottom of Attention behavior rating page)

_____ 0–11 **Severe Attention Deficit**
Cannot function in mainstream classroom or group. Must have constant supervision to succeed. Cannot do sustained tasks without one-to-one monitoring. Cannot follow instructions without step-by-step supervision. Very short work time. Loses the task (off on rabbit trails) after 40 to 90 seconds.

Medication and diet control will probably be required before this student can function in academic and social situations.

_____ 12–25 **Moderately Severe Attention Deficit**
Can function part-time in nonacademic classrooms and groups (activity classes, art, music, crafts) if level of stimulus is controlled. Must have continual supervision to succeed. Can work briefly (2 to 4 minutes) in sustained tasks, but reaches rapid burnout. Can follow simple one-step instructions with continual reminding and supervision. Must have one-to-one instruction to fill in gaps in skills and new information. Must be told and reminded to notice.

Medication and diet control should be considered to help this student succeed and earn praise.

_____ 26–40 **Moderate Attention Deficit**
Can function in mainstream classroom and groups with frequent reminding/supervision. Easily distracted. Wanders off on rabbit trails and must be called back to the task. Must have frequent one-to-one help to fill gaps in skills and new information. Must be guided in following through on instructions. Notices now and then, but needs a lot of reminding to notice and pay attention.

_____ 41–55 **Mild Attention Deficit**
Can function effectively in most situations. Occasionally becomes overly distracted by nearby events. Needs frequent monitoring to finish tasks and stay on schedules. Can be taught to monitor self and bring attention back to task.

_____ 56–60 **No Attention Deficit**

Jordan Executive Function Index for Children
Teacher Response Section, Summary of Behaviors

Organization Behavior
Total Score (Transfer from bottom of Organization behavior rating page)

_____ 0–11 **Severe Organizational Deficit**
Cannot manage own things without help and supervision. Cannot remember where things are, what things are needed for certain tasks, where things were put when last used. Cannot gather up own things without supervision. Cannot remember what to take home or what to bring back to school. Loses things on school bus, at home, in the classroom, in lunchroom, on playground. Loses clothes, books, bookbag, shoes, jackets, wraps. Cannot recall where they were left. Leaves tools and playthings in yard overnight. Cannot clean up own room without direct supervision.

Must be guided/supervised/monitored in order to finish any task. Often called "lazy" and "careless." In continual conflict with adults who do not understand organizational deficits.

_____ 12–25 **Moderately Severe Organizational Deficit**
Must have supervision and help to organize. Can do better if steps are written on notes. Must be reminded to go back to notes/outlines to make sure everything has been finished. Cannot clean up room or do chores without supervision. Cannot manage school things without being reminded. Can learn to follow checklists and outlines if adults maintain supervision and continue to remind.

Must not be expected to organize or stay on schedule without help.

_____ 26–40 **Moderate Organizational Deficit**
Ability to organize is spotty and unpredictable. Needs a lot of reminding and supervision. Responds well to written reminders (notes, outlines). Must be reminded to refer back to notes and outlines to make sure each step has been followed. Tends to be absentminded. Tends to mislay things. Keeps things in loose piles or stacks that often become mixed together. Must have help cleaning out desk/locker/work space. Has cycles of better organization/poorer organization.

_____ 41–55 **Mild Organizational Deficit**
Can develop effective strategies for staying organized and on schedule. Responds well to keeping calendars, outlines of tasks, schedules on paper. Needs to be reminded frequently. Tends to wander off on rabbit trails and forget. Appears to be absentminded and careless.

_____ 56–60 **No Organizational Deficit**

Inhibition Behavior
Total Score (Transfer from bottom of Inhibition behavior rating page)

_____ 0–11 **Severe Problems with Self-Control**
Cannot function successfully in relationships. Severely self-focused and self-centered. Does not notice the needs or wishes of others. Places self first. Things mostly of satisfying own desires. All of personal energy goes toward fulfilling own self-needs. Does not extend affection without demanding something in return. Cannot respond normally to the give-and-take of friendships/family relationships/social relationships. Is irritable, quick tempered, judgmental when pressed to pay attention to others. Attitude is demanding, short tempered, critical of others. Refuses to share. Demands to be first. Wants biggest piece or share for self. Makes insatiable demands on others. Burns others out. Is often rejected by others. Moves from one friend to the next after short term of friendship. Cannot share space peacefully. Usually creates conflict with others. Cannot fit into groups. Tends to be unhappy much of the time. Complains, gripes, finds faults when others see no problem.

This person creates continual conflicts for leaders. Must be handled firmly. Cannot respond to normal suggestions that depend upon noticing others. Continually argues, challenges authority, blames others, indulges in self-pity. Uses others without showing regret or concern.

_____ 12–26 **Moderately Severe Problems with Self-Control**
Has trouble functioning in relationships, but can do so if others are patient and forgiving enough. Must be closely supervised in groups. Triggers frequent arguments/conflicts with peers. Is disliked by certain leaders. Is often rejected by peers and/or adults. Can respond to coaching in how to treat others more kindly, but such lessons do not last. Does not have a natural bent for extending kindness and attention to others.

Leaders must intervene frequently to stop conflict or restore peace. This student requires extra effort from leaders to keep things going smoothly. This person triggers a lot of dislike from peers. A lot of his/her time is spent planning revenge and trying to get even.

_____ 27–41 **Moderate Problems with Self-Control**
Responds to reminding about manners and appropriate behavior. Requires frequent one-to-one guidance in how to behave more appropriately and less selfishly. Can respond well to reminder cues. Responds to guidance/counseling strategies that teach this person how to notice others. Triggers some conflict within group. Has good days/bad days in relationships. Argues a lot over trivial issues. Tends to split hairs over things others take in stride. Is seldom a fully cooperative member of group. Seeks subtle ways to get even with others.

_____ 42–55 **Mild Problems with Self-Control**
Needs frequent reminding about how to interact with others. Responds to guidance about noticing needs/wishes of others. Can learn to put own needs last or postpone wishes until later. Has good day/bad day cycles in relationships. Needs a lot of forgiveness and forgiving.

_____ 56–61 **No Problems with Self-Control**

172

Jordan Executive Function Index for Children
Teacher Response Section

Rating Scale

Mark each of the three total scores on this scale to see the difference between the child's attention, organization, and inhibition behaviors.

Severe			Moderately Severe			Moderate
10	9	8	7	6	5
0 1 2 3	4 5 6 7	8 9 10 11	12 13 14 15 16 17 18	19 20 21 22 23 24 25	26 27 28 29 30 31 32

Moderate		Mild		None
4	3	2	1	0
33 34 35 36 37 38 39 40	41 42 43 44 45	46 47 48 49 50	51 52 53 54 55	56 57 58 59 60

Appendix B
Jordan Executive Function Index
for Adults

This appendix presents the *Jordan Executive Function Index for Adults*. This can be a self-administered questionnaire for adults who read well, if the person is mature enough to give honest responses to each item. For those who struggle to read or who are less mature, the questionnaire can be an oral activity with the instructor, spouse, or some other adult reading each item aloud, and the client helping to choose which column to mark. Scoring is done exactly as described above for the children's version. When possible, it is helpful for two adults to respond to the *Jordan Executive Function Index for Adults*. A spouse, companion, or parent fills out the background information, three pages of questions, Summary of Behaviors, and Rating Scale. The same procedure is followed by a counselor or instructor who knows the adult well.

Self-Response Section

Identifying Information and Background

Name_____   Date _____ _____ _____
                                              year month day

Grade _____ Retained? _____ _____   Birthdate _____ _____ _____
                            yes   no   year month day

If retained, what year? _____   Age _____ _____ _____
                                                   year month day

Adopted? _____ _____ Diagnosed as dyslexic? _____ _____   What age? _____
         yes   no   yes   no

Speech Development _____ _____ _____ Tooth Development _____ _____ _____
                   early on time late   early on time late

Allergies _____ _____ _____ _____ Otitis Media _____ _____
          none   mild   moderate severe   yes   no

Mother's Pregnancy _____ _____ _____
                         normal   difficult   some problems off and on

Birth Length _____ Birth Weight _____ _____
             inches   pounds   ounces

Born Early? _____ _____ If early, how early? _____
            yes   no

Born Late? _____ _____ If late, how late? _____
           yes   no

Diagnosed as ADHD? _____ _____ What age? ____ Medication? _____
                   yes   no

Diagnosed as ADD? _____ _____ What age? ____ Medication? _____
                  yes   no

**On the next three pages, please mark the item before each
statement that is MOST like you MOST of the time.**

Behavior Rating Items

Attention

Never 0	Sometimes 1	Usually 2	Always 3	BEHAVIOR
				Keeps attention focused on the task without darting/drifting off on mental rabbit trails.
				Tunes out (ignores) what goes on nearby in order to keep on doing necessary tasks.
				Keeps on listening to oral information without darting/drifting off on mental rabbit trails.
				Listens to new information, understands it without saying, "Huh?" or "What?" or "What do you mean?"
				Finishes tasks without wandering off on rabbit trails before work is completed.
				Does necessary tasks without needing continual reminding and supervision.
				Can be part of a team or group without wandering off on mental rabbit trails during group activity.
				Follows the rules of games without having to be reminded.
				Can take part in group activities without being called back to attention.
				Remembers what to do after work without being reminded/supervised.
				Remembers phone messages.
				Cleans up own room/workspace without being reminded.
				Does routine chores without being reminded.
				Pays attention to TV shows/movies without wandering off on mental rabbit trails.
				Notices how others respond to his/her behavior. Picks up cues as to how own behavior should be changed.
				Notices details (how things are alike/different) without being told to notice.
				Notices how/where objects are placed and tries not to bump/knock them over.
				Notices how work pages are organized (how lines are numbered, how details are spaced, where written responses should go).
				Follows conversations without losing it or jumping to a different subject before others finish speaking.

Add all of the scores: 0 for Never, 1 for Sometimes, 2 for Usually, 3 for Always

Attention Behavior Total Score _____

Organization

Never 0	Sometimes 1	Usually 2	Always 3	BEHAVIOR
				Keeps track of own things without losing them.
				Gathers up things and gets them back to correct places without having to be reminded.
				Keeps track of assignments/work projects without having to be reminded/supervised.
				Keeps room/desk clean and orderly without being reminded.
				Keeps clothes/personal belongings organized without being reminded.
				Keeps work space orderly while doing tasks.
				Hears or reads instructions, then does the task in an orderly way without supervision.
				Gets things out, then puts them away without being supervised.
				Works with tools/materials, then cleans up/puts them away without being supervised.
				Spaces written work well on page without crowding or making messy.
				Plans ahead/budgets time realistically without needing reminders.
				Has realistic sense of time without needing reminding/assistance.
				Manages own money realistically without help.
				Plans activities, then explains plans to others without help.
				Plans ahead for gifts at Christmas/Hanukkah/birthdays without help.
				Notices sequence patterns (how things should be arranged) without being told.
				Keeps things together in appropriate groups (books on shelves, papers together, shoes in pairs, tools in sets, knives/forks/spoons in correct place) without being reminded/supervised.
				Keeps papers organized in notebooks, folders, files, stacks without supervision.
				Plays by the rules. Wants teammates to follow the rules.
				Does tasks in order from start to finish without skipping around.

Add all of the scores: 0 for Never, 1 for Sometimes, 2 for Usually, 3 for Always

Organization Behavior Total Score _____

Inhibition

Never 0	Sometimes 1	Usually 2	Always 3	BEHAVIOR
				Thinks of consequences before doing what comes to mind.
				Puts off pleasure in order to finish necessary work.
				Follows own sense of right and wrong instead of being influenced by others.
				Puts needs and welfare of others ahead of own wishes/desires.
				Says "no" to own impulses when responsibilities must be carried out.
				Makes an effort to grow up instead of remaining immature or impulsive.
				Tries to change habits/mannerisms that bother/offend others.
				Learns from experience. Thinks about lessons learned the hard way.
				Lives by rules/spiritual principles instead of by whim/impulse.
				Accepts responsibility instead of making excuses/blaming others.
				Asks for help/advice instead of being stubborn.
				Apologizes/asks forgiveness when behavior has hurt/offended others.
				Is recognized by peers and leaders as being mature, unselfish, dependable, teachable, cooperative.
				Stops inappropriate impulses/desires before they emerge so that others will not be bothered/offended.
				Sticks to promises/agreements without being reminded or supervised.
				Goes the extra mile for others without complaining or feeling self-pity.
				Sets long-term goals and works toward them without complaining or quitting.
				Absorbs teasing/rudeness without flaring or becoming defensive.
				Is kind toward others. Avoids sarcasm/hateful remarks/putdowns.
				Resists urge to take things apart, pick at things with fingers.
				Is flexible and creative instead of being ritualized and rigid.

Add all of the scores: 0 for Never, 1 for Sometimes, 2 for Usually, 3 for Always

Inhibition Behavior Total Score _____

Summary of Behaviors
Rating Scale

0 to 11	12 to 25	26 to 40	41 to 55	56 to 60
severe	moderately severe	moderate	mild	none

Attention Behavior
Total Score (Transfer from bottom of Attention behavior rating page)

_____ 0–11 **Severe Attention Deficit**
Cannot function in mainstream classroom or group. Must have constant supervision to succeed. Cannot do sustained tasks without one-to-one monitoring. Cannot follow instructions without step-by-step supervision. Very short work time. Loses the task (off on rabbit trails) after 40 to 90 seconds.

Medication and diet control required before this person can function in academic, social, and work situations.

_____ 12–25 **Moderately Severe Attention Deficit**
Can function part-time in nonacademic groups if level of stimulus is controlled. Must have continual supervision to succeed. Can work briefly (2 to 4 minutes) in sustained tasks, but reaches rapid burnout. Can follow simple one-step instructions with continual reminding and supervision. Must have one-to-one instruction to fill in gaps in skills and new information. Must be told and reminded to notice.

Medication and diet control should be considered to help this person succeed and earn praise.

_____ 26–40 **Moderate Attention Deficit**
Can function in mainstream classroom and groups with frequent reminding/supervision. Easily distracted. Wanders off on rabbit trails and must be called back to the task. Must have frequent one-to-one help to fill gaps in skills and new information. Must be guided in following through on instructions. Notices now and then, but needs a lot of reminding to notice and pay attention.

_____ 41–55 **Mild Attention Deficit**
Can function effectively in most situations. Occasionally becomes overly distracted by nearby events. Needs frequent monitoring to finish tasks and stay on schedules. Can be taught to monitor self and bring own attention back to task.

_____ 56–60 **No Attention Deficit**

Organization Behavior
Total Score (Transfer from bottom of Organization behavior rating page)

_____ 0–11   **Severe Organizational Deficit**
Cannot manage own things without help and supervision. Cannot remember where things are, what things are needed for certain tasks, where things were put when last used. Cannot gather up own things without supervision. Cannot remember what to take home or what to bring back to work. Loses things on bus, at home, at work. Loses clothes, books, wallet, purse, keys, important papers. Cannot recall where they were left. Leaves tools and work things in yard overnight. Cannot clean up own room without direct supervision.

Must be guided/supervised/monitored in order to finish any task. Often called "lazy" and "careless." In continual conflict with others who do not understand organizational deficits.

_____ 12–25   **Moderately Severe Organizational Deficit**
Must have supervision and help to organize. Can do better if steps are written on notes. Must be reminded to go back to notes/outlines to make sure everything has been finished. Cannot clean up own space or do chores without supervision. Cannot manage own things without being reminded. Can learn to follow checklists and outlines if others continue to remind.

Must not be expected to organize or stay on schedule without help.

_____ 26–40   **Moderate Organizational Deficit**
Ability to organize is spotty and unpredictable. Needs a lot of reminding. Responds well to written reminders (notes, outlines). Must be reminded to refer back to notes and outlines to make sure each step has been fol-lowed. Tends to be absentminded. Tends to mislay things. Keeps things in loose piles or stacks that often become mixed together. Must have help cleaning out desk/locker/work space. Has cycles of better organization/poorer organization.

_____ 41–55   **Mild Organizational Deficit**
Can develop effective strategies for staying organized and on schedule. Responds well to keeping calendars, outlines of tasks, schedules on paper. Needs to be reminded frequently. Tends to wander off on rabbit trails and forget. Appears to be absentminded and careless.

_____ 56–60   **No Organizational Deficit**

Inhibition Behavior
Total Score (Transfer from bottom of Inhibition behavior rating page)

_____ 0–11   **Severe Problems with Self-Control**
Cannot function successfully in relationships. Severely self-focused and self-centered. Does not notice the needs or wishes of others. Places self first. Thinks mostly of satisfying own desires. All of personal energy goes toward fulfilling own self-needs. Does not extend affection without demanding something in return. Cannot respond normally to the give-and-take of friendships/family relationships/social relationships. Is irritable, quick tempered, judgmental when pressed to pay attention to others. Attitude is demanding, short tempered, critical of others. Refuses to share. Demands to be first. Wants biggest piece or share for self. Makes insatiable demands on others. Burns others out. Is often rejected by others. Moves from one friend to the next after short term of friendship. Cannot share space peacefully. Usually creates conflict with others. Cannot fit into groups. Tends to be unhappy much of the time. Complains, gripes, finds faults when others see no problem.

This person creates continual conflicts for leaders. Must be handled firmly. Cannot respond to normal suggestions that depend upon noticing others. Continually argues, challenges authority, blames others, indulges in self-pity. Uses others without showing regret or concern.

_____ 12–26   **Moderately Severe Problems with Self-Control**
Has trouble functioning in relationships, but can do so if others are patient and forgiving enough. Must be closely supervised in groups. Triggers frequent arguments/conflicts with peers. Is disliked by certain leaders. Is often rejected by peers and leaders. Can respond to coaching in how to treat others more kindly, but such lessons do not last. Does not have a natural bent for extending kindness and attention to others.

Leaders must intervene frequently to stop conflict or restore peace. This person requires extra effort from leaders to keep things going smoothly. Triggers a lot of dislike from peers. A lot of his/her time is spent planning revenge and trying to get even.

_____ 27–41   **Moderate Problems with Self-Control**
Responds to reminding about manners and appropriate behavior. Requires frequent one-to-one guidance in how to behave more appropriately and less selfishly. Can respond well to reminder cues. Responds to guidance/counseling strategies that teach this person how to notice others. Triggers some conflict within group. Has good days/bad days in relationships. Argues a lot over trivial issues. Tends to split hairs over things others take in stride. Is seldom a fully cooperative member of group. Seeks subtle ways to get even with others.

_____ 42–55   **Mild Problems with Self-Control**
Needs frequent reminding about how to interact with others. Responds to guidance about noticing needs/wishes of others. Can learn to put own needs last or postpone wishes until later. Has good day/bad day cycles in relationships. Needs a lot of forgiveness and forgiving.

_____ 56–61   **No Problems with Self-Control**

182

Jordan Executive Function Index for Adults
Self-Response Section

Rating Scale

Mark each of the three total scores on this scale to see the difference between your attention, organization, and inhibition behaviors.

Severe			Moderately Severe		Moderate
10	9	8	7	6	5
0 1 2 3	4 5 6 7	8 9 10 11	12 13 14 15 16 17 18	19 20 21 22 23 24 25	26 27 28 29 30 31 32

Moderate	Mild		None	
4	3	2	1	0
33 34 35 36 37 38 39 40	41 42 43 44 45	46 47 48 49 50	51 52 53 54 55	56 57 58 59 60

Counselor or Instructor Response Section

Identifying Information and Background

Name _____   Date _____ _____ _____
                                                  year month day

Grade _____ Retained? _____ _____   Birthdate _____ _____ _____
                            yes   no   year month day

If retained, what year? _____   Age _____ _____ _____
                                                  year month day

Classroom Performance

_____	_____	_____
High Achiever	Average Achiever	Low Achiever

_____	_____	_____
No Struggle	Moderate Struggle	Severe Struggle

_____	_____	_____
High Motivation (always motivated)	Average Motivation (good days/bad days)	Low Motivation (seldom motivated)

_____	_____	_____
Fits in well. Liked by peers. Little or no peer conflict.	Some conflict. Not always liked by peers.	Continual conflict. Disliked by peers.

_____	_____	_____
Usually cheerful and happy.	Often moody, touchy, grouchy, irritable.	Seldom cheerful. Usually unhappy. Overly sensitive and touchy.

_____	_____	_____
Outgoing. Active. Eager to cooperate. Ready to lead.	Quiet, passive. Willing to follow and cooperate.	Withdrawn. Did not want to cooperate or participate. Unconnected from group.

On the next three pages, please mark the item before each statement that is MOST like this person MOST of the time.

Behavior Rating Items

Attention

Never 0	Sometimes 1	Usually 2	Always 3	BEHAVIOR
				Keeps attention focused on the task without darting/drifting off on mental rabbit trails.
				Tunes out (ignores) what goes on nearby in order to keep on doing necessary tasks.
				Keeps on listening to oral information without darting/drifting off on mental rabbit trails.
				Listens to new information, understands it without saying, "Huh?" or "What?" or "What do you mean?"
				Finishes tasks without wandering off on rabbit trails before work is completed.
				Does necessary tasks without needing continual reminding and supervision.
				Can be part of a team or group without wandering off on mental rabbit trails during group activity.
				Follows the rules of games without having to be reminded.
				Can take part in group activities without being called back to attention.
				Remembers what to do after work without being reminded/supervised.
				Remembers phone messages.
				Cleans up own room/workspace without being reminded.
				Does routine chores without being reminded.
				Pays attention to TV shows/movies without wandering off on mental rabbit trails.
				Notices how others respond to his/her behavior. Picks up cues as to how own behavior should be changed.
				Notices details (how things are alike/different) without being told to notice.
				Notices how/where objects are placed and tries not to bump/knock them over.
				Notices how work pages are organized (how lines are numbered, how details are spaced, where written responses should go).
				Follows conversations without losing it or jumping to a different subject before others finish speaking.

Add all of the scores: 0 for Never, 1 for Sometimes, 2 for Usually, 3 for Always

Attention Behavior Total Score _____

Organization

Never 0	Sometimes 1	Usually 2	Always 3	BEHAVIOR
				Keeps track of own things without losing them.
				Gathers up things and gets them back to correct places without having to be reminded.
				Keeps track of assignments/work projects without having to be reminded/supervised.
				Keeps room/desk clean and orderly without being reminded.
				Keeps clothes/personal belongings organized without being reminded.
				Keeps work space orderly while doing tasks.
				Hears or reads instructions, then does the task in an orderly way without supervision.
				Gets things out, then puts them away without being supervised.
				Works with tools/materials, then cleans up/puts them away without being supervised.
				Spaces written work well on page without crowding or making messy.
				Plans ahead/budgets time realistically without needing reminders.
				Has realistic sense of time without needing reminding/assistance.
				Manages own money realistically without help.
				Plans activities, then explains plans to others without help.
				Plans ahead for gifts at Christmas/Hanukkah/ birthdays without help.
				Notices sequence patterns (how things should be arranged) without being told.
				Keeps things together in appropriate groups (books on shelves, papers together, shoes in pairs, tools in sets, knives/forks/spoons in correct place) without being reminded/supervised.
				Keeps papers organized in notebooks, folders, files, stacks without supervision.
				Plays by the rules. Wants teammates to follow the rules.
				Does tasks in order from start to finish without skipping around.

Add all of the scores: 0 for Never, 1 for Sometimes, 2 for Usually, 3 for Always

Organization Behavior Total Score _____

Inhibition

Never 0	Sometimes 1	Usually 2	Always 3	BEHAVIOR
				Thinks of consequences before doing what comes to mind.
				Puts off pleasure in order to finish necessary work.
				Follows own sense of right and wrong instead of being influenced by others.
				Puts needs and welfare of others ahead of own wishes/desires.
				Says "no" to own impulses when responsibilities must be carried out.
				Makes an effort to grow up instead of remaining immature or impulsive.
				Tries to change habits/mannerisms that bother/offend others.
				Learns from experience. Thinks about lessons learned the hard way.
				Lives by rules/spiritual principles instead of by whim/impulse.
				Accepts responsibility instead of making excuses/blaming others.
				Asks for help/advice instead of being stubborn.
				Apologizes/asks forgiveness when behavior has hurt/offended others.
				Is recognized by peers and leaders as being mature, unselfish, dependable, teachable, cooperative.
				Stops inappropriate impulses/desires before they emerge so that others will not be bothered/offended.
				Sticks to promises/agreements without being reminded or supervised.
				Goes the extra mile for others without complaining or feeling self-pity.
				Sets long-term goals and works toward them without complaining or quitting.
				Absorbs teasing/rudeness without flaring or becoming defensive.
				Is kind toward others. Avoids sarcasm/hateful remarks/putdowns.
				Resists urge to take things apart, pick at things with fingers.
				Is flexible and creative instead of being ritualized and rigid.

Add all of the scores: 0 for Never, 1 for Sometimes, 2 for Usually, 3 for Always

Inhibition Behavior Total Score _____

Summary of Behaviors
Rating Scale

0 to 11	12 to 25	26 to 40	41 to 55	56 to 60
severe	moderately severe	moderate	mild	none

Attention Behavior
Total Score (Transfer from bottom of Attention behavior rating page)

_____ 0–11 **Severe Attention Deficit**
Cannot function in group. Must have constant supervision to succeed. Cannot do sustained tasks without one-to-one monitoring. Cannot follow instructions without step-by-step supervision. Very short work time. Loses the task (off on rabbit trails) after 40 to 90 seconds.

Medication and diet control required before this person can function in academic, social, or work situations.

_____ 12–25 **Moderately Severe Attention Deficit**
Can function part-time in nonacademic groups if level of stimulus is controlled. Must have continual supervision to succeed. Can work briefly (2 to 4 minutes) in sustained tasks, but reaches rapid burnout. Can follow simple one-step instructions with continual reminding and supervision. Must have one-to-one instruction to fill in gaps in skills and new information. Must be told and reminded to notice.

Medication and diet control should be considered to help this person succeed and earn praise.

_____ 26–40 **Moderate Attention Deficit**
Can function in mainstream classroom and groups with frequent reminding/supervision. Easily distracted. Wanders off on rabbit trails and must be called back to the task. Must have frequent one-to-one help to fill gaps in skills and new information. Must be guided in following through on instructions. Notices now and then, but needs a lot of reminding to notice and pay attention.

_____ 41–55 **Mild Attention Deficit**
Can function effectively in most situations. Occasionally becomes overly distracted by nearby events. Needs frequent monitoring to finish tasks and stay on schedules. Can be taught to monitor self and bring attention back to task.

_____ 56–60 **No Attention Deficit**

Organization Behavior
Total Score (Transfer from bottom of Organization behavior rating page)

_____ 0–11 **Severe Organizational Deficit**
Cannot manage own things without help and supervision. Cannot remember where things are, what things are needed for certain tasks, where things were put when last used. Cannot gather up own things without supervision. Cannot remember what to take home or what to bring back to work. Loses things on bus, at home, at work. Loses clothes, books, wallet, purse, keys, important papers. Cannot recall where they were left. Leaves tools and work things in yard overnight. Cannot clean up own room without direct supervision.

Must be guided/supervised/monitored in order to finish any task. Often called "lazy" and "careless." In continual conflict with others who do not understand organizational deficits.

_____ 12–25 **Moderately Severe Organizational Deficit**
Must have supervision and help to organize. Can do better if steps are written on notes. Must be reminded to go back to notes/outlines to make sure everything has been finished. Cannot clean up own space or do chores without supervision. Cannot manage own things without being reminded. Can learn to follow checklists and outlines if others continue to remind.

Must not be expected to organize or stay on schedule without help.

_____ 26–40 **Moderate Organizational Deficit**
Ability to organize is spotty and unpredictable. Needs a lot of reminding. Responds well to written reminders (notes, outlines). Must be reminded to refer back to notes and outlines to make sure each step has been followed. Tends to be absentminded. Tends to mislay things. Keeps things in loose piles or stacks that often become mixed together. Must have help cleaning out desk/locker/work space. Has cycles of better organization/poorer organization.

_____ 41–55 **Mild Organizational Deficit**
Can develop effective strategies for staying organized and on schedule. Responds well to keeping calendars, outlines of tasks, schedules on paper. Needs to be reminded frequently. Tends to wander off on rabbit trails and forget. Appears to be absentminded and careless.

_____ 56–60 **No Organizational Deficit**

Inhibition Behavior
Total Score (Transfer from bottom of Inhibition behavior rating page)

_____ 0–11 **Severe Problems with Self-Control**
Cannot function successfully in relationships. Severely self-focused and self-centered. Does not notice the needs or wishes of others. Places self first. Thinks mostly of satisfying own desires. All of personal energy goes toward fulfilling own self-needs. Does not extend affection without demanding something in return. Cannot respond normally to the give-and-take of friendships/family relationships/social relationships. Is irritable, quick tempered, judgmental when pressed to pay attention to others. Attitude is demanding, short tempered, critical of others. Refuses to share. Demands to be first. Wants biggest piece or share for self. Makes insatiable demands on others. Burns others out. Is often rejected by others. Moves from one friend to the next after short term of friendship. Cannot share space peacefully. Usually creates conflict with others. Cannot fit into groups. Tends to be unhappy much of the time. Complains, gripes, finds faults when others see no problem.

This person creates continual conflicts for leaders. Must be handled firmly. Cannot respond to normal suggestions that depend upon noticing others. Continually argues, challenges authority, blames others, indulges in self-pity. Uses others without showing regret or concern.

_____ 12–26 **Moderately Severe Problems with Self-Control**
Has trouble functioning in relationships, but can do so if others are patient and forgiving enough. Must be closely supervised in groups. Triggers frequent arguments/conflicts with peers. Is disliked by certain leaders. Is often rejected by peers and leaders. Can respond to coaching in how to treat others more kindly, but such lessons do not last. Does not have a natural bent for extending kindness and attention to others.

Leaders must intervene frequently to stop conflict or restore peace. This student requires extra effort from leaders to keep things going smoothly. This person triggers a lot of dislike from peers. A lot of his/her time is spent planning revenge and trying to get even.

_____ 27–41 **Moderate Problems with Self-Control**
Responds to reminding about manners and appropriate behavior. Requires frequent one-to-one guidance in how to behave more appropriately and less selfishly. Can respond well to reminder cues. Responds to guidance/counseling strategies that teach this person how to notice others. Triggers some conflict within group. Has good days/bad days in relationships. Argues a lot over trivial issues. Tends to split hairs over things others take in stride. Is seldom a fully cooperative member of group. Seeks subtle ways to get even with others.

_____ 42–55 **Mild Problems with Self-Control**
Needs frequent reminding about how to interact with others. Responds to guidance about noticing needs/wishes of others. Can learn to put own needs last or postpone wishes until later. Has good day/bad day cycles in relationships. Needs a lot of forgiveness and forgiving.

_____ 56–61 **No Problems with Self-Control**

190

Jordan Executive Function Index for Adults
Counselor or Instructor Response Section

Rating Scale

Mark each of the three total scores on this scale to see the difference between the adult's attention, organization, and inhibition behaviors.

Severe			Moderately Severe			Moderate	
10	**9**	**8**	**7**	**6**	**5**		
0 1 2 3	4 5 6 7	8 9 10 11	12 13 14 15 16 17 18	19 20 21 22 23 24 25	26 27 28 29 30 31 32		

Moderate		Mild			None	
4	**3**	**2**	**1**	**0**		
33 34 35 36 37 38 39 40	41 42 43 44 45	46 47 48 49 50	51 52 53 54 55	56 57 58 59 60		

References

Ackerman, P. T., Dykman, R. A., & Oglesby, D. M. (1983). Sex and group differences in reading and attention disordered children with and without hyperkinesis. *Journal of Learning Disabilities,* 16, 407–415.

Ackerman, P. T., Dykman, R. A., & Peters, J. E. (1997). Teenage status of hyperactive and non-hyperactive learning disabled boys. *American Journal of Orthopsychiatry,* 47, 577–596.

Alexander-Roberts, C. (1995). *A parent's guide to making it through the tough years with ADHD and teens.* Dallas, TX: Taylor.

American Psychiatric Association. (1968). *Diagnostic and statistical manual of mental disorders* (2nd ed.). Washington, DC: Author.

American Psychiatric Association. (1980). *Diagnostic and statistical manual of mental disorders* (3rd ed.). Washington, DC: Author.

American Psychiatric Association. (1987). *Diagnostic and statistical manual of mental disorders* (3rd ed., rev.). Washington, DC: Author.

American Psychiatric Association. (1994). *Diagnostic and statistical manual of mental disorders* (4th ed.). Washington, DC: Author.

Bain L. J. (1991). *A parent's guide to attention deficit disorders.* New York: Dell.

Barkley, R. A. (1990). *Attention-deficit hyperactivity disorder: A handbook for diagnosis and treatment.* New York: Guilford.

Barkley, R. A. (1995). *Taking charge of ADHD: The complete, authoritative guide for parents.* New York: Guilford.

Barkley, R. A., Spitzer, R., & Costello, A. (1990). *Development of the DSM-III-R criteria for the disruptive behavior disorders.* Unpublished manuscript, University of Massachusetts Medical Center, Worcester.

Bender, L. (1942). Postencephalitic behavior disorders in children. In J. B. Neal (Ed.), *Encephalitis: A clinical study.* New York: Grune & Stratton.

Berlin, R. (1884). Uber dyslexie [About dyslexia]. *Archiv fur Psychiatrie,* 15, 276–278.

Biederman, J., Faraone, S. V., Keenan, K., & Knee, D. (1990). Family-genetic and psychosocial risk factors in DSM-III attention deficit disorder. *Journal of the American Academy of Child and Adolescent Psychiatry,* 29, 526–533.

Blakeslee, S. (1995, March 21). How the brain might work: A new theory of consciousness. *Science Times* (Vol. 1, p. 1). New York: *New York Times.*

Bradley, W. (1937). The behavior of children receiving benzedrine. *American Journal of Psychiatry,* 94, 577–585.

Broadbent, W. H. (1872). On the cerebral mechanism of speech and thought. *Transactions of the Royal Medical and Chirurgical Society,* 15, 145–194.

Bronowski, J. (1977). Human and animal languages. In: *A sense of the future* (pp. 104–131). Cambridge, MA: MIT Press.

Chess, S. (1960). Diagnosis and treatment of the hyperactive child. *New York State Journal of Medicine, 60,* 2379–2385.

Clements, S. D., & Peters, J. E. (1962). Minimal brain dysfunction in the school aged child. *Archives of General Psychiatry, 6,* 185–197.

Cohen, D. J., Paul R., & Volkmar, F. R. (1986). Issues in the classification of pervasive and other developmental disorders: Toward DSM-IV. *Journal of Child Psychology and Psychiatry, 24,* 443–455.

Copeland, E. D. (1991). *Medicines for attention disorders (ADHD/ADD) and related medical problems.* Atlanta, GA: 3 C's of Childhood, Inc.

Copeland, E. D., & Love, V. L. (1991). *Attention please! A comprehensive guide for successfully parenting children with attention disorders and hyperactivity.* Atlanta, GA: SPI Press.

Damasio, A. R. (1994). *Descartes' error: emotion, reason, and the human brain.* New York: Avon Books.

Denckla, M. B. (1985). Issues of overlap and heterogeneity in dyslexia. In D. B. Gray & J. F. Kavanaugh (Eds.), *Biobehavioral measures of dyslexia* (pp. 41–46). Parkton, MD: York.

Denckla, M. B. (1991, March). *The neurology of social competence.* Paper presented at the Learning Disabilities Association national conference, Chicago.

Feingold, B. E. (1975). *Why your child is hyperactive.* New York: Random House.

Galaburda, A. (1983). Developmental dyslexia: Current anatomical research (Proceedings of the 33rd annual conference of The Orton Dyslexia Society). *Annals of Dyslexia, 33,* 41–54.

Geschwind, N. (1984). The biology of dyslexia: The after-dinner speech. In D. B. Gray & J. F. Kavanaugh (Eds.), *Behavioral measures of dyslexia* (pp. 1–19). Parkton, MD: York.

Gilligan, J. (1996). *Violence.* New York: Random House.

Gillis, J. J., Gilger, J. W., Pennington, B. F., & Defries, J. C. (1992). Attention deficit disorder in reading-disabled twins: Evidence for a genetic etiology. *Journal of Abnormal Child Psychology, 20,* 303–315.

Goleman, D. (1995). *Emotional intelligence.* New York: Bantam Books.

Gomez, R. L., Janowsky, D., Zetin, M., Huey, L., & Clopton, P. L. (1981). Adult psychiatric diagnosis and symptoms compatible with the hyperactive syndrome: A retrospective study. *Journal of Clinical Psychiatry, 42,* 389–394.

Green, C., & Chee, K. (1994). *Understanding ADD: Attention deficit disorder.* New York: Doubleday.

Guevremont, D., DuPaul, G. J., & Barkley, R. A. (in press). Diagnosis and assessment of attention deficit hyperactivity disorder in children. *Journal of School Psychology.*

Hallowell, E. M., & Ratey, J. J. (1994a). *Driven to distraction.* New York: Pantheon.

Hallowell, E. M., & Ratey, J. J. (1994b). *Answers to distraction.* New York: Pantheon.

Hinshaw, S. P., Henker, B., & Whalen, C. K. (1984). Self-control in hyperactive boys in anger-inducing situations: Effects of cognitive-behavioral training and of methylphenidate. *Journal of Abnormal Child Psychology, 12,* 55–77.

Hinshelwood, J. (1900). Congenital word-blindness. *The Lancet, 1,* 1506–1508.

Hoffer, E. (1982). *Between the devil and the dragon.* New York: Harper & Row.

Ingersoll, B. D., & Goldstein, S. (1993). *Attention deficit disorder and learning disabilities: Realities, myths and controversial treatments.* New York: Doubleday.

Irlen, H. (1991). *Reading by the colors: Overcoming dyslexia and other reading disabilities through the Irlen method.* Garden City, NY: Avery.

Irlen, H. (1993, September). Personal correspondence.

James, W. (1890). *The principles of psychology* (2 vols.) New York: Henry Holt.

Jamison, K. R. (1995). *An unquiet mind*. New York: Random House.

Jasuja, S. (1995). *Out of chaos! Understanding and managing A.D.D. and its relationship to modern stress*. Palo Alto, CA: Esteem House.

Jordan, D. R. (1972). *Dyslexia in the classroom* (1st ed.). Columbus, OH: Merrill.

Jordan, D. R. (1988a). *Attention deficit disorder*. Austin, TX: PRO-ED.

Jordan, D. R. (1988b). *Jordan prescriptive/tutorial reading program for moderate and severe dyslexics*. Austin, TX: PRO-ED.

Jordan, D. R. (1992). Jordan executive function index for adults. In: *Attention deficit disorder: ADHD and ADD syndromes* (2nd ed.). Austin, TX: PRO-ED.

Jordan. D. R. (1992b). Jordan executive function index for children. In: *Attention deficit disorder: ADHD and ADD syndromes* (2nd ed.). Austin, TX: PRO-ED.

Jordan, D. R. (1996a). *Overcoming dyslexia in children, adolescents, and adults* (2nd ed.). Austin, TX: PRO-ED.

Jordan, D. R. (1996b). *Teaching adults with learning disabilities*. Malabar, FL: Krieger.

Kahn, E., & Cohen, L. H. (1934). Organic driveness: A brain stem syndrome and an experience. *New England Journal of Medicine, 210,* 748–756.

Kauffman, J. M., & Hallahan, D. P. (1995). *The illusion of full inclusion: A comprehensive critique of a current special education bandwagon*. Austin, TX: PRO-ED.

Kelly , K., & Ramundo, P. (1993). *You mean I'm not lazy, stupid or crazy?!* Cincinnati, OH: Tyrell & Jerem Press.

Laufer, M., Denhoff, E., & Solomons, G. (1957). Hyperkinetic impulse disorder in children's behavior problems. *Psychomatic Medicine, 19,* 38–49.

Lehmkuhle, S., Garzia, R. P., Turner, L., Hash, T., & Baro, J. A. (1993). A defective visual pathway in children with reading disability. *New England Journal of Medicine, 328,* 989–996.

Livingstone, M. S., Rosen, G. D., Drislane, F. W., & Galaburda, A. M. (1991). Physiological and anatomical evidence for a magnocellular deficit in developmental dyslexia. *Proceedings of the National Academy of Science, USA, 88,* 7943–7947.

Livingstone, M. S. (1993, October). Personal correspondence.

Llinas, R. (1993). Coherent 40-Hz oscillation characterizes dream state in humans. *Proceedings of the National Academy of Sciences, 90,* 2078–2081.

Loney, J. (1983). Research diagnostic criteria for childhood hyperactivity. In S. B. Guze, J. J. Earls, & J. E. Barrett (Eds.), *Childhood psychopathology and development* (pp. 109–137). New York: Raven Press.

Naglieri, J. A., & Reardon, S. M. (1993). Traditional IQ is irrelevant to learning disabilities—intelligence is not. *Journal of Learning Disabilities, 26*(2), 127–133.

Orton, S. T. (1925). "Word-blindness" in children. *Archives of Neurology and Psychiatry, 14,* 581–615.

Parker, H. C. (1989). *The ADD hyperactivity workbook for parents, teachers, and kids*. Plantation, FL: Impact Publications.

Payne, N. (1994). [Learning disabilities in the workplace]. Unpublished raw data.

Pollan, C., & Williams, D. (1992). [Learning disabilities in adolescents and young adult school dropouts]. Unpublished raw data.

Ramachandran, V. S. (1993). Behavioral and magnetoencephalographic correlates of plasticity in the adult human brain. *Proceedings of the National Academy of Science, USA, 90,* 10413–10420.

Ratey, J. J., & Johnson, C. (1997). *Shadow syndromes*. New York: Pantheon.

Schacter, D. L. (1996). *Searching for memory.* New York: BasicBooks.

Silver, L. B. (1991). The Regular Education Initiative: A deja vu remembered with sadness and concern. *Journal of Learning Disabilities, 24,* 389–390.

Still, G. F. (1902). Some abnormal psychical conditions in children. *Lancet, i,* 1008–1012, 1077–1082, 1163–1168.

Strauss, A. A., & Kephhart, N. C. (1955). *Psychopathology and education of the brain-injured child: Vol. 2. Progress in theory and clinic.* New York: Grune & Stratton.

Tallal, P., Miller, S., & Fitch, R. (1993). Neurobiological basis of speech: A case for the preeminence of temporal processing. *Annals of New York Academy of Sciences, 682*(6), 74–81.

Taylor, J. F. (1994). *Helping your hyperactive/attention deficit child.* Rocklin, CA: Prima Publishing.

Thomas, J., & Adamec, C. (1996). *Do you have attention deficit disorder?* New York: Dell.

Tredgold, A. F. (1908). *Mental deficiency (amentia).* New York: W. Wood.

Warren, P., & Capehart, J. (1995). *You & your A.D.D. child: How to understand and help kids with attention deficit disorder.* Nashville, TN: Thomas Nelson Publishers.

Wechsler, D. (1994). *Wechsler Intelligence Scale for Children–III.* San Antonio, TX: Psychological Corporation.

Weisel, L. P. (1992). *POWERPath to adult basic learning.* Columbus, OH: The TLP Group.

Weiss, G., & Hechtman, L. T. (1993). *Hyperactive children grown up* (2nd ed.). New York: Guilford.

Weiss, L. (1992). *Attention deficit disorder in adults: A practical help for sufferers and their spouses* (2nd ed.). Dallas, TX: Taylor.

Will, M. (1986). *Educating students with learning problems: A shared responsibility.* Washington, DC: U.S. Department of Education, Special Education and Rehabilitative Services.

Wishnie, H. (1977). *Impulsive personality: Understanding people with destructive character disorder.* New York: Plenum Publishers.

Wood, F. (1991, February). *Brain imaging and learning disabilities.* Paper presented at the Learning Disabilities Association national conference, Chicago.

Woodcock, R. W. (1991). *Woodcock–Johnson Psycho-Educational Battery, Revised.* Circle Pines, MN: American Guidance Service.

Zaidel, E., & Zaidel, D. (1979). Self-recognition and social awareness in the disconnected minor hemisphere. *Neuropsychologia, 8,* 41–55.

Zametkin, A. J., Nordahl, T. E., Gross, M., King, A. C., Semple, W. E., Rumsey, J., Hamburger, S., & Cohen, R. M. (1990). Cerebral glucose metabolism in adults with hyperactivity of childhood onset. *New England Journal of Medicine, 323,* 1361–1367.

Index

AADF (Adult Attention Deficit Foundation), 155
Abusive behavior, 81, 101–102, 150
Ackerman, Peggy, 3–4
Adamec, Christine, 150
ADDA (National Attention Deficit Disorder Association), 155
Addiction, 97, 112, 122, 143
Aggression, 1, 4, 10, 28, 32, 35, 47, 80–84, 88–92, 101, 141, 145, 147, 154
Alexander-Roberts, Colleen, 150
Allergies, 79, 145–148
An Unquiet Mind, 111
Anger, 82–83, 88–92, 98, 100, 120, 144–145, 150, 153
Anosognosia, 14
Answers to Distraction, 150
Antisocial Personality Disorder, 98
Anxiety, 53, 89, 97, 122, 124, 143
A Parent's Guide to Making It Through the Tough Years, 150
Arguing, 86, 89–91, 98–99
Arithmetic, 30, 51, 53–54, 70–71, 73, 130, 131, 137–138, 151
Asperger's syndrome, 116–122
Attention burnout, 75–76, 77–78
Attention-control systems, 7–8, 70
Attention Deficit Disorder
  ADD, 4–5, 13, 16–17, 45–61, 63–95, 97
  ADD+H, 4–5, 20, 46
  ADD–H, 4–5, 46
  ADD/ADHD Severity Scale, 20, 80
  ADHD, 5, 13–14, 16–17, 19–44, 46, 63, 95, 97
  Diagnosing ADHD, 21–23, 46
  Percent of population, 19, 46, 103, 110, 130
  Residual ADHD, 91–92
Attention Deficit Disorder in Adults: Practical Help for Sufferers and Their Spouses, 150
Attention surplus disorders, 97, 109–114, 122–124
  Anxiety Disorder, 124
  Intermittent Rage Disorder, 123–124

Autism, 97, 115–116
Avoidance behavior, 78–80
Awkward motor coordination, 85, 117

Barkley, Russell, 4, 14, 17, 23–26, 40, 46, 97, 130, 140, 150
Bender, Lauretta, 3
Berlin, Reinhold, 131
Bierderman, Joseph, 17
Biofeedback training, 81
Bipolar I Manic/Depressive Illness, 110–111
Bipolar II Manic/Depressive Illness, 110–111
Blaming others, 29–30, 32, 68, 99–100, 121
Body language, 28, 117
Boredom, 26–28, 53–56, 65–66, 70, 89, 99
Boring behavior, 118–121
Bradley, William, 2
Brain blood flow, 26–27, 131
Brain cell firing
  Firing rhythms, 11–12, 26, 123–124
  Timing, 11–12
Brain imaging, 6, 8, 19–20
  Brain electrical activity mapping (BEAM), 6
  Computed tomography (CT), 6
  Magnetic resonance imaging (MRI), 6, 125
  Positron emission tomography (PET), 6, 125
  Single photon emission computed tomography (SPECT), 6
Brain language. *See* Inner voice
Brain monitoring, 13, 109
Brain structure
  Auditory cortex, 8, 131–132
  Axon, 9–10, 13, 122, 124, 141
  Corpus striatum, 7
  Dendrite, 9–10
  Frontal lobes, 11, 24, 26, 32, 76, 140
  Inferior parietal lobe, 7
  Left brain, 8, 10, 12–13, 27, 34, 109–110, 114, 124
  Medial geniculate nucleus, 131–132
  Midbrain. *See* Limbic system
  Midline reticular nucleus, 7
  Motor cortex, 11–12, 26–76

Myelin, 9, 13
Neuron, 9
Occipital lobe, 11–12
Parietal lobe, 11–12, 33, 50, 98, 125–126, 132
Prefrontal cingulate, 7
Premotor cortex, 26–27
Right brain, 9–10, 12–13, 34, 109–110, 114, 124
Sensory cortex, 11
Superior temporal cortex, 7, 26
Synapse junction, 9–10
Tectum mesopontine reticular formation, 7
Temporal lobe, 11–12
Transcortical motor area (TCM), 27
Visual cortex, 8, 125
Brain sugar metabolism, 26, 131
Bronowski, Jacob, 14, 24–25
Bullying behavior, 81–83, 101–102
Buzsaki, Gyorgy, 11

Capehart, Jody, 45
CHADD (Children and Adults with Attention Deficit Disorders), 91, 155
Checklists
  ADD Behaviors, 57–61
  ADHD Behaviors, 40–44
  Jordan Executive Function Index for Adults, 175–191
  Jordan Executive Function Index for Children, 157–173
Chee, Kit, 45, 150
Chess, Stella, 3
Chronicles of Narnia, 86
Cohen, David, 103
Cohen, Leonard, 2
Color application, 125–126
Commonsense reasoning, 6, 14, 32
Comorbidity, 97
  ADD/Anxiety Disorder, 124
  ADD/Asperger's syndrome, 116–122
  ADD/Chronic depression, 54–57, 114–115
  ADD/High functioning autism, 115–116
  ADD/Passive/Aggressive Personality Style, 120
  ADD/ADHD/Irlen syndrome, 125–130
  ADD/ADHD/Learning disabilities (dyslexia), 130–135
  ADD/ADHD/Visual perceptual disorder, 124–130
  ADHD/Attention surpus disorders, 122–124
  ADHD/Bipolar I Manic/Depressive Illness, 110

ADHD/Bipolar II Manic/Depressive Illness, 110
  ADHD/Conduct Disorder, 101–103, 140
  ADHD/Hypomanic Personality, 111
  ADHD/Intermittent Rage Disorder, 123–124
  ADHD/Multiplex Developmental Disorder, 103–109
  ADHD/Oppositional Defiant Disorder, 98–101, 140
Conduct Disorder (CD), 24, 80–84, 97, 101–103, 140
Confrontation, 80–83, 88–92, 98–103, 120–122
Confusion, 11, 47–48, 53, 71, 78–80, 120, 133
Consequences, 14, 33, 79, 87, 88–92, 113, 153–154
Controlling behavior, 81, 120
Counseling, 84–87, 88–92, 98, 119, 154
Criticism, 32–33, 66–67, 69, 119, 123
Cytotoxic. *See* Food intolerance

Damasio, Antonio, 5–6, 26, 33
Damasio, Hanna, 5
Daydreaming, 4–5, 12, 48, 53, 70, 78, 106, 114–115
Decision making, 1, 80–84, 88–92, 98–99, 102
Delayed maturity, 3, 87, 91–93, 151–152
Delusional thinking, 111
Delinquent behavior, 81, 89, 101–103, 130
Denckla, Martha, 116, 121, 139
Denhoff, Ernest, 3
Depression, 10, 15, 54–57, 90, 92, 114–115, 140–141, 144, 147
Descartes' Error, 6–7, 26
Diagnostic and Statistical Manual of Mental Disorders
  DSM-II, 3
  DSM-III, 4, 36, 63
  DSM-III:R, 5, 36
  DSM-IV, 5, 21–23
Diet control, 83–84, 145–148
Dinklage, David, 103
Discipline, 67, 80, 148–150, 153–154,
Disinhibition, 24–25
Disruptive behavior, 1–3, 11, 16, 24, 31–33, 63–95, 97–101, 106, 109–114, 120, 140–141, 145
Distractibility, 2, 11, 29, 52, 74–75, 90, 94, 97, 113–114
Disturbed emotional expression, 108–114
Do You Have Attention Deficit Disorder?, 150
Doodling, 53–56, 79
Driven to Distraction, 151

Drug/alcohol usage, 17, 92
Dykman, Roscoe, 3–4
Dyscalculia, 138
Dysgraphia, 76–77, 138
Dyslexia, 13, 130–135, 140
    Auditory dyslexia, 131–133
    Visual dyslexia, 133–135
Dyslexia in the Classroom, 131

Eccentric behavior, 116–122
Elation, 110–111
Electroencephalogram, 3
Embarrassment. *See* Shame
Emotion, 5–6, 8, 14
    Activated emotions, 15, 53
    Basal emotions, 6, 8, 53, 123
    Centers of emotion, 6, 8, 31
    Higher emotions, 6, 8, 31
    Negative emotions, 13, 53
    Positive emotions, 13
Emotional bonding, 82–83, 85, 92
Emotional highjacking, 124
Emotional Intelligence, 124
Emotional sensitivity, 32–33, 64, 66, 68, 89, 122–124
Emotional volatility, 1, 108–109
Encaphalitis lethargica, 2
Escape behavior, 53–57
Executive function, 139, 141, 157–191
External self, 122–124

Failure, 68–69, 78–80
Family patterns, 17, 40, 150
Fantasy. *See* Make-believe thinking
Fear, 8, 53, 64
    Fight-or-Flight response, 53, 123
    Nightmares, 55–57, 83
    Phobia, 55, 108
Feelings, 6, 7–8, 14–15, 25
Feingold, Ben, 145–148
Filtering information, 6–7, 11, 131
Food intolerance, 79, 83–84, 97, 143, 145–148
Forgetfulness, 48, 74, 86, 90, 92–95, 115, 154
Full inclusion, 139

Galaburda, Albert, 5, 131
Genetic factors, 4
Geschwind, Norman, 5, 131
Gilligan, James, 123
Gillis, Jacquelyn, 17
Goleman, Daniel, 124
Gomez, Richard, 4
Gray, Charles, 11

Green, Christopher, 45, 150
Grief, 108–110, 150
Guevremont, David, 103
Guilt, 81, 101

Hallahan, Daniel, 139
Hallowell, Edward, 150–151
Hechtman, Lily, 2
Helping Your Hyperactive/Attention Deficit Child, 150
Helplessness, 74, 78–80, 123
High risk behavior, 81, 110, 113
Hinshaw, Samuel, 4
Hormone development, 88
Hostile behavior, 80–83, 88–92, 101
Hygiene, 49, 57, 93, 107, 116–117, 119, 149
Hyperactivity, 1–4, 28, 35–36, 46, 80–84, 88, 141, 144, 147, 150, 154
Hyperkinetic Impulse Disorder, 3, 46
Hyperkinetic Reaction of Childhood Disorder, 3
Hyperlexia, 25, 112, 114
Hypomanic personality, 97, 111–114

Immaturity, 34–35, 53–54, 68, 87–88, 151–152
Impatience, 88–92, 103–104
Impulse control, 5, 64, 123
Impulsivity, 1–4, 25–26, 28, 30–31, 88–92, 97, 114, 141
Inappropriate behavior, 2, 53–54, 87–92, 98–103, 106–108, 113, 118
Inattention, 1–2, 4, 69–80, 92–95, 97, 114
Information highways to the brain
    Bloodstream, 11
    Viscera, 9, 29, 30
Inherited ADHD/ADD, 17, 40
Inner voice, 14–15, 24–25, 78, 31
Insatiable behavior, 10, 32, 68, 80, 83, 99
Insecurity, 84–92
Intelligence, 5, 35, 82, 111, 118, 124, 137–139, 141–142, 151–152
Internal self, 122–124
Interrupting behavior, 99, 119
Irlen, Helen, 125
Irlen syndrome, 125–130
Irregular motor coordination, 85, 108
Irregular classroom performance, 36–38
Irregular social skills, 85, 105–108
Irregular thinking, 103–105
Irritable behavior, 88–92, 100, 143–144

James, William, 1, 97
Jamison, Kay, 111

Johnson, Catherine, 14–15, 25, 97, 110–111, 123, 151
Jordan Executive Function Index for Adults, 139, 175–191
Jordan Executive Function Index for Children, 139, 157–173
Jordan Written Screening Test, 135
Jumping mental tracks, 20–21, 33–34, 103–105

Kahn, Eli, 2
Kauffman, James, 139
Kelly, Kate, 150
Keyboard writing, 86–87
Koch, Christof, 11
Kopell, Nancy, 11

Language usage, 2, 13, 71–73, 103–108, 131, 137–138
Laufer, Morris, 3
LDA (Association for Children and Adults with Learning Disabilities), 155
Learning disabilities, 4, 13, 16, 76, 130–135
Legal status of LD, 137–138
Lehmkuhle, Stephen, 125
Lewis, C. S., 86
Lifestyle, 17, 36, 49, 54, 91, 98, 101
Limbic system, 6–7, 9–12, 16, 25, 30–33, 48, 50, 53, 98, 123–126, 131, 139, 141, 144
  Amygdala, 6, 9–10, 12, 16, 31, 53, 98, 123
  Basal ganglia, 6, 31, 53
  Brain stem, 6, 9–10, 12, 48, 50, 98, 125–126, 132
  Cerebellum, 9–10, 12
  Diencephlon, 3
  Hippocampus, 9–10, 12, 98
  Hypothalamus, 9–10
  Medulla, 6, 31, 53, 98
  Pons, 6, 31, 53
  Tectum mesopontine reticular formation, 7
  Thalamus, 9–10
Livingstone, Margaret, 125
Llinas, Rodolfo, 12
Logic, 6, 8, 14, 24–25, 30, 32, 118, 123–124, 139
Loney, Jane, 4
Loose mental images, 49–50, 74

Magnicellular pathway, 125–126
  Magno cells, 125–126
  Retina, 125–126
  Parvo cells, 125–126
Make-believe thinking, 52–56

Fantasy thinking, 34, 64, 79, 86, 104, 114–115, 122
Magical thinking, 34, 64
Role playing, 34, 64, 85–86, 122
Wishful thinking, 114–115
Marriage, 92, 95, 150
Math. *See* Arithmetic
Medication, 2, 8, 10, 15, 140–146
  Adderall, 141, 144
  Anafranil, 145
  Antiaggressives, 145
  Antidepressants, 140, 144
  Antiobsessives, 144–145
  Aurorix, 145
  Aventyl, 144
  Benzedrine, 2
  BuSpar, 144
  Catepres, 145
  Cortical stimulants, 8, 10, 140–144
  Cylert, 10, 83, 143, 145
  Dexedrine, 141, 143–145
  Dextroamphetamine, 2, 143–144
  Effexor, 145
  Elavil, 144
  Inderal, 145
  Levoamphetamine, 2
  Low dosage strength, 141, 143
  Luvox, 145
  Manic/Depressive Illness, 111
  Norpramine, 144
  Obsessive/Compulsive Disorder, 15
  Pamelor, 144
  Paxil, 145
  Petrofrane, 144
  Prozac, 145
  Selective serotonin reuptake inhibitors (SSRIs), 145
  Serzone, 145
  Side effects, 143–145
  Tenex, 145
  Tofranil, 144
  Tryptonal, 144
  Welbutrin, 144
  Zoloft, 145
Memory, 5, 8, 14
  Changes in memory, 15–16
  Emotional memory, 15
  Engrams, 15, 23
  Long term memory, 10, 29, 63, 74
  Memory images, 14, 16, 78
  Memory and attention deficits, 16, 78
  Permanent memory, 29, 33, 78
  Recall, 33

Mental rabbit trails, 5, 64
Midbrain. *See* Limbic system
Minimal Brain Damage (MBD), 3–4, 46
Minimal Brain Damage syndrome, 2–3, 46
Misunderstanding, 20–21, 67–68, 104–108
Monitoring. *See* Supervision
Monopolar depression, 97
Mood swings, 1, 3, 109–114, 147
Multiplex Developmental Disorder (MDD), 97, 103–109

Naglieri, Jack, 139
Narcissism, 15
Neurotransmitters
  Acetylcholine, 9–10
  Dopamine, 9–10, 140–141, 144
  Norepinephrine, 9–10, 141, 144
  Serotonin, 9–10, 144–145
Noisy brain, 14–15, 25–26

Obsessive behavior, 118–119
Obsessive/Compulsive Disorder, 15–16, 54, 144
Oglesby, David, 4
Opposition Defiant Disorder (ODD), 24, 80–84, 88–92, 97–101, 140
Optimism, 13–14, 109–110, 114, 124
Oral language, 8, 3, 70, 90–91, 117, 131
Orton Dyslexia Society, 155
Orton, Samuel T., 125
Out of Chaos! Understanding and Managing A.D.D. and Its Relationship to Modern Stress, 151
Outgrowing ADD/ADHD, 36–40, 87, 92–93
Overcoming Dyslexia in Children, Adolescents, and Adults, 16, 130–131
Overfocused behavior, 89–90, 123–124
Overinterpreting, 104–108

Parenting skills, 81, 87, 88–92
Parker, Harvey, 141
Passive/Aggressive Personality Style, 47, 120
Passive behavior, 4–5, 20, 46–47, 79, 86, 120
Perseveration, 2, 105–108
Personal space, 28, 31, 49, 86, 93, 99, 116, 120–121, 149–150, 153
Personality/Mood Disorder, 98
Pessimism, 13–14, 109, 114, 124
Peters, John, 3
Phillips, Allan, 45
Phobia. *See* Fear
Phonemes,
  Hard/fast consonants, 131–132

Soft/slow consonants and vowels, 131–132
Pollan, Carolyn, 130, 140
Poor eye contact, 50, 106, 113
Poor leadership ability, 121–122
Poor listening, 20, 29, 32–33, 50–51, 69–70, 78, 89–90, 148–149, 151–154
Poor organization, 20–21, 31, 49, 70, 74, 82–83, 86, 89, 148, 151, 154
Poor social behavior, 4, 21, 24, 31, 63–69, 86, 116–122, 147–148
Praise, 8, 69, 116, 141
Pressure to hurry, 71–73, 86
Privacy, 28, 86–87, 101, 113, 115
Procrastination, 78–80, 86–87, 93–94
Prosody
  Sing-song speech, 85
  Flat tone of voice, 117–118
Psychotherapy, 81, 154

Rage disorders, 97
Racing thoughts, 21, 88–91, 112–114
Ramachandran, Vilayanur, 13, 110
Ramundo, Peggy, 150
Ratey, John, 14–15, 25, 31, 97, 110–111, 123, 150–151
Rationalizing behavior, 121–122
Reading, 4, 8, 20, 32, 77–78, 130–131, 137–138, 151–152
Reading by the Colors, 125
Reardon, Sean, 139
Rebellious behavior, 80–84, 88–92, 98–99, 140–141, 145
Rebound from medication, 88, 143
Regular Education Initiative (REI), 139
Rejection, 89, 100, 118
Resentful behavior, 88–92, 100, 120
Restless behavior, 20, 65, 70, 89, 144
Revenge behavior, 83, 100–101
Ribary, Urs, 12
Ritual behavior, 86, 107–108, 113, 120–122

Safety, 53, 151–154
Schacter, Daniel, 8, 15, 33
Schizophrenia, 103, 122
Score discrepancy model, 137–139, 151–152
Searching for Memory, 8, 15
Self-centered behavior, 64–65, 88–92, 112
Self-correcting, 13, 109, 135
Self-defense, 67, 88–92, 100, 123–124
Self-esteem, 68–69, 74, 112, 123
Self-focus, 32, 88–92, 98, 114
Self-gratification, 65, 88–92, 98, 113
Self-regulation, 23–25, 34, 63–95

Sense of humor, 64, 93, 106, 118
Sensory perception, 107–108
Sequence, 8, 24, 49–50, 52, 76, 103–108, 124, 131–132
Severity scale
 ADHD, 20–21
 ADD, 80
Sexuality, 150
Shadow Syndromes, 14, 97, 110, 151
Shame, 53, 69, 73–74, 89, 122–123, 152
Sidetracking, 105–108
Silver, Larry, 139
Skill Development, 49–50, 66, 69–80, 86–87, 94–95
Sleep deprivation, 112
Slow processing, 48, 69, 86, 117–118
Social blindness, 28, 86, 103–108, 117–118
Social signals, 28, 103–108, 117–118
Social skills, 6, 28, 32, 63, 86, 116–121, 148–150
Solomons, George, 3
Special education, 2, 4, 137–139
Spelling, 8, 13, 71, 76, 130, 138, 151
Standard Ritalin Dosage Chart, 141
Still, George, 1, 97
Strauss, Arthur, 2
Stress, 10, 123, 151–152
Structure, 148–150
Stubbornness, 63, 88–92, 120, 154
Suicide, 57, 110, 115
Supervision, 20–21, 29–30, 87–95, 148–150
Support team, 92–93

Tag-along syndromes, 97–135
Taking Charge of ADHD: The Complete, Authoratative Guide for Parents, 17, 24, 40, 150
Tallal, Paula, 131
Taylor, John, 150
Telling lies, 16, 69, 99–101
Temper tantrums, 21, 32, 80–82, 88–92, 98, 119, 123, 145, 147
Thomas, James, 150
Time awareness, 24–25, 49
 Chronological order, 104

Tardiness, 49, 74, 89–90, 94
Time blind, 24–25
Time-limited tasks, 73, 78, 117–118
Tolkien, J. R. R., 86
Tone deafness. *See* Auditory dyslexia
Tredgold, Alfred, 2, 97

Underachievement, 4, 55, 141–142
Underarousal, 26–28, 140–144
Understanding ADD, 45, 150
Unfinished tasks, 29–30, 49, 75, 86, 113
Unidentified Bright Objects (UBOs), 13–14, 103, 114, 122, 124
Unpredicatable resonse, 71–73

Violent behavior, 1, 10, 80, 123, 145, 147
Visual acuity, 124, 133
Visual perception, 11, 124–130

Warren, Paul, 45
Wechsler Adult Intelligence Scale–R (WAIS–R), 142
Wechsler Intelligence Scale for Children (WISC–III), 36, 137–138
Weisel, Laura, 130, 140
Weiss, Gabrielle, 2
Weiss, Lynn, 150
Why Your Child Is Hyperactive, 146
Williams, Dorothy, 130, 140
Wishnie, Howard, 122
Withdrawal behavior, 57, 70, 114–115
Wood, Frank, 6, 26, 131
Woodcock-Johnson Psycho-educational Battery, 137–138
Word blindness, 124–130
Word sounding, 8, 77
Workplace, 21, 32–33, 87–95, 150–151
Writing, 71–73, 76–77, 113, 131, 141

You and Your A.D.D. Child, 45
You Mean I'm Not Lazy, Stupid or Crazy?, 150

Zaidel, Erin, 6, 13, 109
Zametkin, Alan, 6, 26–27